The Wreckage of Intentions

ALEMBICS: PENN STUDIES IN
LITERATURE AND SCIENCE

Mary Thomas Crane and Henry S. Turner, Series Editors

THE WRECKAGE OF INTENTIONS

Projects in British Culture, 1660–1730

DAVID ALFF

PENN

UNIVERSITY OF PENNSYLVANIA PRESS

PHILADELPHIA

Published by
University of Pennsylvania Press
Philadelphia, Pennsylvania 19104-4112
www.upenn.edu/pennpress

Printed in the United States of America on acid-free paper
10 9 8 7 6 5 4 3 2 1

Library of Congress Cataloging-in-Publication Data
Names: Alff, David, author.
Title: The wreckage of intentions : projects in British culture, 1660–1730 / David Alff.
Other titles: Alembics: Penn studies in literature and science
Description: 1st edition. | Philadelphia : University of Pennsylvania Press, [2018] | Series: Alembics | Includes bibliographical references and index.
Identifiers: LCCN 2017010475 | ISBN 978-0-8122-4959-0 (hardcover : alk. paper)
Subjects: LCSH: English literature—17th century—History and criticism. | English literature—18th century—History and criticism. | Industrial development projects—England—History—17th century. | Industrial development projects—England—History—18th century. | Scientific literature—England—History—17th century. | Scientific literature—England—History—18th century. | England—Civilization—17th century. | England—Civilization—18th century.
Classification: LCC PR431 .A39 2017 | DDC 820.9/004
LC record available at https://lccn.loc.gov/2017010475

For Katie, as always

Contents

Introduction

What Is a Project?

In 1652, an anonymous London pamphlet proclaimed the end of famine. The twenty-four-page *Designe for Plentie* reasoned that England could secure "food in the time of want" by forcing its landholders to plant twenty apple, pear, walnut, or quince trees on every "five pounds *per annum*" of arable soil.[1] According to this treatise, a law for compulsory arboriculture would restock the Commonwealth in the wake of civil wars that ruined tillage and emptied larders.[2] "Woodwards" would patrol nurseries, fine defaulters, and schedule "common dayes" when parishioners would harvest the trees.[3] These statutory labors would supply produce, timber, firewood, and juice, which could be fermented into cider. "Universal plantation" promised to barrel so much cider that England could stop brewing beer, a beverage that devoured bread barley while seeding "drunkennesse, disorder, and dangerous plots."[4] Fruit groves would transform "waste and wilde places" into a veritable "Garden of God" that could fill stomachs and dazzle eyes.[5] Beauty, abundance, civility, and even a taste of prelapsarian bliss all seemed within the grasp of this single law.

Despite its euphoric imagery and breathless reasoning, *Designe for Plentie* concedes that its vision may not materialize. The author bemoans the "sluggishnesse" of his countrymen, likening them to a cat who hungers for fish, "yet her foot in water will not weat."[6] He simultaneously fears detractors who would dismiss communal orcharding as a "vain and trifling" notion, a specious enterprise unworthy of state support.[7] To shake apathy and forestall censure, *Designe* characterizes itself as a practical measure for the benefit of all Commonwealth citizens: "we have thought it our dutie to present an Assay of Plenty, which we call (*A Designe or Project for Plenty*) yet not a project of any private advantage to us; but of publique good and plenty unto this Nation."[8] *Designe* anchors its self-justification to three nouns—assay, "designe," project— that in the seventeenth century denoted both kinds of writing and modes of

action. "Assay" frames the fruit scheme as a composition that subjects propositions to trial in the spirit of Montaigne's *essai*. The author distinguishes his
"try" at advancing the "publique good" from venal pursuits of "private advantage," fashioning *Designe* as a tested article of national improvement rather
than a vehicle for personal gain. "Designe," the first word of the title, gives the
impression of an elegant plan combining forethought and reason. The pamphleteer claims selfless motives *and* painstaking methodology to make credible
his glimpse into future plenty.

The final term is "project." Given its position behind the conjunction *or*,
"project" at first sounds like the mere complement and trailing echo of "designe." But then five words later "project" returns to displace "assay" and "designe" both: the "Assay of Plenty" becomes a "project . . . of publique good."
"Project," in these two sentences, harbors universal plantation's lofty but tenuous prospects: its singular ability to happen or not. The word reappears in the
next sentence, following a pledge that fruit mandates will strengthen the realm
if Parliament ratifies them: "Otherwise we shall but term it (*The Embrio of
Plenty, and the untimely Birth of good Desires*) which had it come to perfection,
might have yielded both pleasure and profit to many. And such a *Project* also
it is, as is not without . . . good Reasons to speak for it; whereof we shall desire
to make all rationall man partakers."[9] *Designe* promises a radiant future while
mourning its foreclosure. The author compares his project to premature human life at the same time he grieves its miscarriage: "had it" been completed,
the plantation scheme "might have" benefited England, he reflects, entombing
seeming opportunity in the past tense. But in the next sentence, *Designe*
emerges from its gloomy report of prospective failure to again revel in present
possibilities: "such a *Project* also it is." The italicized, capitalized word "*Project*"
insists that "universal plantation" remains a viable plan. The invocation of "this
project" reinscribes eternal plenty within a subjunctive future achieved through
the reader's action.

But what is a project? Today, few readers will think twice about this word,
which feels familiar, even self-evident in the context of our goal-oriented,
enterprise-driven modernity. Such habituation was not yet possible in 1652,
when "project" referred not only to the capacity of human ambitions to raise
society, but also to alchemical procedures, optical displays, informational
charts, and physical motions. One could hatch a project, in the sense of a
scheme, jot down thoughts within a table called project, or map the project or
schema of a book.[10] "Project" was an even more versatile verb: things one could
project included light on a surface, a philosopher's stone in a cauldron, a

three-dimensional figure on a two-dimensional plane, and any object—or projectile—through space. These denotations, alive if sometimes obscure to-day, derive from *project*'s heterogeneous etymology, whose strands include the Latin *prōiectum*, for a protruding object, and *proicere*, meaning to throw or propel, and the Middle French *projetter*, meaning to plan. The English word first appeared around 1450, though it would not see widespread use until the middle sixteenth century, the same period in which the Italian *progetto* and Spanish *proyecto* gained currency. It was in the 1500s that "project," in its nominal and predicate forms, began to signify the work of conceiving and delivering future outcomes through discrete efforts.

By the early seventeenth century, "project" could refer also to the writing that proposed new enterprise. *Designe for Plentie* was just one of many works from this era that identified as a project according to the English Short Title Catalogue. Early modern Britain saw "projects" of war and diplomacy.[11] The word adorns petitions to abolish doctrinal tests and refine etiquette, to build libraries and administer lotteries.[12] William Penn proposed *One Project for the Good of England* (1679) to unify fractious Protestants against the common enemy of Roman Catholicism. The anonymous *New Project to Make England a Florishing Kingdom* (1702) singles out Catholics and Jacobites as national enemies and proposes an oath of abjuration to uproot them. Commercial projects endeavored to bolster England's mercantile economy, cultivate rural land, sanitize London, popularize new commodities, and explore overseas territories.[13]

These visionary attempts to reform and redirect British society often raised objections, especially among those who had a stake in maintaining the status quo or who advocated alternative schemes, including their own. In the late sixteenth and early seventeenth centuries, "project" began to connote deceit, hazard, and upheaval. The word could be used to praise the usefulness of inventions in agricultural and mechanical arts or condemn untoward schemes contrived to aggrandize their authors at the public's expense.[14] Distinguishing between projects that were benevolent and malicious, actionable and impossible, posed a stiff challenge to crown officials, legislators, parish officers, investors, and readers in general, who parsed a burgeoning mass of proposals through increasingly pejorative terminology.

"Project" took on a decidedly negative feel in the early Stuart era, when courtiers purchased royal patents in order to launch manufacturing projects that promised to cheapen staples like salt, starch, soap, bricks, and coal. Upon award, most of these fraudulent industrialists abandoned their pretenses of improving trade and instead sought to monopolize it, using patent protections to gouge consumers and amass fortunes.[15] Less overtly egregious but equally controversial in the period were a string of patent-backed land improvement initiatives, like fen drainage, which sought to convert the flooded peats of eastern England into arable tillage. This venture promised to raise the value of Anglian soil but also enriched their investors to the detriment of commoners who derived their livelihoods from the partly flooded landscape.[16] Projects became so suspect in the early 1600s that a need to identify and make culpable those behind them motivated the coinage of new terms: a "projector" (1596) was an author of projects, while "projection" (1611) and "projecting" (1616) signified the act of creating new schemes.[17]

Reviled for masking private greed in the language of civic uplift, the scheme-hawking projector continued to haunt discussions of national improvement long after the Caroline era that made this figure notorious. For instance, the English Commonwealth's confiscation and repurposing of royalist land presented new opportunities for suspect projects.[18] Walter Blith, author of *The English Improver Improved* (1652), the Interregnum's most important compendium of agricultural proposals, conceded that "there is such a scandall & prejudice among many of you against new projections."[19] Blith had no patience for unfounded ideas in husbandry, though he attempts to redeem the inventive agrarian by characterizing God as the "first projector of that great designe, to bring that old Masse and Chaos of confusion unto so vast an Improvement."[20] Conceiving of his own manual as a divinely endorsed effort to reform postbellum England from the ground up, Blith believed that applying written knowledge to the land would perpetuate the work of creation and advance the Republic's grand political experiment. England needed new projects, he argued, even if their authors were not always upstanding citizens.

By the Restoration, "project" and its lexical derivatives conjured memories of both Caroline patent seekers and the architects of the failed Republic. In this atmosphere, the Royal Society of London, which was chartered by Charles II but steeped in the protocols of Interregnum scientific correspondence networks, faced critics like Henry Stubbe, who rallied his readers to "oppose these projectors," claiming that even a peasant would dismiss the Royal Society's "superlatively ridiculous" ventures as "but projecting."[21] Thomas Sprat anticipated these attacks in his *History of the Royal Society* (1667), which boasted that the society funded itself through member contributions so they would not be "contemn'd, as vain *Projectors*."[22] Early modern scientists sought to distinguish their work from England's tarnished tradition of scheming at a time when the word "project" came to name an attack on the handling, financing, and authorization of natural knowledge.

In 1688, the Whig coup that replaced James II with William of Orange and Mary Stuart catalyzed a new period of speculative activity that the Cripplegate haberdasher and brick maker Daniel Defoe called a "Projecting Age."[23] The formative event of this inventive era was the War of the Grand Alliance, which disrupted trade between England and the Continent, forcing the kingdom to develop self-sufficient agriculture and industry, as well as a modern financial infrastructure capable of subsidizing foreign military campaigns. The establishment of a central bank, national debt, lotteries, and recoinage in the 1690s encouraged a new generation of adventurers to seek profit through instruments like the joint-stock company. Defoe, who went bankrupt during these heady years farming cats to make perfume and financing marine salvage expeditions, acknowledged the benefits and perils of projects. His *Essay upon Projects* (1697) distinguishes between ventures that "tend to the Improvement of Trade, and Employment of the Poor, and the Circulation and Increase of the publick Stock of the Kingdom," and those "fram'd by subtle Heads . . . to bring People to run needless and unusual hazards."[24] Defoe celebrated the era's projecting spirit while warning readers that the proposal could serve as an edifice for deceit. His entrepreneurial career and reflective writings exemplify England's continuing ambivalence toward schemes and their claim on the public imagination.

By the time Defoe died in 1731 projection had become such an obvious, even inescapable approach to forging the future from at-hand resources that there was no longer any need to talk of a "Projecting Age." The first decades of the eighteenth century saw projects graduate from a volatile release of ambition in response to particular historical circumstances to a reconciliation of resources and possibility that would be routinized and then taken for granted within the writing of governmental ministers, legislators, merchants, scientists, authors, and ordinary subjects. In Georgian Britain, even those like Jonathan Swift who sought to curb the freewheeling energies of improvement schemes often imagined their interventions as projects of a sort. The audacious enterprise that Defoe declared the singular theme of his era in 1697 had, by the time of his death, become a pervading, usually unremarked context for comparing present-day Britain to what it could become.

Whether worthwhile or foolhardy, fiscal or technological, crown-backed or republican, what all these early modern British projects shared was a written plan for action and the possibility of action itself. What I mean by "written plan" is a document, like *Designe for Plentie*, proposing that certain people do certain things. "Action" signifies the happening of those things through "physical movements" that "extend mind into world," as Jonathan Kramnick defines it.[25] What distinguishes projected action from other forms of action is that it belongs to the future, and thus does not necessarily need to leave behind evidence of its planning. *Designe for Plentie* prescribes acts of legislation, labor, surveillance, and prosecution, packaged together as a bill of instructions for eliminating famine. But universal orcharding never took hold. No fruit bill came before the Commons. No woodward ever claimed parochial office. All that remains of the defunct *Designe* is its proposal, an embryonic plan that failed to become anything other than words and desire.

This book claims that even unenacted words mattered to the extent they tested new ways of being a society. Projects could "benefit the world even by their miscarriages," according to Samuel Johnson, who praised authors for charting original courses in commerce and statecraft no matter how feasible.[26] Projection records a thinking through of possibility, even when those possibilities remain ultimately shut. In this vein, it shares with works of early modern natural philosophy a tendency to use hypothetical events and imaginary settings to report on reality. Amos Funkenstein has shown that despite their commitment to empirical witnessing, practitioners of the new science employed counterfactual conditionals to "explain nature even when they do not describe it."[27] A conclusive demonstration of inertia, for example, would require a frictionless, obstruction-free universe, an "unobservable if not downright counterfactual setting."[28] To circumvent the physical limitations of reality, natural philosophers developed imaginary experiments as a "tool for the rational construction of the world," or as Elizabeth Spiller puts it, they made "fictions function as practices for the production of knowledge."[29]

Designe for Plentie tests its food supply scheme in the laboratory of an idealized future, wherein the shining virtues of parochial stewardship and Christian charity illuminate the need for cooperative planning. It creates a fictional world in order to adjust its readers' "imaging and understanding of reality," and thereby rally them to political action.[30] Similar to utopia—another rhetorical mode that presents "fictional alternatives" to the actual world—*Designe*'s horticultural vision activates a reform agenda that seeks to "transcend the merely feasible."[31] Imaginative proposals functioned as fictions insofar as they prescribed unreal phenomena through an artifice of rhetorical verisimilitude. It is no coincidence that Defoe's "Age of Projects" shared the late seventeenth and early eighteenth century with what Catherine Gallagher calls the "rise of fictionality," wherein a set of "believable stories that did not solicit belief" found conceptual stability and nonfactual credibility in the novel.[32] At first glance, projection's solicitation of trust seems to cross the novel's program of training readers in "an attitude of disbelief" through its depiction of "gullibility, innocence deceived, rash promises extracted, and impetuous emotional and financial investments."[33] But Gallagher shows how this interrogation of faith cultivates in readers a sense of "cognitive provisionality," training them to take part in speculative activity in an age when "no enterprise could prosper without some degree of imaginative play."[34] Both novels and project writing invited readers to explore hypothetical worlds for immediate pleasure and the promise of moral or monetary gain.

But projection was distinct from counterfactual science, utopia, and novelistic world making in that it endeavored not just to describe reality or modify behavior, but to make real the precise vision it advanced. Where literary genres serve to "mediate and explain intractable problems," in Michael McKeon's famous phrase, the project purports to solve them, or at least to explain away that which makes a given dilemma seem insurmountable.[35] *Designe for Plentie* makes the future constructible through human action precisely by framing itself as stirring prophesy and an implementable plan. In claiming that "such a *Project* also it is," the author instructs readers not to dismiss his pamphlet as mere description of what is and could be, but rather to create the very future its language portends.

This book examines the workings of such imperative enterprise and asks how, in the hands of early modern British readers, its former potential for action sometimes materialized, more frequently lapsed, and was usually forgotten. *Wreckage of Intentions* reads old proposals word for word to investigate the generation of futures that seldom got to exist. My study of visionary schemes and schemers uncovers the strategies of rhetorical persuasion, publication, and embodied action that made projection a unique and controversial cultural practice during the seventeenth and eighteenth centuries. Approaching projects through the language, landscapes, data, and personas that they left behind reveals how writers sought to make proposed endeavor seem plausible in the context of the future, and how such argumentation was (and remains) vital to the functions of statecraft, commerce, science, religion, and literature.

At stake in the study of projection is an understanding of how eighteenth-century authors applied their faculties of imagination to achieve finite goals. The functional quality of their writing—their subordination of rhetorical creation to material objectives—may at first appear to discount projection's literary and intellectual value. Jason Pearl traces a critical preference for escapist utopias over "timidly incremental or naively grandiose" projects on the grounds that the former seem like a more transcendent literary achievement.[36] Against this tacit consensus, I find mere "blueprints" to offer an unusually resourceful form of invention refined by the demands of enlisting investors, lobbying politicians, and selling goods—argumentative burdens that weighed less heavily on utopia. If projects seem incremental or naive to us, I argue it is because we are consuming them long past their expiration date. Old proposals confront problems that sometimes no longer exist with solutions that today can seem neither necessary nor desirable. Bound to the expectations of their present, projects often do little to accommodate us belated readers, struggling to grasp the world they sought to remake.

But it is through this disorienting anachronism that projection offers a unique entry point to history. By interpolating present-day readers as residents of early modernity, the proposal invites us to believe in a certain idea of the future that is by now historical (or, more often, counterfactual history). The expired scheme asks us to *not* know what is to come—to "play the stranger" to a world of enterprise whose fate we already know.[37] Rekindling the eighteenth-century projector's long-extinguished imaginary therefore requires a recalibration of the interpretive practices that we normally bring to bear on this period. Given that the archives of projection generated so much obvious failure, it would be no hard task to pick apart their contents, ridicule their assumptions, disprove their expectations, trace their Whiggism, and unmask their profit motives. In short, I could bring to bear the full forces of ideology critique to uncover projection's submerged commitments and presumptions of mastery. And when it is illuminating, I do just this. But more often, what this book attempts is not the critique of projects, but rather the revival of their former possibility by reimagining what once was dreamt as a sign of that culture's understanding of itself and its capacity to change. Mine is a hermeneutics of salvage that gathers historical evidence in order to reanimate old enterprise. What this resuscitation contributes to eighteenth-century studies and culture studies more broadly is a demonstration of how to think with the past's inadvertent posterity in the moment it tried to build an unknowable here-to-come that we are used to viewing through hindsight.

The specific past futures that I study originated between 1660 and 1730, a period when "project" retained its old associations with Caroline monopolists and parliamentary state building while amassing new connotations derived from discourses of science, finance, exploration, and technology. I argue that it was during these decades that projects became ubiquitous, assuming a foundational role in the making of Anglophone culture that they did not previously possess or have since relinquished. It was after the Restoration that projection engendered an adequately broad and self-reflexive discourse for Defoe to declare it the spirit of his age. By the 1720s, projects came to seem less like a notorious invention than an unavoidable practice and unquestioned social fixture. While authors continued to debate the value of particular schemes, they were less prone to attacking the project itself as a vehicle for ambition.[38] Defoe's "Age of Projects" never really ended, though we have grown oblivious to its experience over the last three centuries. This book scrapes away the sediment of familiarity to remember the project as an eighteenth-century inheritance we use and inhabit daily.

Projects as Literature

My investigation of projects employs methods of literary inquiry, in particular close reading, genre criticism, book history, performance studies, and historicist analysis. Project writing belongs to the domain of rhetorical and literary criticism, I argue, because it attempts to make worlds out of words, words with the potential to remake the actual world. Borrowing the terms of structural linguistics, we can understand projecting as an act of signification in search of a referent. Until the moment that action is conjured out of language, when a proposal either becomes fact or burns out the fuel of its hopes, the project resides neither in nor outside of the material reality it would re-create. Bruno Latour equates this limbo stage with fiction in *Aramis*, a postmortem investigation of a twentieth-century project to build an automated transit system in Paris. "A technological project is a fiction," he explains, "since at the outset it does not exist, and there is no way it can exist yet because it is in the project phase."[39] Project for Latour is a mode of expression as well as the "phase" that Aramis inhabited when it hung between implementation and its ultimate scuttling.

As a discipline that knows its way around fiction, literary studies is well suited to grasp the imaginary ontology of projects that existed in made-up stories, fleeting fabrications, and predictions later proven false. Scholars of literature are also trained to recognize how arguments, like those made by projectors, could be cunning and self-aware. Though few of the proposals I have read display belletristic mastery, many employ conceits, modes of

emplotment, and perspectival shifts that we have come to associate with poems, novels, and drama. Even some of the period's most prosaic pitches for
land banking and clover cultivation recycled passages from Virgil and staged
dialogues between made-up discussants. They fawned over patrons in dripping
panegyric and burst with dedicatory puff made of heroic couplets. Although
most projects never became pleasing aesthetic objects, many at least sought to
gratify the tastes of culturally literate readers.

The formal challenge of making unreal things seem real, or at least realizable, burdened project proposals with two incongruous missions: to deliver a
believable report of practical ideas and to provoke readers with revelation. Proposals likened themselves to established enterprise at the same time they strove
to appear fresh, even altogether newfangled. On the one hand, projects could
not be "bright ideas appearing out of the blue" as Joan Thirsk observes, but
instead "clustered in places where facilities already existed to give the enterprise
a promising start."[40] In this vein, Defoe presented a project to renovate England's deteriorating highway system as an example of what Maximillian Novak
calls the "rediscoveries of ancient devices."[41] Defoe summons memories of Britain's Roman colonizers, excellent road makers who built a durable network of
stone causeways across the island, to shame officials into renovating the kingdom's rutted and mire-prone dirt tracks. His plan entailed the reclamation of a
neglected legacy rather than a dauntless adventure in new public works.

On the other hand, projects had to offer an unthought-of solution to
persistent trouble. They needed to break with tradition to position themselves
as unique interventions—as writing that outsmarted a problem's existing proposal literature. Like the eighteenth-century prose form that came to exemplify
novelty, so much so that it derived its name from that word, project writing
sought to be "critical, anti-traditional, and innovating."[42] These are the words
of Ian Watt, who endows the novel with narrative procedures that conveyed
"truth to individual experience," an individual "free from the body of past assumptions and traditional beliefs."[43] But unlike novels, which recorded past
events, it was a view of the future that project proposals tried to make realistic.
In pursuit of what we might call future realism, the projector surfaces inherited
assumptions about society and its management. This exfoliation becomes credible through its ability to seem like disinterested testimony. The fictional qualities of proposals authorized projectors to guide readers through future
prospects by inscribing such hypothetical events within "some 'reality' that is
cut off from the actual historical continuum."[44]

Project writing uses distinct rhetorical conventions for visualizing the future as the direct result of present action. In promoting an as-yet unrealized vision, the proposal *Designe for Plentie* equates civic virtue with delight in nature, likens stewardship to statecraft, and even suggests that orcharding will play a consequential role in man's redemption as it did in his fall. These devices help the author bridge the temporal and modal chasm between a forthcoming paradise of fruit and the moment of postbellum worry in which it was conceived. The challenge of suturing an indicative present to a subjunctive future forced projectors to become nimble rhetoricians. *A Designe for Plentie* warrants close reading not just for its provocative recommendations, but for its use of language to create belief.

Projection also invites literary analysis because so much of its historical evidence is contained within writing we understand as "Literature" with a capital "L"—poems, plays, novels, and songs. Projectors' representations of the future engrossed a variety of authors in the late 1600s and early 1700s, whose creations usually illuminated the fissures between the conception and realization of schemes. Jane Barker's Galesia declares in response to the sudden death of her suitor, Brafort, "human projects are meer Vapours, carry'd about with every Blast of cross Accidents."[45] Milton's Beelzebub upbraids the Congress of Pandemonium for "projecting peace and war" in book 2 of *Paradise Lost*.[46] Galesia characterizes courtship projects as the trifle of indifferent fate. Beelzebub perceives how oratorical projects license idleness, a want of the very action they endorse. The term, for Barker and Milton, implies a lacking response to grave ordeal.

Authors relished making a stock fool of the harebrained and vainglorious projector. Jonathan Swift's *Tale of a Tub* (1704) presents Lord Peter, a "projector and virtuoso" who schemes to purchase continents, cure splenetic worms, and establish "*a Whispering-Office*, for the Publick Good and Ease of all such as are Hypochondriacal, or troubled with the Cholick."[47] Two decades later, Swift's Gulliver would visit the Academy of Projectors, where he witnessed experimenters scheming to extract sunlight from cucumbers, weave garments from cobwebs, and transform excrement into food.[48] Gulliver's experiences at Lagado comport with Alexander Pope's description of an even more ludicrous institution, the court of Dullness in *The Dunciad*, overrun by "wild enthusiasts, projectors, politicians, inamoratos, castle-builders, chemists, and poets."[49] That Pope places projectors in the company of poets within a poem draws attention to the fixation of both figures on illusory outcomes and writing's potential complicity in the denial of reality.

Projectors routinely paraded across the seventeenth-century stage in comedies and masques either as self-deluding dimwits or calculating villains. The chief antagonist of Ben Jonson's *The Devil Is an Ass* (first performed in 1616) is Meercraft, a projector who plies his victims with schemes to manufacture leather gloves from dog skin, distill wine from raisins, and drain the Great Fen. Meercraft's name puns on his prospective activities ("mere" in the British sense of "lake," and thus also "lake craft") and on his embodiment of empty artifice ("merely craft"). The protagonist of Richard Brome's *The Court Beggar* (1653) is an aspiring projector, Andrew Mendicant, who invests in schemes to monopolize peruke sales, tax sartorial accessories, and construct a "floating Theatre" out of Thames barges.[50] John Wilson's 1665 play *The Projectors* targets the Royal Society for defrauding its patrons with unworkable experiments. Wilson's play features a "projecting knight," Sir Gudgeon Credulous, and a diabolical schemer, Jocose, who seduces him with the promise of fictitious whirligigs to drain the sea, devices to "stop up the Rivers," and a "*Horse-Wind-Water-Mill.*"[51]

In eighteenth-century novels, an itch for projects could also afflict more complex literary personas: not projector caricatures, but rounded protagonists who also happened to project. Defoe's Robinson Crusoe reflects that while managing a plantation in Brazil, "my head began to be Full of Projects and Undertakings beyond my reach; such as are indeed often the Ruine of the best heads in Business."[52] Crusoe subsequently abandons his tobacco fields to sail for Guinea, where he has planned to buy slaves and increase his estate. This luckless journey ends in shipwreck on an island off Trinidad, where Robinson embarks on new "Projects and Designs" of survival, including his ultimate "Project of a Voyage to the Main."[53] Projects for Crusoe epitomize both the dangers of overreaching one's station and the virtues of self-reliance in the face of danger. His adventures reflect Defoe's ambivalence toward projects, which he concluded were as likely to bring about "publick Advantage" as "needless and unusual hazards."[54]

Samuel Richardson took a darker view of projection in novels that punish those who scheme to shape the conditions of their being. Pamela Andrews conjures "designs," "stratagems," "enterprises," "plots," "contrivances," and "projects" to escape Mr. B's advances, which she terms "wicked Projects for my Ruin."[55] She calls her plan to flee B's Lincolnshire estate by faking suicide and scaling the garden wall a "projected Contrivance."[56] Like Crusoe, Pamela conspires against a "ruin" that is the result of projects, not her own, but rather B's lustful designs. Unlike Defoe, Richardson's didactic plot forecloses on intended action: Robinson eventually reaches the mainland and returns to Europe—if not in the way he originally envisioned—but the bolting Pamela retreats when confronted by two grazing cows she mistakes for possessed bulls. Pamela struggles to escape entrapment; she attempts but cannot effect her liberation from external forces. In a tragic case of captivity, Clarissa Harlowe laments her subjugation to the plans of her family and suitors when she begs "that I may not be sacrificed to projects, and remote contingencies," but she succumbs to Lovelace, who exclaims that "success in projects, is every thing."[57] One person's scheme supplies another's contingency according to Richardson, who makes "project" encompass both acts of heinous privilege and the struggle to withstand them.[58]

Defoe and Richardson tested the efficacy and wisdom of projects. Other literary authors conceived of their compositions *as* projects, acknowledging their participation in the speculative economies that resembled those they mocked. Jonson's *The Devil Is an Ass* appears to condemn project-crazed Jacobean court culture when it renders Meercraft a contemptible villain. But then, in the epilogue, Jonson refers to his play as "a Project of mine owne," framing his dramatic authorship as its own enterprise of public entertainment, social reform, and profit potential.[59] Of Milton's *Paradise Lost*, Andrew Marvell reflected, "I liked his project, the success did fear."[60] David Hume chastises "the vulgar, quacks and projectors" for their "magnificent pretensions" but also touts the virtues of pride for giving "us a confidence and assurance in all our projects and enterprizes."[61] These "projects and enterprizes" likely included *A Treatise of Human Nature* itself, which Hume subtitled "an attempt to introduce the experimental method of reasoning into moral subjects."[62]

Projects in the 1600 and 1700s were both a popular theme in writing and a metaphor for understanding authorship as its own enterprise for accruing fame and righting an imperfect society. But overwhelmingly, literature from this period lends the impression that projects held, in Novak's words, "a distinctly unsavoury connotation, being associated with unscrupulous schemes for getting money."[63] Therefore, it is crucial to distinguish between critical depictions of projection and actual projects under proposal or in progress. Lagado's inmates and Lord Peter should not stand in for the self-reflexivity and sophistication of actual projectors, the subtlety of their rhetoric, the diversity of their addressees, and their understanding of the world as unreaped potential. Canonical literature has a tendency to flatten cultures of projection, rendering their authors transparently self-interested if not altogether criminal. In order to historicize rather than uncritically inherit these assumptions, my study keeps projects—proposals and the actions they incited—at the center. It was the temerity of visions like *Designe for Plentie*'s, I argue, that made projection such a controversial idea in early modern Britain, and an enduring basis for public debate and literary invention.

Projects Against History

The word "project" marks a historical attempt at becoming, an arrival of potential distinct from the stage at which an ambition ultimately succeeds or fails. To see *Designe* as a project is to return to the moment of its conception, when no one could know for sure what "universal plantation" might do to English soil and society. By accepting the author's premise that "such a *Project* it is," we recognize how this proposal imagined itself as a viable course of action at the moment it circulated. Approaching projects like *Designe for Plentie* today not as retrospective dead ends (things that did not happen) but rather as once-live opportunities (things that could have happened) compels us to share this uncertainty ourselves by screening what Richard Scholar calls "the hindsight that turns signs of a future story into the origins of the future that is *our* present."[64] In the case of *Designe*, escaping the trap of anachronism means considering fruit fiats as a conceivable element of the future, even if that future is now past, and we know it bore no fruit.

When read in light of their former potential, old proposals reveal a past in process. These writings can vitalize our conception of history by showing the impact of undertakings that were intended but unachieved. Even fantastical schemes for draining the Irish Channel and raising silk worms in Middlesex challenge what Michael Andrew Bernstein calls the "triumphalist, unidirectional view of history."[65] Such teleological perspectives underwrite not only much-questioned "Whig" narratives positing constitutional monarchy as the zenith of British civilization, but also the tendency of eighteenth-century scholars to find in this period the birth and rise of empire, capitalism, the novel, the self, the public sphere, the nation, and enlightenment. It is not my aim to contest claims of origin and upsurge, but to suggest that their preponderance implicates our desire to make the past a history of modernity—to find prefigurations of our ourselves and our experiences in the 1600s and 1700s. This pursuit founders on projection and the many thousands of schemes that failed to produce recognizably modern institutions and practices. While the proposals I examine invariably aspire to progressive ideals (to rise, discover, enlighten), their history is riddled with commercial busts, epistemological cul-de-sacs, and abandoned infrastructure. Projects simultaneously harbored the possibility of improvement and debris. They manifested forward-looking intention but also anticipated a form of wreckage incongruous with the positivist narratives we construct to explain this era and connect it to our own.

The archives of early modern projects reveal a society simultaneously making and unmaking itself through the ongoing generation of chancy schemes. *Wreckage of Intentions* suggests that this (un)making has a rhetorical form and material history. Failed enterprises encapsulate what Reinhart Koselleck calls "since-superseded future," a nonexistent temporality that can nonetheless ventilate a past thick with multiple possibilities, including unenacted plans that challenge progressive accounts of human development.[66] Projects instance since-superseded futurity, indeed constitute one of this imaginary ontology's most observable units. Old projects reframe the past as an ongoing "present" brimming with former potential. Inhabiting this past is, according to Michael Bernstein, "not merely to reject historical inevitability as a theoretical model. Far more important, it means learning to value the contingencies and multiple paths leading from each concrete moment of lived experience, and recognizing the importance of those moments not for their place in an already determined larger pattern but as significant in their own right."[67] Bernstein and Gary Saul Morson use the term *sideshadowing* to refer to interpretive modes that admit not just "actualities and impossibilities," but also "a *middle realm* of real possibilities that could have happened even if they did not."[68] This "middle realm," I suggest, is identical to Latour's "project phase," a duration when an aspect of the future can be thought but not yet experienced. *Wreckage of Intentions* surveys some of seventeenth- and eighteenth-century Britain's paths untaken or not fully taken. It traces what Herbert Butterfield, archcensor of teleologies, calls the "crooked and perverse . . . ways of progress," while rejecting the assumption that progress need always be found (let alone in linear form).[69] In dwelling on what Morson calls the "presentness of the past," I propose the project's evocation of past presentness as a means of unstreamlining the histories we inherit and make.[70] Old plans enable us to recover history as a scatter plot of lived experiences and to appreciate how each unconstellated moment implied futures that we can recollect and learn from today.

The Project Itself

The project was a popular vehicle for voicing public opinion and personal ambition in early modern Britain. Its writings fashioned distinctive rhetorics of persuasion that migrated into some of the era's most popular and canonical literature. Its proposals index a world of defunct possibility that shapes and shadows histories of the real. And yet, the project is hard to grasp as a distinct, history-bearing idea. The word can feel less like a salient topic than a mere topical container—the context for discourse rather than its matter. Despite its breadth of usage and colorful history, "project" has failed to achieve the status of a cultural keyword or enduring episteme.[71] Why is this?

Part of what makes projects so hard to track is that action in potential is ephemeral. Many plans anticipated becoming real, but most remained fantasy. While *Designe for Plentie* imagined prodigiously, it failed to fashion anything beyond the matter of a pamphlet. Visiting its universally planted world today requires a willingness to veer off the course of empirical history to engage with the counterfactual world that the author imagined. *Designe*'s instructions form just one unenacted proposal among thousands of obsolete plans for poor relief, academies for women, vineyards in Cambridgeshire, fisheries in the North Sea, and a host of newly invented domestic goods. Other projects, such as those related to New World settlement, engendered more striking triumphs (and telling debris).[72] Still other schemes left nothing except for passing accounts of their expired potential.[73] When a select few ventures managed over time to establish institutions in fields like experimental science, banking, and postal delivery, their project status—their former ability to come or not come into being—might be forgotten, allowing once-uncertain endeavor to harden into the empirical fact of achievement.[74] Successful enterprise sometimes spawned imitation or ramified into subsidiary schemes whose authors reckoned new sets of contingencies by taking for granted the improvements that came before them. The project remains elusive today because it is always turning into something else—including the origin of further projecting—or into nothing at all.

Confounding matters is the fact that proposal authors, who were aware of projection's stigma, referred to their labors by "other termes of Art," like "invention," "improvement," and "public works."[75] In so doing, they facilitated the absorption of their ventures into the respectable status quo they set out to reform. For example, the early modern drainage of Anglian fenland began as a string of faltering projects before it eventually rendered a landscape so dry and full of farms as to conceal these past struggles and enfold itself into grand narratives of progress, reclamation, and modernization. Jeremy Bentham identifies as a project anything that ever made England "more prosperous than at the period immediately preceding it" and attacks Adam Smith for not acknowledging how England benefited from once-degraded schemes.[76]

Remembering old projects as "projects"—that is, as writing and potential action—therefore means assessing the cultural impact of a broad spectrum of enterprise, from ventures that flopped to ones so proficient in creating the conditions of the future, even our present, that it is hard to recall how these pursuits were ever under development or in doubt.

Another obstruction to seeing the "project itself" arises from presumptions built into our methods of humanities research. The bounding of scholarship by disciplinary field and time period tends to highlight the contents of specific schemes while taking for granted the availability of the project as a vehicle by which ideas for future action circulated and materialized. Today it is common to see "project" fused prepositionally to finite subject matter—husbandry projects of the Elizabethan era or forestry projects from the Restoration. But it is rare that someone confronts projection decoupled from its discrete implementations the way writers like Defoe, Bentham, and Smith did.[77] Aided by technologies of database keyword searching, we are well outfitted to latch onto taggable particulars of the past but can struggle to grasp structures of thought so massively pervading and deeply embedded within society that they go unnoticed, even unnamed. Projects, in their ubiquitous invisibility, both overwhelm and escape the digital tools and specialized modes of scholarly thought we expect to presence them.

The experience of calling for *Designe for Plentie* at a rare books library illustrates the dissonance between the self-conception of old proposals and modern efforts to classify them. *Designe*'s author refers to his work as a project (as well as a design and assay), but the English Short Title Catalogue files this pamphlet under the subject headings "Fruit trees—England—Early works to 1800" and "Food supply—England—Early works to 1800." These textual strings indeed touch on the central concerns of this Commonwealth orcharding pamphlet. But they also reflect habits of organization that overlook *Designe*'s self-understanding as an instrument of social reform. The proposal's will to remake the world through trees is absent from these tags. This means furthermore that the search string "project" will likely miss *Designe*, which includes the term only a few times in its body text, as well as many other projects that, for various reasons, did not identify as such.

Topic-driven bibliography captures a mass of empirical particulars but does not return the project as an indexable concept. The taxonomies that organize our archives have made it difficult to see that even projects with dissimilar contents can share the same formal features and self-conception. Like Watt's realism, which "does not reside in the kind of life it presents, but in the way it presents it," what made project writing recognizable was not its coverage of a particular subject, but rather its methods for locating future solutions to various needs.[78] The privileging of searchable content over pervasive forms has given projection a fragmentary critical literature in which "project" means different things to different readers. Projects were agro-industrial initiatives in the Tudor and Jacobean period for Joan Thirsk.[79] Novak associates them with the "age of Newton and Newtonism or the 'Augustan Age.' "[80] Christine Gerrard regards projectors as speculators who "floated shares in new enterprise on a stock market."[81] John Brewer confers the title on civilians who put forward unsolicited proposals for government reform and "usually received short shrift from the incumbent officials they sought to displace."[82]

These definitions treat projection as the offshoot of historical developments in agriculture, experimentation, finance, and court patronage. Taken alone, none can show how "project" performed multiple services for speakers ranging from Renaissance courtiers and Commonwealth sequestrators to Restoration experimenters and Hanoverian bureaucrats—to anyone who wanted to categorize and shape perception of these figures. To deny the project's own historical subjecthood hazards underestimating what one Caroline writer called the "protean" character of the projector, who disguised himself as "a decaied Merchant, a broken Citizen, a silent Minister, afore-judgd Atturney, a busy Solicitor, a cropeard Informer, a pickthank Pettifogger, or a nimble pated Northern Tick."[83] *Wreckage of Intentions* seeks to recover the wide range of personas and pursuits that belonged to the early modern word "project" by connecting ideas of enterprise scattered across scholarly fields ranging from the history of science and technology to theories of state formation to studies of Restoration theatrical satire. Retrieving projects beyond their idiosyncratic deployments entails scanning the horizons of seventeenth- and eighteenth-century print culture for the traces of old enterprise, and then scrutinizing those traces. Methodologically, I alternate between what Brad Pasanek calls the desultory reading of "page images and passages indexed and made available in large electronic text collections," and minute examination of how particular proposals and their critiques solicited readers.[84] This negotiation of reading up close and at a distance, of individual works in the context of many, can begin to draw the project out of history and restore the singularity it possessed therein.

A final impediment to seeing the project as a distinct history-bearing concept—as well as a stimulus to do so—is the difficulty of establishing critical distance from a subject that is inescapably central to modern society. Project terminology endures to ubiquity today in the form of client projects, art projects, book projects, housing projects, infrastructural superprojects, and the projects of self-fashioning dramatized in television series like *The Mindy Project* and *Project Runway*. The project has become so fundamental to modern ways of life that it has become ungraspably abstract, proliferating almost imperceptibly within entrepreneurial rhetorics and managerial modes of thought, as well as philosophical discourses ranging from Heideggerian ontology and Freudian psychoanalysis to Sartrean existentialism and Marxist definitions of value.[85] The astonishing versatility of projects is neatly demonstrated by Howard Eiland and Kevin McLaughlin, translators of Walter Benjamin's *Passagenwerk*, who assembled Benjamin's unfinished reflections under the title—among countless options for English renderings—*Arcades Project*. This usage appears to signify the work's incompletion, perhaps even its status as a "blueprint for an unimaginably massive and labyrinthine architecture."[86] Benjamin appears to encourage this conception of *Passagenwerk* by imagining within it a dream city comprising "building plans, street layouts, park projects, and street-name systems that were never developed."[87] "Project" signifies both futuristic planning related to the growth of Paris into a nineteenth-century capital, as well as a program for redeeming past opportunity scattered within the "rags" and "refuse" of history.[88] Like my own project of projects, Benjamin's reflective collage culls the debris of old possibility for cultural insight—in his case, for evidence of how commerce, technology, and urban development created the conditions for modern bourgeois experience.

Projection's idiom has proven so resilient that it threatens to impede investigation by conflating the object of study with the instruments of its analysis.[89] In this vein, Georges Bataille grudgingly conceded that projection had become an insuperable employment of modern philosophers when he described his *Inner Experience* as a "projet contre projet," a manifesto for "existence without delay" that ironically (but inevitably) took form as a book project.[90] Given this problem of immersion, a theoretical goal of this book is to establish the project as an investigable form. In looking back to seventeenth- and eighteenth-century Britain, I seek to dislodge an aspect of present experience so given we hardly notice it.

The overall goal of *my* project is to restore the remarkable early modern life of an idea today mired in anodyne ubiquity. The hollowness of modern projects, their signification of everything and thus nothing, is the result of gradual naturalization. The first step toward representing projects as a touchstone cultural concept is to return them to the categories of thought and expression in which they existed for authors of the seventeenth and eighteenth centuries. We should remember that the word "project," as noun and verb, engendered a distinctive kind of writing in the 1600s and 1700s, as well as a form of print and mode of performance: text, the matter containing it, and embodied attempts to realize its vision.

In this spirit, my chapters confront the project's conceptual slipperiness by dividing the idea into concrete stages: the articulation, circulation, undertaking, and reception of ideas for new enterprise. Project authors composed persuasive arguments to render their schemes plausible and attractive. They worked alongside stationers to disseminate new proposals through print. They enacted written designs through performances known as undertakings. Finally, these attempts at reforming society stimulated public response. The idea of projects in seventeenth- and eighteenth-century Britain encompassed acts of writing, print, and performance. Therefore, my approach combines techniques of rhetorical analysis, book history, performance theory, and genre criticism to illuminate the multifaceted phenomenon of projection, from some of the era's most ephemeral schemes to a few of its most enduring.

Chapter 1 shows how projects began as words. It identifies the rhetorical strategies that enabled Andrew Yarranton's 1677 pamphlet *England's Improvement by Sea and Land* to foresee the nation's perfection through the establishment of a land registry, the dredging of canals, and the building of textile mills. This work employs several signature conventions of projection, including the comparison of a troubled present with better futures, the reconciliation of profit motives with the public good, and the representation of the Dutch Republic as a menacing threat and economic model. It is Yarranton's occupation and evacuation of different conceits that makes his tract a striking example of how authors justified the work of reforming society. As a former captain in the New Model Army and suspected Presbyterian conspirator, Yarranton used projects to legitimate himself as a moderate reformer fit to voice an Anglican kingdom's future interest. Close reading of *England's Improvement* reveals how an especially resourceful projector manipulated language to solicit readerly belief in his ideas and talents.

Chapter 2 argues that print played a crucial role as an enabling medium of projection. It investigates a series of stationery artifacts generated by Aaron Hill's star-crossed attempt to manufacture and market beech seed oil in Georgian England. The beech oil venture rose to prominence and then disintegrated between 1714 and 1716, one of many entrepreneurial busts in an era renowned for Agricultural Revolution. Hill's failed enterprise left a paper trail that included patent petitions, investment tracts, newspaper advertisements, and Tory panegyric. This study in project print culture shows how the material requirements of different documents shaped the experience of projects for authors, readers, and potential participants. In so doing, it intervenes in modern academic debates over the role of mediation in historicist scholarship by asking how nonaction governs the materiality of its proposal and the conditions under which it can be read today. While issues of publication concerned all aspirant industrialists of the early 1700s, beech oil makes a particularly intriguing case study because so many of its founding documents survive, a low attrition due to Hill's reputation as a prominent poet and playwright.

Recognizing that successful projects eventually needed to become more than paper and ink, my third chapter builds on the insights of performance theory to show how new enterprise was enacted through a process called "undertaking." This study of projected action concentrates on efforts to drain eastern England's Great Fen during the middle seventeenth century. Approaching this land improvement enterprise through evidence of its once-embodied labors enables us to ask what can be known about projects once they make the leap from words in pamphlets to bodies toiling on land. This analysis of enactment offers an extended view of the final stages of a project from the vantage not only of its architects, financiers, and victims, but its laborers. The view from the ground—as opposed to the page—reveals how the performance of new enterprise could never follow the straightforward line that its proposal drew.

My final two chapters show how the reception of new enterprise spurred the innovation of eighteenth-century literary forms. Chapter 4 argues that British georgic, a popular mode of poetry that celebrated agricultural tasks like hop picking and sheep shearing, derives its tendency to aestheticize rural ways of life not only from Virgil, as scholars have assumed, but also from seventeenth-century husbandry manuals that taught readers how to undertake improvement projects within the ambit of their own property. I demonstrate that agricultural project proposals, typically undervalued as prosaic and evidentiary, presaged georgic's survey of a virtuous English heartland to anchor illustrations of domestic prosperity and imperial dominance.

My final chapter argues that projectors played a formative role in the development of prose satire, a literary genre bearing its own commitments to social reform. It turns to the most famous scene of projection in eighteenth-century fiction: the Academy of Lagado in Swift's *Gulliver's Travels* (1726). While scholars have long argued that the third book of *Gulliver's Travels* satirizes specific scientific, financial, and political projects from the seventeenth and eighteenth centuries, I contend that Swift's Academy of Projectors also critiques the linguistic strategies of projection itself. Drawing on an established literary tradition of antiproject plays and pamphlets, *Gulliver's Travels* pastiches popular conventions of proposal writing to demonstrate how even the most misguided ventures could be rendered attractive through the rhetorical dexterity of their authors. For Swift, a perennial opponent of English schemes for Irish improvement, project pastiche offered a mode of subversive mimicry revealing how the certitude of state planners derived from illusory device.

Wreckage of Intentions opens with a vision of plenty. It closes by asking what Daniel Defoe's *Tour thro' the Whole Island of Great Britain* can tell us about the afterlife of abandoned enterprise. In the *Tour*'s third letter, Defoe enters the New Forest of Hampshire and finds there a plot of land he had projected to populate with refugees from the Rhenish Palatine in 1709. This settlement scheme came to nothing, leaving the author to rehearse his once-hopeful plans fifteen years later while walking through the exact wilderness he petitioned to improve. Defoe invests "this place" with foreclosed potential, an example of where an unfinished venture left its imprint on a literary record but not actual land. In assessing the signifying nonmatter of this wilderness, I ask why unenacted projects became an enduring obsession for period writers and hypothesize how such anecdotes could spur cultural historiographies better equipped to accommodate the unreal. I contend that an obsession with projection's counterfactual histories is not something we impose on the long eighteenth century, but a possibility for salvage inscribed within its former blueprints.

Chapter 1

Improvement's Genre

Andrew Yarranton and the Rhetoric of Projection

> He begins with a Petition.
> —Thomas Brugis, *The Discovery of a Proiector*, 1641

Early modern projects began as words that formed proposals to enhance society and make money. These written attempts at imagining and inspiring better worlds exhibited an array of persuasive devices, narrative scaffolds, grammatical tics, and habits of diction that constituted the project as a distinctive genre. There was no textual formula for initiating a project. There were, however, certain rhetorical tendencies that characterized the conception of new enterprise. This chapter shows how projectors devised argumentative strategies to shape England's future during the reign of Charles II. It concentrates on the frustrations of one man, Andrew Yarranton, who proposed projects both to modernize a late Stuart society he thought backward, and to stabilize his own position within partisan conflicts stemming from the civil wars. This story begins with Yarranton's rousing call for national improvement. It ends with his murder in a bathtub. What this tragedy makes visible is an idea of how projection worked as a process of rhetorical persuasion. By identifying the linguistic patterns that made projects recognizable in the seventeenth century, this chapter lays the groundwork for later examinations of the print forms that carried proposals, the actions that realized them, and the responses they provoked.

When twenty of his majesty's ships entered Dover Roads on May 25, 1660, the naval spectacle marked the end of Charles Stuart's restless exile as well as Parliament's tumultuous experiments in republicanism. Monarchy had returned to Britain, and with it the Anglican Church, public theater, and regal court life. The two decades following "the coming over of the king" also saw epidemic plague and devastating fire.[1] England would wage two costly wars against the States-General of the Netherlands. The slave-trading Royal African Company languished in the face of Dutch competition, and the Royal Fishery, a state-financed attempt to control the North Sea herring trade, collapsed altogether. Charles II proved a popular and dexterous leader but was so cash-strapped that he struck a secret alliance, the Treaty of Dover, with France's Louis XIV in return for two million crowns. His brother, James, Duke of York, shocked the nation by converting to Roman Catholicism, inciting calls for his exclusion from the succession.

Despite these trials, royalists argued that the Stuart Restoration had ushered an unprecedented era of sectarian healing and commercial growth. John Dryden compared Charles to a morning star that shone through England's "sullen Intervall of Warre" to illuminate "time's Whiter series."[2] His *Annus Mirabilis* (1667) interprets English victory over the Dutch fleets at the Battle of Lowestoft and London's spirited response to the Great Fire as evidence that "now, a round of greater years begun."[3] Another royalist, Thomas Sprat, claimed that "since the Kings Return" Parliament had passed more acts for beautifying London, repairing highways, digging canals, and founding industry "than in divers Ages before."[4] Citing the "present prevailing *Genius* of the *English* nation," Sprat credits the king with organizing unprecedented civic efforts to recuperate a land supposedly left to waste during the Commonwealth and Protectorate eras.[5] Restoring monarchy, he suggests, had not merely returned England to an antebellum age but had elevated it to a new and better state.

Stirring pronouncements of rupture and return often compensated for the fact that the Restoration's most enthusiastic acolytes and celebrated achievements first gained momentum during the Interregnum. Dryden lauded England's rebirth after processing in Cromwell's funeral.[6] Sprat was the spokesman for a Royal Society that institutionalized models of knowledge production and correspondence outlined a decade earlier by Samuel Hartlib and his circle.[7] The 1660s and 1670s were not an age of revolution. Given the compromises required to bring Charles back from the Hague, the era was actually more conducive to what Paul Slack calls "gradual, piecemeal change, not necessarily determined by any overarching theory or ambition."[8] The ideas belonging to the word "improvement" held that England need not behead a king, dissolve a parliament, or invoke the imminence of end times to achieve progress.

Rather, it could better itself incrementally through reforms compatible with the broad political latitudes of the Stuart settlement.[9]

Forward-thinking and incremental, improvement often materialized through projects, finite ventures meant to put England's resources to better use. A project marked an attempt at improvement in the 1600s; indeed, it served as a popular vehicle by which the abstract ideals of social uplift could translate into concrete change. But in an era when improvement ideology was gaining widespread legitimacy as "a familiar item in English public discourse," projects bore the lingering stench of patent monopolists, quack doctors, chartered dilettantes, and courtier parasites from the Tudor and early Stuart eras.[10] Improvement required projectors to implement its progressive rhetoric through discrete investments of money, time, and labor. Projectors needed "improvement" as a slogan that could make reputable their schemes by affiliating them with Restoration England's universal desire for betterment.

One man who exemplified the tensions between the scandalizing ambition of projection and the respectable compromises of improvement was Andrew Yarranton. A native of Worcestershire, Yarranton applied his relentless energies to cutting canals, forging iron, making linens, and marketing clover as a fodder crop. He lobbied for England to establish a land registry, observed German tinplate manufacturing, and studied Dutch mercantile policy. For his innovations in industrial planning and finance, Yarranton has been credited as a pioneering navigations engineer, an early modern railroader, and even the inventor of political economy.[11] But when Charles Stuart stepped ashore at Dover Beach in 1660, Yarranton was also a veteran of Cromwell's army and former sequestrator of royalist land. In 1662 he would be arrested for disobeying his lord lieutenant and later was accused of plotting to overthrow the king. Like his contemporary projector-improver Carew Reynell, who fruitlessly pursued patronage appointments, Yarranton struggled to keep pace with his age and so went about imagining a future that would vindicate his beliefs and talents.

This future found fullest expression in Yarranton's *England's Improvement by Sea and Land* (1677), a 216-page pamphlet that claimed to "chal[k] out the Way" for England to secure and strengthen itself during an "unsteady Age."[12] Yarranton's tract indeed charts a new direction for English society through a series of projects, though the image of a chalk line belies the work's great length, complexity, and confusion. *England's Improvement* consists of prose paragraphs, dialogues, letters, legislation, maps, and diagrams. It addresses topics ranging from land banking and forestry to firefighting, factory management, grain storage, and naval strategy, sometimes breaking off discussion of one subject to circle back to another.[13] Yarranton's frenetic display of knowledge makes *England's Improvement* a mesmerizing but wooly case study in projection and improvement, a bricolage transformation of professional fluency into persuasive resource. *England's Improvement* was one proposal "amongst others" of the 1670s as Yarranton himself noted, but its length, digressiveness, and confessed incompletion both invite and embarrass systematic explanations of how project writing worked.[14]

Paul Mantoux calls *England's Improvement* a "curious book in which were jumbled together the observations, plans and dreams of [a] whole life with a host of new and daring ideas."[15] Sifting through this "jumble" of dreamscapes and self-promotion reveals two recurrent themes: Yarranton's desire to ingratiate himself to the Stuart government that once made him an outlaw, and his anticipation of a world of merchant power, central banking, and land capitalization that would ultimately divert power from the crown, eventually rendering its holder inconsequential to debates over the national economy. These contradictory ambitions—to participate in and outlast Restoration society—compelled Yarranton to develop a rhetoric of persuasion that could smooth over political difference, including his own vexation with the state. Project writing provided him with a set of argumentative conventions for framing futuristic desire as disinterested advice, and for envisioning an alternative world in which the way "chalkt out" is acknowledged as the only viable path for moving society forward.

By approaching Yarranton's schemes as acts of writing, this chapter challenges material-bound definitions of the term "project" coined by economic historians. Joan Thirsk's much-cited formulation equates "project" with a "practical scheme for exploiting material things."[16] While some projects proved capable of moving matter, many others were completely infeasible. Daniel Defoe considered the Tower of Babel the quintessential project, "too big to be manag'd, and therefore likely enough to come to nothing."[17] Projects often originated from nothing as well. That seventeenth-century improvers like Yarranton wrote at all underscores their inability to command "material things" through illocutionary power—projectors *proposed* enterprise because they lacked the land, money, and muscle to execute it themselves. Their schemes manifest the "wants of some ingenious persons" according to Carew Reynell, an improver and sinecure seeker who associated projecting with desire and privation in the context of his own frustrated career.[18] An anonymous author of the 1690s invited Londoners to "Reflect on the vast Number of Projectors in and about this City, how bare-bon'd they are, that is, how few of 'em are Rich?"[19] This image of scarcity attributes projects not to practical knowledge but to the hunger of threadbare visionaries.

Projection, as Reynell and Yarranton understood it, was an articulation of want: a voicing of ambition and inventory of deficits. It addressed those equipped to put plans into action (monarchs, parliaments, patrons, and readers in general), even if those addressees rarely moved to execute unsolicited schemes. Even well-received proposals sometimes stimulated nothing beyond the creation of more text. The speaker of the satirical ballad *The Nevv Projector; or, The Privileged Cheat* (1662) boasts of his "protection," a certificate granting him security from competing inventors and immunity from criminal charges.[20] Self-satisfied with his possession of this document, the projector shows no inclination to invent anything. Thomas Brugis likewise dismisses projection as the generation of "petitions" and "references" to "procure a *Patent*," writing empowered to legitimate writing.[21] Brugis and the balladeer reduce projects to their illusive textuality, a dissembling rhetoric whose point is to aggrandize the author while deferring action in the world.

England's Improvement was no mere piece of patent graft or stockjobbing. To the contrary, its words convey the complex experiences of an author who struggled to participate in Stuart culture while imaginatively reworking that society to accommodate his ambition. How *England's Improvement* conceives itself as improvement's instrument while defying projection's stigma is a question of language that we can answer only by examining the text itself. A close reading of Yarranton's proposal reveals a projector more deliberative and self-questioning than the feckless opportunist Brugis implicates. His persona, moreover, reflects a world of Restoration scheming governed by a broader range of motives and attitudes than antiproject satirists were typically willing to acknowledge. However, the preponderance of skeptical attacks on new enterprise can obscure this complexity, making it difficult to retrieve the actual projector from the scandal that swirled around his title: the historical actor seems always hidden behind literary caricature.

Indeed, for all the fanciful origin myths conferred on projectors, there have been few serious attempts to explain their existence in relation to actual events and institutions. Thomas Macaulay made one such attempt. His *History of England* (1848) dates the rise of projection to the years 1660–88, when the growth of commercial wealth outpaced the opening of investment opportunities in land, banks, and joint-stock companies. The projector, Macaulay concluded, was the "natural effect" of "redundant capital," someone who identified

conduits for money otherwise "hidden in secret drawers and behind wain-
scots."[22] Adam Smith also attributed projectors to financial imbalance. He
scorned them as the offspring of high interest rates, which discouraged "sober"
investment while inspiring rash ventures by "prodigals and projectors" willing
to borrow on usurious terms.[23] Smith cites Peruvian mines, national lotteries,
and John Law's Mississippi Company as conspicuously "unprosperous
projects."[24]

Writing of his own age (and of himself), Daniel Defoe identified the
quintessential projector as a merchant who pursued new sources of income
between 1688 and 1697, when the War of the Grand Alliance disrupted trade
with the Continent. He finds the projecting spirit strongest in those stymied
traders who "prompted by Necessity, rack their Wits for New Contrivances,
New Inventions, New Trades, Stocks, Projects, and any thing to retrieve the
desperate Credit of their Fortunes."[25] Defoe would subsequently broaden this
finite definition to include anyone who had ever planned, promoted, built,
invented, or reformed something for personal gain or society's advantage, beginning with Noah's ark. Defoe's "Age of Projects" referred both to the wartime
improvisations of late seventeenth-century merchants, and the recurrence of
industrious behavior throughout all human history.

Macaulay and Smith conceive of projectors as the mechanism and by-
product of economic forces. Defoe also circumscribes the agency of proposers
by stereotyping them either as heroic pioneers or victims of circumstance—
social roles rather than flesh-and-blood people. This chapter's concentration
on the career and writing of Andrew Yarranton works against the reduction of
projector to placeholder by foregrounding an actual human who brought
schemes to public notice. However, intensive focus on one figure begs the
question of how "projector" came to name a multiplicity of people who inaugurated a self-conscious age of enterprise. It would be impossible to formulate
a coherent category, "projector," that accommodates all of early modern England's entrepreneurs, pamphleteers, engineers, and experimenters. However,
comparing the biographical details of a subset of projectors, the improvement
propagandists of Yarranton's age, takes a step in that direction by delivering a
more realistic and fine-grained portrait than the one we have inherited from
critics and historians.

Perhaps most formative among these shared biographical details was the
fact that Yarranton's contemporaries lived through a rapid succession of disparate political regimes between the reign of Charles I and the Hanoverian Dy-
nasty. While some projectors, like Carew Reynell (1636–90), remained devout

royalists throughout their careers, others, like Yarranton (1619–84), trimmed their sails to prevailing political winds to ensure their proposals were heard. This was no easy task. The improver Josiah Child (1631–99) served as deputy treasurer of the Protectorate navy at Portsmouth but later lost the lucrative right to sell beer and victuals to the fleets because James Stuart suspected him of supporting Shaftesbury. Hugh Chamberlen (1664–1728), author of *Several Matters Relating to the Improvement of Trade* (1700), lost his post as physician to Charles II under suspicions of Whig loyalties (a misgiving he would validate by later joining Monmouth's Rebellion). The builder and insurance salesman Nicholas Barbon (1637–98) bore the infamous name of his father, Praisegod Barbon, the Millenarianist politician from whom Cromwell's "Barebones Parliament" took its title, but he showed few signs of a radical Puritan upbringing. Projectors of Yarranton's age sought to mitigate or capitalize on their pasts, a self-reckoning that often had the adverse effect of increasing their notoriety. Successful schemers needed to establish meaningful ties with ruling parties and monarchs without foreclosing opportunities for action under future governments.

Projectors hailed from the city and country, though most seem to have lived in southern England. Many enjoyed privileged upbringings, either as the sons of London merchants (Samuel Fortrey and John Bellers), or by inheriting rural estates (Reynell). Few seem to have been exceedingly rich or completely destitute, and therefore most showed some desire to make money. Projectors were seldom as penurious as their critics suggested, though a number, like Roger Coke and Daniel Defoe, faced the prospect of debtor's prison in the wake of failed ventures.[26] Several seventeenth-century improvers attended Oxford or Cambridge, many training to become physicians or lawyers. A few, such as Barbon and Richard Weston, were educated at Leiden and Utrecht and in Flanders, and like Yarranton, drew on their experiences abroad to propose improvements in England.

Yarranton would stress his involvement with the political and economic affairs of a realm he proposed to modernize. But he was a veritable outsider compared to other projectors who were elected to Parliament (Barbon, Mackworth, Child) and fellows to the Royal Society (John Houghton, Chamberlen). A small number of projectors were knighted, including Humphrey Mackworth, Hugh Chamberlen, and, to Defoe's lasting chagrin, the shipwreck explorer William Phips.[27]

A projector's proximity to power often shaped what (s)he sought through writing. Some proposed schemes in order to obtain governmental office, such as Reynell, who had designs on joining the Board of Trade, and Samuel

Fortrey, who succeeded in becoming Clerk of the Deliveries of the Ordnance seven years after his *England's Interest and Improvement* (1663) appeared. Others wrote pamphlets to advance business interests. Nicholas Barbon's advocacy of free trade and house construction would complement the insurance office he opened in 1680. Mackworth wrote an improvement tract, *England's Glory* (1694), before later organizing the joint-stock company Mineral Manufactures of Neath (1713). Other projectors insisted that they wrote out of a genuine interest in the public good, and there is often little evidence to refute these claims. What John Evelyn hoped to gain from his anti-air-pollution pamphlet *Fumifugium* (1661), or Moses Pitt sought to make from his prison reform treatise *The Cry of the Oppressed* (1691) is probably irreducible to profit and fame.

As a former republican official, for-hire engineer, and energetic pamphleteer, Andrew Yarranton personified all these motivations. His fraught career in projects epitomizes the difficulty of existing within a society while trying to change it. His *England's Improvement* was one proposal "amongst others" but foregrounded projection's universal need for authorial self-fashioning, whose terms and stakes we can grasp only by turning to Yarranton's own words.

Possessing Dutch Progress

The first word of Yarranton's title, *England's Improvement by Sea and Land* (Figure 1), designates England as either an object or agent of improvement. The possessive adjective "England's" implies that the kingdom can receive improvement, that its lands and people could be put to better use. The word alternatively endows England with the capacity to pursue improvement, to enhance itself through collective action. What England has, according to Yarranton, is a series of deficiencies and the power to remedy them. The pamphlet's textual content belongs to one author, "Andrew Yarranton, Gent."; but its enacted outcomes will become the entire nation's grammatical possession. Improvement denotes both a pursuit and a destination, a program for controlling the future and an attribute of the future itself. Yarranton forges consensus support for his plans by addressing England as a single, unified entity in the style of William Carter's *England's Interest Asserted* (1669), Samuel Fortrey's *England's Interest and Improvement* (1673), and Roger Coke's *England's Improvements* (1675). Like Yarranton's *England's Improvement*, these works pledge to salvage new utility from existing assets; their titles entitle England to unreaped benefits while imagining the nation as a "seamless whole."[28]

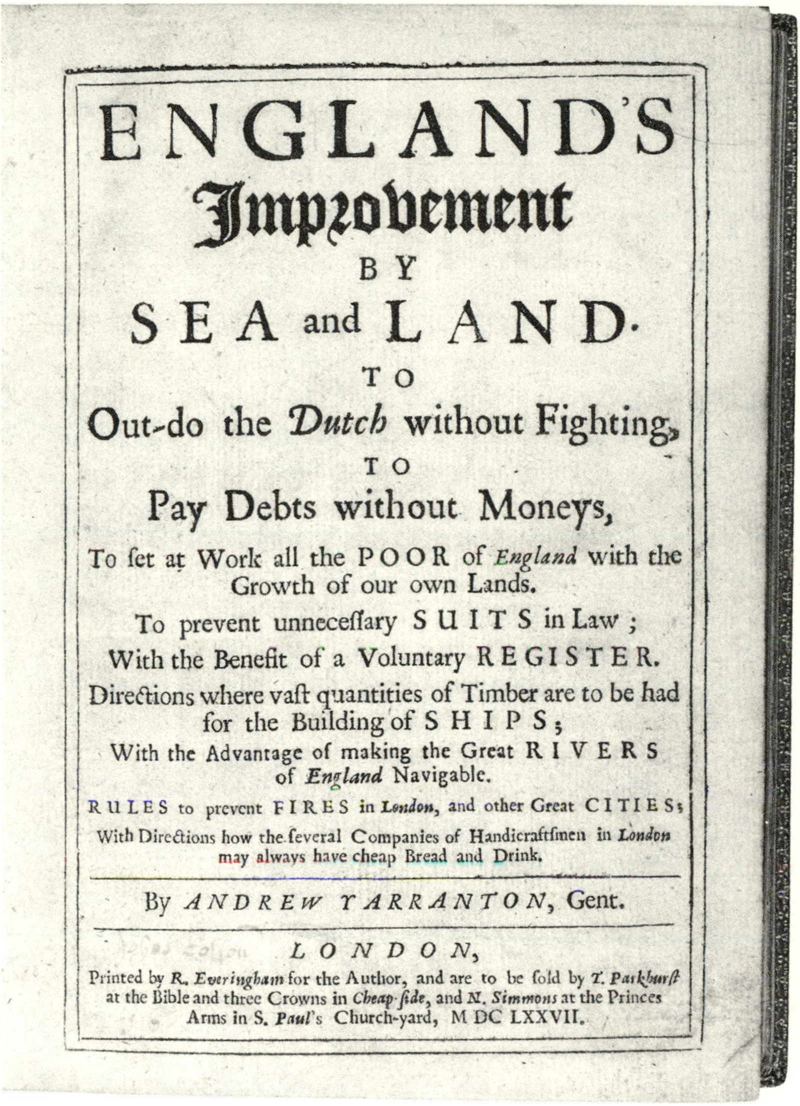

ENGLAND'S
𝕴𝖒𝖕𝖗𝖔𝖛𝖊𝖒𝖊𝖓𝖙
BY
SEA and LAND.
TO
Out-do the *Dutch* without Fighting,
TO
Pay Debts without Moneys,

To set at Work all the POOR of *England* with the
Growth of our own Lands.

To prevent unnecessary SUITS in Law ;
With the Benefit of a Voluntary REGISTER.

Directions where vast quantities of Timber are to be had
for the Building of SHIPS ;

With the Advantage of making the Great RIVERS
of *England* Navigable.

RULES to prevent FIRES in *London*, and other Great CITIES;

With Directions how the several Companies of Handicraftsmen in *London*
may always have cheap Bread and Drink.

By *ANDREW YARRANTON*, Gent.

LONDON,
Printed by R. *Everingham* for the Author, and are to be sold by *T. Parkhurst*
at the Bible and three Crowns in *Cheap-side*, and *N. Simmons* at the Princes
Arms in S. *Paul's* Church-yard, M DC LXXVII.

Figure 1. Title page of Andrew Yarranton's *England's Improvement by Sea and Land.*
RB 148563, Huntington Library, San Marino, California.

England's Improvement divides the proleptic possession of future value into discrete activities. "By Land," improvement entails harvesting timber to build ships, making shallow rivers navigable, fireproofing cities, employing poor subjects, and supplying London with "Bread and Drink." These measures would strengthen England "by Sea" by stimulating exports, relieving debt, and positioning the kingdom to surpass its Continental trade rival, the Dutch Republic, "without fighting." Yarranton introduces these measures through infinitive sentence fragments—to out-do, to pay, to set at work, to prevent—phrases that seem to insist on a course of action without assigning that action an agent. The paradoxical injunction "To Pay Debts without Moneys," for instance, arrests readers without specifying a payer or payee. Yarranton's ambiguity is deliberate. His title evokes outcomes without specifying means to lure readers into the pages of the pamphlet, where he describes at great length concrete solutions to the kingdom's most debilitating problems.

"People confess they are sick," observes Yarranton in a prefatory letter; "trade is in a Consumption, and the whole Nation languishes."[29] By portraying England as a victim of consumptive disease, *England's Improvement* proposes itself as a bill of treatments, and its author as caregiver to the tuberculin national body politic. England's lack of vitality stems from dysfunction at home and competition from abroad. First, Yarranton censures his readers for failing to take advantage of "our Climate, the Nature of our Soil, and the Constitution of Both our People and Government," arguing that temperate weather and mild rule oblige industry.[30] The kingdom's fortunate "our" implies an active "we" who must labor in gratitude for God's blessings. This sentiment echoes the rhetoric of contemporary improvers whose projects claimed to uncover the "means by which the fertility hidden by God in the soil could be unlocked."[31] "Divine providence" endowed England with "all in the most profitable advantages," according to Samuel Fortrey.[32] Samuel Coke set out to describe "the benefits which may arise to my native Country, from those Natural Endowments wherewith God has adorn'd it above any other."[33] "Great-Britain is acknowledged by all the world to be Queen of the Isles, and as capable to live within it self as any Nation," argued Reynell.[34] Therefore, he reasons, Britons should "add to it and give some advance, by our own Art and Industry."[35] Yarranton likewise portrays improvement as the distinctly English labor of realizing the "unparallel'd Advantages" of a providential birthright.[36]

The second impetus to improve loomed across the North Sea in the form of the Dutch Republic, a state that came to dominate global trade in the seventeenth century despite lacking England's prodigious geography. The enterprising Dutch, who built their compact republic on diked polder, fashioned fleets from Norse timber, and secured credit with astounding facility, stoked English envy and puzzlement. "*Holland* hath not much of its own store," noted Fortrey, and yet by "industrious diligence" furnish themselves with "whatsoever the world affords and they want."[37] How, asked an incredulous Nicholas Barbon, could such a "little tract of Ground" derive the "great Advantage and Profit that Trade brings to a Nation" at the same time that blessed England languished?[38] Fortrey and Barbon express astonishment at Holland's seeming ability to create "wealth out of nothing" by attracting "goods with the new power of quick sales, easy exchanges, and ready cash."[39]

By 1677, Anglo-Dutch rivalry had triggered three "bloody Wars," in Yarranton's words, draining conflicts that made English merchants "g[o] by the worst," while occasioning moments of national humiliation, like the "sad news" of the "Dutch burning our Ships at Chattam."[40] After "spending some time" studying the Dutch Republic's "Laws, Customs, publick Banks, Cut Rivers, Havens, Sands, Policies in Government and Trade," Yarranton arrives at the unrousing conclusion that England "could not beat the Dutch with fighting."[41] Holland's perceived invincibility was partially the result of marine topography: the shoal-lined Frisian archipelago blocked English fleets from pursuing Dutch ships. Where the Dutch Republic's shallow-bottomed fluyboats could navigate to port during sieges, English ships were forced to anchor in the channel, exposed to "all Storms and accidents that the seas and our Ships are lyable to."[42]

Even when the Commonwealth navy smashed the Netherlands during the first Anglo-Dutch War (1652–54) on the strength of superior fleets and a crippling blockade, the English victory proved short-lived. The resilient Dutch economy, supported by banks that issued low-interest loans and a land registry that enabled citizens to efficiently assess and collateralize their land, soon regained the upper hand. Rejecting military aggression as futile, even catastrophic, as demonstrated by Michiel de Ruyter's 1667 raid on the English fleets docked in the Medway, Yarranton plotted to transpose Anglo-Dutch conflict from an arena of war to one of trade, scheming ways for England to "out-do" a country that had enshrined commercial knowledge as a national virtue.

England's Improvement's major intervention was to understand the Dutch Republic not simply as a menacing threat, but as a model for economic reform. Yarranton attempts to demystify Dutch power so that England could emulate its practices and match its wealth, to "write by their Copies and do the great things they now do."[43] To this end, he criticizes those improvers who commit the "common mistake of the world" in attributing Holland's prosperity to vague notions of "a great cash in Bank," and thereby misidentify the particular mechanisms that made such accumulation possible. According to Yarranton, these devices included social institutions ("laws, customs, publick banks") and topographical features, both natural ("havens, sands") and man-made ("cut rivers"). With few natural advantages of its own, the Dutch Republic molded its land and culture to accommodate the circulation of goods and capital, from the financial infrastructure of banks to the public works of canals and harbors.[44]

Yarranton's report of Dutch innovation holds England accountable for its failure to achieve lasting prosperity, for not converting its tillage, timber forests, mineral deposits, and people into advantage "at Sea." Yarranton proposes "peeping abroad" to locate the means by which England could access the wealth lodged in its soil and subjects to become "great, beyond any Nation in the World."[45] The title's injunction to "To Out-do the *Dutch* without Fighting" begets a counterintuitive mandate for England to imitate its rival and thereby capitalize on long-neglected natural assets. Holland provided Yarranton with a shining example of what England could become, a place where the futuristic projects he was proposing had already been profitably realized (often to England's detriment). *England's Improvement* would teach readers how to apply Dutch practices to "our own Climate and Constitution," and in so doing, to learn from foreign merchants and officials how to become better at being English.[46]

The Projector's Persona

No project could be more credible than was its projector. This is why writers like Andrew Yarranton took extraordinary measures to portray themselves as trustworthy handlers of land, labor, and money. Projectors often legitimated themselves by impugning rival schemers. Walter Blith lamented that pamphleteers with "pretences of great abilities" had brought a "scandall upon Ingenuity" in the Commonwealth era.[47] His *English Improver Improved* (1652) outlines several schemes for increasing the value of rural land, while vindicating ingenuity itself as a virtue despite its corruption by talentless braggarts. Self-legitimation would prove especially hard for Andrew Yarranton, whose career included a stint in the parliamentary army, a sinecure in the Protectorate, the oversight of several aborted river navigation projects in Worcestershire, and multiple arrests for treason after the Restoration. *England's Improvement* therefore excerpts select moments from Yarranton's checkered career to frame his Dutch-styled improvement program as an expression of "love to my Country."[48]

Yarranton concentrates these biographical details within four dedicatory letters that preface *England's Improvement* and an "account of my education," which comes at the end of the tract. He begins to establish a prudent and public-minded authorial persona in his letter addressed to Arthur Annesley, the Earl of Anglessey and Lord Privy Seal, and Thomas Player, Chamberlain of the City of London. That Yarranton chose two addressees for this letter reflects his desire to promote *England's Improvement* both in the court of Charles II and among the merchants of the City. He suggests that Annesley could "advocate for it to the Prince," while Player could procure the pamphlet "a favourable Reception among those honourable Gentlemen of the City, whose Wealth and Grandeur are the chief support of Trade, and consequently of England."[49]

This selection of emissaries showcases Yarranton's proximity to court and commercial power, as well as his mindfulness to the disparate interests of urban traders and royal courtiers. When the Text Acts (1661, 1673) made Anglican oaths compulsory for holding clerical appointments and public office, capable nonconformists assembled in the commercial world of London's ports and exchanges. Yarranton's own delegate to the "Gentlemen of the City," Thomas Player, held office under Cromwell and later became an outspoken Whig. The Anglo-Irish Annesley, by contrast, was a staunch Stuart loyalist and future Treasurer of the Navy. Yarranton entrusts *England's Improvement* to men who had taken opposite sides during the civil wars and would later become factional opponents. He models in letters an act of political compromise that serviced both sides of a debate in the hopes of offending no one.[50]

Projectors routinely tried to surmount (or hedge) partisan conflict during the seventeenth century, especially in periods when it was unclear who held what power. In 1652, the year before the Commonwealth became a Protectorate, Blith dedicated his *English Improver Improved* to Lord General Oliver Cromwell, nobles and gentry, the courts and universities, soldiers, husbandmen, and the "Cottager, Labourer, or, meanest Commoner." This panoply of dedicatees reflects the inscrutable political terrain of the early Commonwealth, and Blith's aversion to offending potential stakeholders. Blith's "English," like Yarranton's "England's," incorporates an array of figures to make its ideas sound like popular consensus among readers who might otherwise share no common political ground. In an example from the late Stuart era, John Evelyn dedicated his *Fumifugium* (1661) both to Charles II and the parliament that

restored him, perhaps uncertain which institution was better equipped to execute his project to cleanse the capital of air pollution. Demonstrating respect
for king and commons appeared to be a prerequisite for convincing either
entity to consider the proposal.

Yarranton's first dedicatory letter, to Annesley and Player, and his second,
to Thomas Hickman-Windsor, Baron Windsor and later the first Earl of Plym-
outh, place him in imagined dialogue with powerful political operatives who
were also titled elites. Printed at the front of *England's Improvement*, this correspondence was meant to impress readers with the author's epistolary connections. Projectors flaunted their attachments whenever possible by imagining
influential public figures as readers and patrons. For instance, Fortrey addressed *England's Interest and Improvement* to Charles II and bragged of his
intimacy with the monarch in his capacity as gentleman "of his Majesties most
Honourable Privy Chamber."[51] John Smith allied himself with experimental
science when he dedicated *England's Improvement Reviv'd* to William
Brouncker, president of the Royal Society.[52] Samuel Coke curried royalist favor
by devoting his *England's Improvements* (1675) to Prince Rupert of the Rhine.[53]

Yarranton's dedicatory epistles do more than drop names; they imply that
their author has established relationships with men capable of enacting his
proposals. Yarranton addresses Windsor because the baron had once employed
him as an engineer to render navigable a segment of the River Avon, an enterprise that supposedly delivered "general Advantage" to the public.[54] Yarranton
thanks Windsor for "the great Incouragement your Lordship hath been pleasure to afford me, in those indefatigable Pains you have taken in the Survey of
several Rivers" and uses the occasion of thanksgiving to boast of past accomplishment.[55] By addressing a satisfied patron, *England's Improvement* legiti-
mates itself as a trustworthy reform vehicle born of credentialed experience.
Yarranton invokes Windsor to draft himself a letter of commendation.

The third prefatory letter addresses another one of Yarranton's former em-
ployers: a commission of Worcestershire metal makers who sent him to Dresden in 1667 to report on the Saxon manufacture of tinplate. Yarranton recalls
that this assignment required "studious prying into the curious intreagues of
Trade and thriving Politicks of our Neighbour Nations."[56] The plural form of
"nations" and the mention of intriguing "trade" and "thriving Politicks" alludes
to the fact that after investigating German forges, Yarranton proceeded on
through Flanders and Holland, where he marveled at the United Provinces'
extensive inland canals, vigorous commerce, and prosperous citizens. Where
the Worcestershire iron mongers tasked Yarranton with importing industrial

knowledge, *England's Improvement* conveys his greater ambition to "make practicable here at home" the policies and institutions that made Dutch society so prosperous. Yarranton acquired not only German trade secrets in 1667, but the conviction that cultural advancement required "finding out abroad."[57]

In the middle of this letter, Yarranton apologizes to his readers for telling a "long story, that little or nothing concerns them."[58] The insertion of an unconcerned "them" confirms that this message was intended for audiences beyond its ostensible recipients, the members of the Worcestershire syndicate. Yarranton imagines that his correspondence will be heard and overheard: that his former colleagues will support his improvement agenda, and that the reader at large will be impressed that the author completed an industrial fact-finding mission out of "pure love to your Country."[59] Perhaps to make up for this gratuitous self-promotion, Yarranton addresses his final dedicatory letter to that same general reader. In it, he pledges to "drive away the great fears and complaints rooted in the hearts of the People, as the decay of Trade, the growing Power of the French, and much more."[60] The credibility of this promise depends on Yarranton's reputation as fashioned through his epistolary appeals to power.

The letters offer a flattering but incomplete depiction of their author's adventures. Yarranton touches briefly on his experiences as a traveler and consultant throughout *England's Improvement*, but it is not until the pamphlet's final pages that he inhabits completely the biographical mode in the form of a "short Account of my Education and Improvement."[61] The postscript suggests that Yarranton advocates improvement because he was himself its product. This narrative of experience is meant to distinguish *England's Improvement* from the "notions of a hot Brain" as a work of reasoned counsel rather than baseless enthusiasm.[62] "I was an Apprentice to a Linnen Draper when the King was born," he begins, recollecting an adolescence spent in the village of Astley, Worcestershire, during the 1630s. Yarranton locates in his youth the origins of the current Stuart regime, identifying as "King" an infant who would not take the throne for another thirty years. Finding the cloth trade "too narrow and short for my large mind," Yarranton abandoned the shop to pursue what he calls a "Country-Life."[63] This rustic interlude ended with the English Civil Wars, which brought heavy fighting to the West Midlands, capped off by Cromwell's victory at Worcester in 1651. Yarranton recalls that "I was a soldier," but he omits the fact that it was the New Model Army in which he enlisted (and through whose ranks he rose to become a captain), probably out of fear that old republican allegiances could undermine his pamphlet's consensus-building efforts.[64] While *England's Improvement* forgets its author's allegiance, its critics would be quick to remind "Captain Y" of his commission in Cromwell's forces.[65]

We learn that Yarranton built an iron forge and surveyed several major rivers after the war.[66] But the account is again most illuminating for what it excludes. *England's Improvement* does not mention that between 1651 and 1653 Yarranton served as a commissioner of sequestration in Worcester, in charge of confiscating and reapportioning lands owned by Charles I and his supporters. In an undated letter, he identifies twenty Caroline loyalists in Hereford and Gloucester whose lands were "sequestrable," the kind of assessment that conceivably earned Yarranton powerful enemies following the Restoration.[67] These seizures transferred the estates of Stuart loyalists into new hands, often New Model Army veterans and London merchants eager to experiment with innovative forms of husbandry. The new corps of "rational and often progressive land managers" discarded the ornamental and recreational vestiges of the bygone Caroline era in order to make the land return greater profits, whether by testing new crops or harvesting game parks for timber.[68] As commissioner, Yarranton toured former royalist strongholds that had become some of England's most "economically backward" regions.[69] Like Blith, another sequestration commissioner, Yarranton witnessed with his own eyes the rise of a new landowning regime, a motley crew of traders and soldiers that strove to become new model agrarians.

Yarranton also took a progressive hand to his own affairs. He purchased confiscated land in the Wyre Forest in 1651 and built an iron forge there. He oversaw an unfinished project to expand the slender River Salwarpe into a navigable channel between Worcester and the Severn River. Yarranton applied himself to studying "the great weakness of the Rye-lands," a region in Worcestershire, Gloucestershire, Herefordshire, Shropshire, and Staffordshire whose soil was exhausted by overcultivation, and proposed planting clover there to feed cattle and replenish the land.[70] Yarranton initially promoted clover through an earlier pamphlet, *Yarranton's Improvement by Clover*. No copy of this work survives, but Yarranton composed a revised edition in 1663, fittingly titled *The Improvement Improved, by a Second Edition of the Great Improvement of Lands by Clover*, and had it published by the local bookseller Francis Rea. Yarranton credits himself with discovering concrete methods to enrich land in a period he knew that many Restoration readers had come to associate with the vast social ambitions and broken promises of Commonwealth.

Here the account cuts off with terse insistence that "what I have been

doing since, my Book tells you at large."[71] This abrupt conclusion charges
England's Improvement with delivering a biographical account of Yarranton's
last twenty years. This deferral relieves Yarranton from having to explain how
the Stuart Restoration stalled his varied and energetic career. The *Calendar of
State Papers* fills in some of these gaps, documenting Yarranton's arrest in 1662
and subsequent jailing under suspicion of plotting a Presbyterian uprising.[72]
Yarranton would at one point face charges of treasonous speech, but a jury trial
exonerated him of all charges. This verdict appeared to put Yarranton's legal
troubles behind him, but as demonstrated in later critical responses to *England's Improvement*, criminal exculpation could not silence insinuations that
he was a dangerous radical and unrepentant regicide.

England's Improvement sets out to mend many bridges. It reconciles Yarranton to the Stuart settlement through its call for incremental reform, even
claiming that it is the "Wealth, Strength, and Honour" of Charles II that are
"the chief things aimed at in this Undertaking."[73] The pamphlet makes a dedicatee of the same Baron Windsor by whose authority the Lord Lieutenant of
Worcestershire arrested Yarranton for insubordination in 1662. It invokes the
Worcestershire metal makers who dispatched Yarranton to Dresden in 1667
and in so doing gave the former parliamentarian a chance to resuscitate his
embattled reputation. *England's Improvement* remembers (and strategically
forgets) Yarranton's life to characterize him as a loyal subject who associated
with respectable moderates. Conversely, the dedicatory letters and "short Account" make personal experience the basis for civic action, showing how Yarranton derived his powers of authorship from being a participant in history.
It is *England's Improvement*'s enfolding of biographical account into public
exposition—its positioning of Yarranton within the society he sought to reform—that permits a Presbyterian dissenter and onetime republican fugitive
to voice an Anglican kingdom's future interest.

Storied Ventures

Yarranton eases readers into the fraught business of imitating Dutch society by
making his recommendations appear self-evident and inoffensive. Having
taken part in some of country's most divisive conflicts and having suffered
through decades of personal turmoil, he maintains that *England's Improvement*
manifests universal values through uncontroversial means. Among Yarranton's
strategies for making projects seem widely appealing is the telling of stories

that portray societal reform through digestible plots. *England's Improvement* incorporates several narrative fragments that render compelling the causal links between present action and the future it creates. For instance, Yarranton likens his country's quest for commercial gain to a romantic contest between England and the Netherlands for the hand of trade: "To beat the *Dutch* with fighting, so as to force them from their beloved Mistress and delight (which is trade and Riches thereby) hath been the design of the most of their Neighbours for this forty years last past."[74] By personifying trade as a fickle paramour, *England's Improvement* converts recondite social problems into the matter of an amorous tale. Yarranton depicts war as the use of force to abscond with "Trade" to "better Ports, and healthfuller Air," a tactic pursued without success by Spain during the Eighty Years War (1568–1648), France during the Franco-Dutch War (1672–78), and England during the first and second Anglo-Dutch Wars. But violent kidnapping provides only a temporary advantage, claims Yarranton, because trade always returns to the venue of most vigorous exchange, even the "dull and flegmatick Air" of Holland.[75]

England can possess trade only by furnishing her with "all that she can desire." These conjugal comforts included a property register, navigable rivers, a bank, a "Court of Merchants," and the construction of "lumberhouses" (i.e., pawn shops) where "poor people may have Moneys lent upon Goods at very easie interest."[76] These institutions would entice trade to abandon the Netherlands and "come and settle her self with us," predicts Yarranton, who emplots improvement as noncoercive seduction, an expenditure of civilian labor preferable to the ravages of war.[77] Yarranton's story of Anglo-Dutch conflict treats commerce not simply as an object to be seized, but as an independent agent capable of denial and consent. His courtship allegory reframes commercial rivalry as a contest of hospitality.

Yarranton dedicates his longest tale to lobbying for the establishment of a land registry, a national office that would keep track of who owned what lands under what terms. *England's Improvement* identifies land registration as the cornerstone of Dutch prosperity, a long-standing tradition of centralized record keeping that enabled Hollanders to verify property claims, and thereby borrow against their estates.[78] In England, by contrast, "no man can know a Title by his writings" and therefore must resort to cobbling together parish-held deeds and liens to certify property rights. Yarranton suggests that starting a registry would encourage the pursuit of land-backed loans, which would, in turn, transform England's rural acreage into exchangeable value, injecting "riches, strength, and trade" into a countryside that held so much of its wealth and wealth-creating potential in the soil. Registration would be the mechanism by which English subjects could obtain credit to improve their estates and parishes could amass the funds necessary to commission Dutch-styled public works. Registration would, according to Yarranton, unleash "all delightful Golden Streams of Banks, Lumber-houses, Honour, Honesty, Riches, Strength and Trade."[79]

Yarranton dramatizes the consequences of England's lack of a registry through the story of a fictitious family ruined by its pursuit of a loan. The protagonist is the family father, who owns an ancestral estate worth "a Thousand pounds a year" and owes "Four thousand pounds" in costs associated with outfitting his son in business and paying his daughters' dowries.[80] The high value of the land and modest balance of debt suggest that this man should have no trouble obtaining and repaying a loan. But without clear title to his property of the sort registration would provide, the landholder cannot submit his property as security, even though "the Estate hath been in the Family Two hundred years."[81] He is forced to consult a "scrivener" to acquire a mortgage and to cosign that bond with "coventers," a process that often failed according to Yarranton, leaving the mortgager unable to repay his debt and without means to set his sons and daughters "into the World."[82]

This particular landholder does manage to secure a loan, but the terms are harsh. Yarranton interjects his own voice in this narrative frame to ask the reader to ponder the dire repercussions of scarce credit and predatory creditors: what would happen if the estate were to fall on "bad Times, or decay of Tenants, great Taxes, or the Eldest Son matching contrary to his Father's will, or oftentimes it is worse, he is so debaucht no one will match with him?"[83] In these unhappy cases, the mortgager stands no chance of satisfying his coventers, despite residing on lands worth significantly more than the original debt. "Sheriff, Bayliffs, Solicitors, and Lawyers" inevitably descend on the estate and it is "torn to pieces."[84] The former owner, now an unlanded debtor, must plead before "the *Fleet* or *Bench*" and suffer the humiliation of debtor's prison.[85]

This upsetting tale transforms a proposal for clerical transparency into familial tragedy, complete with the confiscation of homestead, fractured paternal-filial relations, and incarceration. "O *Pity*, and *Sin*," Yarranton exclaims, "that it should be so in brave *England!*"[86] Outside England, the same transaction is less harrowing. A loan seeker in Dutch Friesland, Yarranton explains, can call on his sons trading in Venice, Hamburg, Nuremberg, and Danzig to acquire credit because "every Acre of Land in the Seven Provinces trades all the world over, and it is as good as ready Money; but in *England* a poor Gentlemen cannot take up Four thousand pounds upon his Land at six in the hundred interest although he would Mortgage a Thousand pounds a year of it."[87] Although this particular Friesland merchant's holdings command only £100 a year (one-tenth the annual returns earned by his English counterpart), he is able to borrow at a lower interest rate and at less personal hazard. Land registration, according to Yarranton, made Dutch soil an internationally exchangeable commodity in an era when English estate holders could not prove titles to the satisfaction of parish justices.

Yarranton presents Anglo-Dutch commercial rivalry through the experience of individual economic actors, characters endowed with human hope, judgment, and emotion. His storytelling recasts diplomacy as romance, and malfunctioning debt instruments into a crisis of familial integrity—fictions that enabled even those readers who did not understand Yarranton's proposals to support them. Another writer who invested macroeconomic phenomena with affective resonance was Blith, who campaigned for timber cultivation in Commonwealth England by telling the story of an aged widow: "I have heard of a poor woman that had two or three ash-trees in her Garden hedge, & a strong wind came and blew the Ash Keys all over the Garden, that at the Spring, her Garden was turned from that to a hopfull plantation of Ashes as green as a leek above the ground, the woman was at a great debat, to loose her Garden she was loth, and to destroy so hopefull a crop she was unwilling."[88] The germination of ash seeds presents a gripping dilemma: the "heard of" woman must decide whether to maintain her garden, a crucial chore given her poverty, or cultivate the accidental nursery, which might return greater sustenance, but only after the trees came to maturity and someone purchased their timber. The woman recognizes that over time the trees would prove more lucrative than vegetables, but she is hesitant to risk her livelihood in pursuit of future gain. Blith distinguishes between the conservation of private uses and the exchange of commodities, in this case through a timber trade that would likely dispose of the ash trees in London's shipyards. The woman, in other words, must decide whether to maintain her austere existence or become the "English Improver" that Blith heralded: "at last she resolved to let them grow, and now her garden is turned into a nurcery, and she is turned a planter, and hath ever since maintained it to that use, and made many times more profit than she did before."[89] The parable of the ash keys rewards public-minded plantation. Remitting the fruits of the land to a national economy yields "profit," an exchangeable surplus unavailable in the subsistence paradigm.

Blith's triumphant conversion of garden plot to literary plot furthermore suggests that even the most precarious members of society, here a "poor woman," can contribute to the Commonwealth, helping to furnish England's navy at a time when war with the Netherlands first loomed on the horizon.

Projectors like Blith and Yarranton recognized the power of allegories and anecdotes to make improvement concrete and personal. The ruined mortgager and reluctant orcharder solicit pity and admiration, even when the economic impasses they personify do not pertain to individual readers. Their narratives also stand in for explicit argumentation, limiting the instances in which Yarranton needed to make bald claims about the future, claims that would tip off his audience to the fact that they were reading a work in the disreputable project mode. Whenever possible, Yarranton tries to appear as if he is describing rather than disputing, composing narrative rather than building polemic. These performances reflect Yarranton's anxieties over the usefulness of language for enlisting readers to his cause, anxieties he processes paradoxically by renouncing rhetoric altogether. A signature of project writing, I will now show, was a disavowal of projects and writing. Inspection of *England's Improvement* reveals a text at war with its medium.

Writing Against Language

England's Improvement derives legitimacy from its imagined interlocutors, who range from connected elites to the general reader. This unrequited correspondence liberates Yarranton to discuss his own improvement agenda with affable modesty: "I here not only present with these my weak Endeavors, for the vigorous Improvements of those unparalel'd Advantages, which the situation of our Climate, the Nature of our Soil, and the Constitution of both our People and Government affords us, in order to the making us every way great, beyond any Nation in the World."[90] Yarranton contrasts the "weak endeavors" of his prose with the possibility of "vigorous" improvement and "unparalel'd" advantage that the proposal raises. He confesses to feeble exposition through the possessive adjective "my," while insisting that this scheming could make the entire realm "great." Yarranton characterizes *England's Improvement* as the unassuming vehicle for momentous change. It is a "humble Petition" meant to give rise to "so Glorious a Work."[91] The topos of modesty was an essential tool for projectors, who downplayed their rhetorical acumen to forestall skeptics who would portray them as cunning wordsmiths brandishing empty ideas.

Many authors found that the most direct way to refute charges of rhetorical deceit was to disclaim persuasive advantage altogether.

Yarranton discounts his writerly talents by calling *England's Improvement* a "humble petition" and "weak endeavors." At one point, he breezily reduces his 216-page manifesto to "these few Sheets."[92] Fortrey likewise characterizes his *England's Interest and Improvement* as an "unworthy Treatise," claiming he felt "ashamed" that King Charles (his dedicatee) might waste time reading such an "undeserving paper."[93] Barbon calls his *Discourse on Trade* a "rough sketch." John Blanch brushes off his *Interest of England Considered* (1694) as "this little Essay," diminishing the proposal's supposedly paltry substance to the status of mere attempt.[94] Mary Astell claims that her *Serious Proposal to the Ladies* (1694) needs not "the set-offs of *Rhetorick* to recommend it, were I capable, which yet I am not, of applying them."[95] Humphrey Mackworth performs a particularly jarring devaluation of his work when he likens *England's Glory, by a Royal Bank* to "this little Brat."[96] These self-deprecating authors attempt to shift the reader's attention from the rhetorical instrument of the proposal to the action it foresees, and in so doing to disown the act of proposing itself.[97]

Yarranton rejects the artifice of writing to assert the underlying value of his ideas. The purpose of his rhetoric was to remove the semblance of persuasion, and thereby return readers to the unmediated object Thirsk calls a "practical scheme for exploiting material things."[98] Yarranton's professions of verbal inelegance actually exhibit deft understatement—he disclaims an argumentative mode to reinforce arguments, suggesting that there was substance to his proposals beyond the words they contained. Modesty functions as a mode of self-authorizing performance in *England's Improvement*, as Yarranton's "humble petition" refashions itself into the "unanimous Prayer of the Nation in General."[99] The generic transposition of "petition," an individual plea to the state, to "prayer," a request of God made on behalf of the nation, demonstrates how claims to plain speech facilitate the acquisition of political power.

A purported plain style could also distinguish new proposals from projection's history of misspent eloquence, a notorious legacy personified by Elizabethan monopolists, Jacobean and Caroline patentees, and Commonwealth social planners. Yarranton understood it was crucial for *England's Improvement* to appear not to belong to the degraded project tradition and therefore solicits "shelter" of Annesley and Player so that they could shield him from "the Arrows of Obloquy and Envy, that are usually shot at the Projector, be the Undertaking never so noble."[100] Yarranton confesses that others will call him a projector and denounce his ideas out of prejudice or jealousy. The archery metaphor implies that these obligatory assaults relied on tonal bluster and specious clichés, and often missed their mark, injuring some of England's most capable and public-minded improvers.

Yarranton decries the perfunctory malice shown toward new enterprise and denounces those who rail against "my Project, as most will call it" despite its potential benefits.[101] He nonetheless capitulates to this hostile readership by spurning project terminology. With the exception of one reference to an earlier river navigation scheme as "my projection," Yarranton always substitutes less insidious synonyms like "Design" and "Undertaking," terms that imply the possibility of action beyond proposal language without conjuring projecting's incriminating historical associations.[102] Yarranton's denial of projects reflects the influence of writers like Blith, who wanted to be accounted a "poor and faithful Servant to his Generation" and not be "Scandalized as a Projector."[103] His self-conception also anticipates a distinction later drawn by Aaron Hill, the eighteenth-century poet and beech oil inventor, who claimed "the Business we are now upon, is no *Project*, 'tis a *Discovery*."[104] To escape its own wordy realm of projection, *England's Improvement* organizes its diction and syntax to renounce fine rhetoric and proposing both.

Projection's Passive Voice

Trepidation over language manifested at the level of syntax. For example, later in the pamphlet, Yarranton proposes to increase England's power at sea by establishing a navigable waterway in Ireland. Turning his attention to the Shalela Wood of Leinster, Yarranton decries the "great shame it was that such quantities of Timber should ly rotting in these Woods, and could not be come at, the Mountains and Boggs having so lockt them up."[105] These were not any old trees, but sturdy oaks, some mast worthy, that could boost the English navy's ship-building efforts. It was no coincidence that this timber stood on land in the County of Wexford that Charles II had granted to his loyalist supporters, including Yarranton's dedicatee, the Earl of Anglessey. When Yarranton predicts that the unimproved land "will never bring the Owners Twenty thousand pounds," he laments both the nation's forfeiture of ship timber and his patron's loss of revenue. The solution, he perceived, was in deepening the River Slane (today called the Slaney), which meandered through southeastern Ireland on its way to the sea at Wexford: "But if the *Slane* were made Navigable and the Rivulets running into it, these great quantities of Timber might be

employed in building Ships for the Royal Navy."[106] The conditional statement
exemplifies Yarranton's dedicatory pledge to exploit "our Climate, the Nature of
our soil, and the Constitution of our People and Government," in this case by
making "our" encompass the colonized County of Wexford. *England's Improvement* implies an Ireland that is also England's, and hence improvable. From early
in his career, Yarranton recognized the value of traversable rivers, likening them
in *England's Improvement* to veins: "let them be stopt, there will then be great
danger either of death" or injury.[107] He was so confident in his project to make
the Stour River navigable through part of Worcestershire that he purchased
adjoining mines in the hopes that barges would one day carry his coal to forges
downstream. Making the Slane navigable, he argued, would allow England to
build ships at "three fifths of what the King now pays," and these ships would
be well positioned to "preserve the West *India* Trade" or sail into the Mediterranean and thereby give "great comfort to all Trade that is used in those seas."[108]
It was all a matter of getting to those oaks.

Yarranton summarizes the project through a single sentence that transforms a natural substance ("Timber") into a manmade product ("Ships")
through an act of industry ("building"). This rough grammatical formula for
projection transforms a direct object into an indirect object through the use of
a gerund. What's missing is a subject, an entity responsible for this foretold
action. Passive voice construction permits *England's Improvement* to extol a
complex work of river engineering without calling on anyone in particular to
discharge its labor. Perhaps Yarranton feared that such an act of naming would
divert the reader's attention from England, the ostensible beneficiary of improvement, to an individual undertaker who might stand to profit (especially
if that undertaker wound up being the polarizing surveyor and engineer Andrew Yarranton). Passive voice enables the projector to talk about improvement without hazarding to assign it a grammatical agent or human face.

Modern writing pedagogy discourages use of the passive voice on the
grounds that it conveys diffidence, inaction, even deception. In *England's Improvement*, passive construction propels Yarranton's schemes forward by attributing them a sense of inevitability. His grammar helps create the conditions
for believing in his project, which derives plausibility from the fact that it at
first obliges nobody to do anything. Yarranton's sentence is in the conditional
mode, but no one is responsible for satisfying any conditions—things simply
will "be." Yarranton evinces similar passive certainty in his later proposal to
forge metal in Hampshire using iron stone buried at the mouth of the Stour
River and timber from the New Forest: "If two Furnaces be built around

Ringwood to cast Guns, and two Forges to make Iron, and the Iron Stone to be brought from the Harbour mouth out of the Sea up the River to the Furnaces, and the Charcole out of *New Forest* to the works, there being sufficient of decayed Woods to supply four Iron-works for ever; by these means the King makes the best of everything, and builds with his Timber being near and convenient."[109] Furnace construction appears straightforward in this syntax. Forges will "be built" and raw iron "brought" through actions that later solidify into "means" of instrumental value. The omission of subjects makes Yarranton sound authoritative, not evasive. Eventually he attributes action to Charles II, a sovereign who "makes the best of everything," but in reality makes nothing.

Yarranton proposes to establish linen manufacturing in Warwick, Leicester, Northampton, and Oxfordshire through yet another passively voiced future-conditional sentence, except here, *England's Improvement* transmutes the lack of specified agency into a positive gain: the creation of jobs. "And so it will be," proclaims Yarranton: "There the Flax will grow, and be manufactured easily and cheap; part whitened there, and the Thread and part of the Flax sent down the Navigable Rivers to the several Towns to be woven and spun. And so there will be employ for the great part of the Poor of England. In such Towns where it meets with a settled voluntary Register, thence never will it depart."[110] The cloth spinning project presumes the execution of Yarranton's other schemes for navigations and land registration. Once in place, these enterprises enable the linen industry to run itself: flax "will grow," "be Manufactured," "be sent down" rivers. A former draper's apprentice, Yarranton predicts that central England would one day surpass Germany as Europe's largest producer of cloth. He suggests that nimble-fingered children would make the best linens workers, following the example of German industrial schools that taught youngsters how to spin flax, weave bone lace, and make toys. "There the Children enrich the Father," Yarranton lamented, "but here begger him."[111] In the world of *England's Improvement*, "employ" is improvement's product rather than its animating force. Yarranton transforms children from cost burdens into wage earners, a measure that would stimulate population growth in the region.

Given its capacity to make a speculative future feel like an inevitable extension of the present, passive syntax appears frequently in project writing. The subtitle of Coke's *England's Improvements* promises to disclose "How the Kingdom of England May be Improved." Fortrey professes "no doubt but the people, and riches of the kingdom might be greatly increased and multiplied" if land were enclosed, mines expanded, and a fishery established.[112] "*England*, may be enriched," declares William Carter, by banning the exportation of raw

wool.[113] His *England's Interest Asserted* declares that "Cloathing must be purged
from its Corruption," in a syntactical construction that identifies neither what
qualified as "Corruption" nor who would take responsibility for decontami-
nating the trade.[114] Reynell treats England as a passive object in his assertion
that "this Nation might be greatly advantaged by cutting of Rivers, and making them Navigable."[115] The kingdom, according to Reynell, possesses the
means of advancing itself, so there is no need to identify the agents who would
actually carry out the work.

After denying the efficacy of its words, *England's Improvement* appears also
to refuse the agency of its author. This maneuver permits Yarranton to invert
the means and ends of his project, imagining labor not as a prerequisite for
projects but as projection's salutary outcome. Passive voice also makes it possible for *England's Improvement* to synchronize projects of industry, engineering,
and policy reform within a single sentence, producing a momentary sense of
coherent organization within a long and varied pamphlet.

Schemes and Schemas

England's Improvement sprawls across two hundred pages and several fields of
professional knowledge, from Irish forestry to London fire prevention. Incorporating such dissimilar material into a single piece of writing challenged Yarranton to make "improvement" encompass many actions and yet remain a
legible ideal. He conceived of *England's Improvement* not as a miscellany of
separate proposals, but a methodical plan for concerted action. This was the
goal at least. In its published form, Yarranton's pamphlet feels neither methodical nor self-contained. To the contrary, *England's Improvement* tries readers
through its lengthy digressions and deadening repetition. The text speeds
through some proposals—particularly those having to do with London—
while lavishing minute detail on others. Yarranton defers to knowledgeable
experts in some passages, addresses uninformed readers in others, snipes at
known enemies and imagined critics elsewhere. While the pamphlet resists
front-to-back reading, it nonetheless establishes a kind of order between the
projects it unveils. When, for instance, *England's Improvement* presents linen
as the product of synchronized efforts to register land and cut rivers, it suggests
that projects create their own conditions of possibility. This idea of reciprocity
enables Yarranton to depict momentous changes in society as the result of incremental measures. Yarranton links one scheme to the proliferation of others

in his description of how a land registry would reshape rural England: "the free Lands of England being put under a Voluntary Register by Act of Parliament: From the Credit whereof spring Banks, Lumberhouses, with all Credits necessary to drive Trade, Cut Rivers, the Fishery, and all things else that Moneys are capable of; and it will drive away the great fears and complaints rooted in the hearts of the People, as the decay of Trade, the growing power of the French, and much more."[116] The prepositions "by," "from," and "with" establish causal bonds between each measure. Appropriately enough, the former navigations engineer employs a hydrographical metaphor to liken the land registry to a spring that feeds the streams of lumber mills, river embankments, trade, and a fishery. The metaphor breaks off with the more literal suggestion that new institutions will enhance England's global stature, neutralize the threat of French invasion, cheer a fearful and quarrelsome populace, and "much more." Improvement is imagined as the outflow of interdependent enterprises whose benefits exceed articulation. The land registry will do much good, and through its tributary schemes, "much more."

Yarranton's prepositions and water imagery establish spatial relations between projects to imply their harmonious interworking. Other projectors asserted improvement's reciprocal nature more directly. Samuel Fortrey observed with aphoristic brevity that "people and plenty are commonly the begetters of the one of the other, if rightly ordered."[117] Carter identifies a "Connexion of Trades one to another," predicting that England's short-sighted exportation of raw wool would bring the poor to "desperate straits" and make them "uncapable of paying rent."[118] The cloth maker Joseph Trevers incorporates English commerce through the trope of the "body politique," in which "one member depends upon another, and is serviceable to the other" producing "natural Harmony and Correspondence, even so doth one Trade, or occupation closely, and necessarily depend upon another."[119]

Thirsk traces a similar course of mutual causation in the writings of fen improvers. She observes that a growing market for coleseed oil in the early seventeenth century "was linked with drainage projects, which gave fresh encouragement to yet another group of inventors and projectors—those who were commending their designs for windmills and drainage engines."[120] A hunger for oil drives the mechanical inventions that would eventually turn the fens into plantable land. One oil projector, John Taylor, employs the same logic of "fresh encouragement" in his *Praise of Hemp-Seed* (1620), which recounts how hemp cultivation both demanded and returned "labour, profit, cloathing, pleasure, food, Navigation: Divinity, poetry, the liberall Arts, Armes, Vertues

defence, Vices offence, a true mans protection, a thiefs execution. Here is
mirth and matter all beaten out of this small seede."[121] An entire civil society
congeals in the kernels of this crop, claims Taylor, who reasons that hemp
could nourish commoners, inspire artists, and punish criminals. Likewise,
Richard Weston's *A Discours of Husbandrie Used in Brabant and Flanders* (1650)
argues that implementing horticultural methods "not practised in *England*"
would catalyze trade and create new employment opportunities.[122] Weston
advises Commonwealth cultivators to plant the signature crops of the continent's lowlands, including flax, turnip, and clover. Then these planters could
"send for som Workmen out of *Flanders*, that understand the Manufacture of
Linnen Cloth, and make your own *Flax* into Linnen Cloth."[123] The profits
derived from finishing textiles would return "publick benefit to the Kingdom"
in the form of profits that would subsidize the repair of highways and the
construction of canals. Weston's *Discours* promises to make English subjects
better farmers, then industrialists, and finally, sponsors of public works. His
agricultural projects pledge to capitalize on English land and expand the range
of lives that the countryside could sustain.

Yarranton often makes the culmination of one project the impetus for
another, though he does not always do this. For instance, *England's Improvement* employs a paragraph break to mark the shift between his discussion of
the registry and plan to log Irish and English forests:

> And if this doth not convince the Reader, that hereby we shall beat
> the *Dutch* without fighting, and pay our Debts without Moneys, I
> have no more to say.
>   Besides the Advantages aforesaid, let me tell you that I have
> found out two places, one in *Ireland*, the other in *England*: In that
> in *Ireland* are great strange quantities of Timber to build Ships, and
> places to build them.[124]

Language and typography place the logging proposals "besides" the purported
benefits of the property register, rendering these two ideas adjacent but apart
from one another. The new timber scheme nonetheless abides by its own internal logic of self-necessitation: "great and strange quantities of wood" become
accessible only when workers make the Slane and Avon Rivers passable to ships.
A cache of fleet-ready timber needs reengineered rivers to become boats. Conversely, the future navigability of the Slane and Avon depend on their proximity
to forests, whose wood motivates the moving of land and water.

Yarranton depicts the project through a crude map (see Figure 2). The top of the map displays forest groves owned by English aristocrats, including Anglesey, who would stand to profit from the extraction of Irish timber. The bottom shows a finished ship under English ensign sailing out the broad-mouthed Slane River past Wexford into the open sea. The forest's status as ships in potential could not be more obvious. The absence of dockyards, logging camps, and any other traces of labor implies that Irish forests, like Alexander Pope's Windsor Forest, might simply "rush into [the] Floods" on their own accord.[125] Yarranton's syntax lacks the prosodic compression of Pope's later scene, but it relies on a similar animating conceit: "those Woods may with ease and at very cheap Rates be brought down the *Slane* to *Wexford*."[126] Cartography and grammar conspire to reduce rural wilderness to its industrial possibilities, possibilities that the single outbound ship implies are already being exploited.

Yarranton's chain of projects stretches beyond the text of *England's Improvement*. The multitude of benefits (and beneficial projects) signaled by the phrase "much more" would eventually motivate him to compose a "Second Part" to *England's Improvement*, published in 1681. This continuation contained, among several additional proposals, "advice" for employing "Six thousand young Lawyers, and Three thousand Priests . . . who now have neither practice nor cure of Souls."[127] Yarranton recognizes that the institution of a land registry would clear parochial court dockets, deny lawyers lucrative casework, and make England sufficiently prosperous and self-content to repel the enticements of Roman Catholicism.[128] Despite his tongue-in-cheek concern for jobless lawyers and papists, Yarranton nonetheless demonstrates his willingness to deal with the repercussions of his scheming and to solve, even fancifully, problems of his own making. The patterns of causation that drew together Yarranton's projects outstretch the document that originally called them into being.

Universal Interest

Yarranton purports to voice collective values through the first word of his title, "England's," his strategically addressed dedicatory letters, and passively voiced predictions. He advances schemes that benefit broad constituencies, transforming the need for labor into a beneficial occasion of "employ." A desire to employ the poor, to make enterprise serve its undertakers, was "one of the axioms of project writing," according to Samantha Heller, who demonstrates

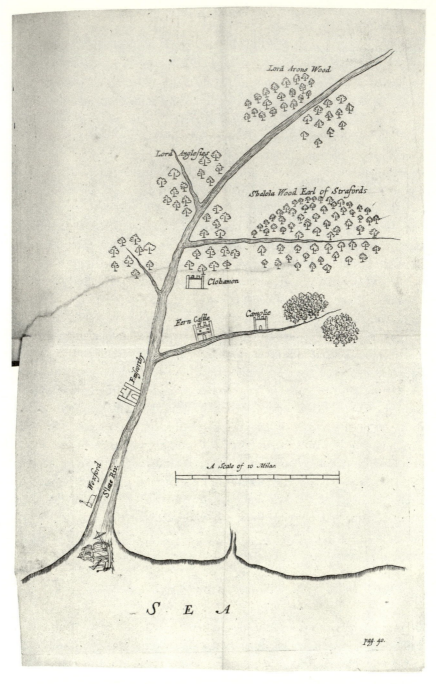

Figure 2. Map of Slane River from Andrew Yarranton's *England's Improvement by Sea and Land.* RB 148563, Huntington Library, San Marino, California.

how economic planners of the sixteenth century promised to make use of England's idle and destitute subjects.[129] The inventor Hugh Plat (1552–1608) typifies this caring rhetoric when he sets out to "procure great loue and securitie to the rich, sufficient maintenaunce and reliefe to the poor, some credit to the Author and no small benefite to the whole realm of England."[130]

Poor relief remained a central concern of projectors a century later. Reynell was one of several improvers who proposed a herring fishery on the grounds it would employ a staggering half million subjects.[131] The fishery, he explained, was just one example of public enterprise that England could profitably undertake if "the Rich hoard not up their Money, but employ the poor people in general works, as building of Houses, Colledges, Bridges or the like."[132] Nicholas Hawksmoor goes so far as to suggest that his proposal for a hospital in Greenwich would prove advantageous even if it never served a patient, because even "vain Projects" like Egypt's pyramids and Trajan's pillar were useful in that they "employed vast Numbers of the Poor, in Building."[133]

Reynell and Hawksmoor exploit images of poverty to promote their schemes. They make a persuasive resource of scarcity. Similarly, Yarranton's proposal to establish a network of granary banks, seven-story brick buildings that would protect corn from vermin, aligns poor relief with industrial growth.[134] Granaries, he predicts, would benefit "all the people that are imployed in these Manufactures," by supplying them with "bread sufficient, without a charge to the Publick, and thereby the Commodities will be manufactured cheap."[135] A reason to feed the hungry is that it cheapens goods, argues Yarranton, who charges his project to "cheat the Rats and Mice, to feed the Poor, to preserve the Tenant, to pay the Landlord, to bring us several Manufactures, to prevent Law-Suits, to fetch out all Moneys now unimployed into Trade; and it will be, if done, as the Blood in the Body, it will so circulate in a few years, that Corn will be to *England* better than ready Moneys; and to have this so, is undoubtedly every Mans interest in the Kingdom."[136] This procession of infinitive statements explains how the erection of storehouses would monetize grain into currency "better than ready Moneys." Yarranton predicts that corn, when secured from pests and freely distributed, would function as a unit of exchange similar to registered lands. The circulation of grain as money would ensure the availability of bread while stabilizing tenant-landlord relations, serving "undoubtedly every Mans interest in the Kingdom." All men hold "interest" in this project because they belong to the same body, Yarranton's simile suggests, and depend on the same flow of blood.

Virtually all improvers aligned their proposals with some notion of the public good. But only certain works, like Yarranton's, were comprehensive enough to claim "every mans interest." Projects "should be made as Universal as possible," declares the like-minded Reynell, "and that it be universal, all particular Parishes ought to be employ'd in it."[137] Both Reynell and Yarranton solicit readers who are poor and rich, rural and urban, Anglican and nonconforming to fashion their proposals as expressions of universal interest. Though the bulk of his proposals belong to the countryside, Yarranton maintains the importance of cities as centers of trade, showing how the fruits of the fields busied the ports of London. Yarranton addresses the dangers of urban life most explicitly through a proposal to fight conflagrations, like the Great Fire of 1666, by constructing a system of semaphores and roping water cisterns to sleighs.[138] The publication details of *England's Improvement* themselves imply the reciprocity of capital and country: the colophon indicates that the work was composed by a Worcestershire native, Yarranton, published by a freeman in the London Company of Stationers, Robert Everingham, and sold in bookstalls in Cheapside and St. Paul's Churchyard.

England's Improvement stages unanimity across vocation and region in a fictive "Dialogue betwixt a Clothier, a Woollen-draper, and a Country-Yeoman at Supper upon the Road." This didactic conversation opens when the draper (a rural wool supplier) asks the urban clothier, "what News from *London*, old friend?"[139] "A bad Trade still," laments the clothier, who blames the decline of his business on the rise of factors, drawers, and packers, an ambitious class of functionaries who allegedly seized control of England's textile industry by setting themselves up as merchants and creditors. A third party, the yeoman, soon enters the conversation, interjecting that the health of his estate relied on the unfettered trade of drapers and clothiers, because "every Acre of my Land rises price, according as the Woollen Manufacture flourishes."[140] The draper, in turn, salutes the yeoman for his "fellow-feeling in our misery," an expression of solidarity through shared financial hardship.

The decline of clothiers, drapers, and yeomen recalls the sorrow of Yarranton's benighted mortgager. Their dialogue foregrounds the mutual dependence of pastoral labor and port markets, suggesting in this particular case that the traffic between Salisbury and London sustains both places. "Fellow-feeling" expresses a collective desire to restore England's wool trade to its rightful directors.

Yarranton's discovery of universal interest finds an urban-focused counterpart in Nicholas Barbon's 1685 pamphlet, *Apology for the Builder*. Barbon, a London-based insurance purveyor, calls for the construction of houses in

London, a project that would stimulate tax revenue (and policy sales). His proposal addresses rural landholders who feared that a larger metropolis would drain the countryside of workers and raise the cost of labor. Like Yarranton, Barbon shows how urban trade consumes rural outputs, "Stones, Bricks, Lime, Iron, Lead, Timber . . . the Commodities of the Country."[141] The city vents and constitutes the matter of quarries, forests, pastures, and tillage, claims Barbon, who observes that new buildings would provide "habitations and live-lihood for the Supernumerary and useless Inhabitants of the Country," specif-ically, the younger sons of gentry and the children of peasants.[142] A growing city, *Apology* concludes, puts surplus goods and bodies to work.

Barbon characterizes building as an ancient vocation derived from the paternal obligation to shelter family. It is, he claims, the fundamental chore of a society committed to growing its population humanely: "New Buildings are advantageous to the King and Government. They are instrumental to the pre-serving and increasing of the number of the Subjects; And numbers of Subjects is the strength of a Prince: for Houses are Hives for the People to breed and swarm in, without which they cannot increase."[143] Barbon compares London houses to teeming hives, colonies "instrumental" to the growth and mainte-nance of society. This trope, perhaps drawn from Virgil's depiction of commu-nally industrious bees in *The Georgics*, draws together city and country respectively as the tenor and vehicle of a metaphor. *Apology* uses the figure of the hive to unearth the city's rural roots.

Barbon invents his own metaphors while neutralizing others. He addresses a particularly nefarious "*simile* from those that have the Rickets, fansying the City to be the Head of the Nation, and that it will grow too big for the Body," accusing that simile's authors of themselves being rickets victims deluded by their search for companionable forms.[144] Barbon refuses this comparison and installs his own in its place: London is not the head of England, but rather "the heart of a Nation, through which the Trade and Commodities of it circulate, like the blood through the heart, which by its motions giveth life and growth to the rest of the Body."[145] London, in this comparison, is no longer a peripheral bulging but a central pump that propels goods throughout England. The heart metaphor accommodates urban and rural interests, reconstituting the capital within a functional body politic. Barbon himself acknowledges the impact of his tropes, remarking "this *simile* is the best."[146]

Yarranton's dialogue and Barbon's metaphoric surrogation authorize their proposals to voice universal interest. Both projectors endeavor to comfort read-ers by addressing them as improvement's beneficiaries rather than its bystanders or victims. Recitations of shared values simultaneously marginalize detractors by depicting them as contrarian outsiders contriving to "shake their Interests."[147] Yarranton imagines his future critics as improvement's enemies, civic outlaws rather than reasonable opponents. *England's Improvement* attempts to manage its own reception. This rhetorical self-fashioning would unravel in 1677, when Popish plots, Titus Oates, and possibility of exclusion made universal interest appear to be Yarranton's most risible idea.

Improvement's Readers

In 1679, there appeared an anonymous pamphlet mocking Yarranton and his ideas. *A Coffee-House Dialogue; or, A Discourse Between Captain Y——— and a Young Barrester of the Middle Temple* stages a conversation between Yarranton ("Captain Y," rewritten into his republican past) and a lawyer skeptical that "so good an Effect might be so easily wrought" from projects.[148] Captain Y badgers the attorney with outlandish claims that resemble but also exaggerate Yarranton's original proposals: "we may beat the *Dutch* without fighting, pay Debts without Money, make all the Streets in *London* Navigable Rivers, harbour all the King's Great Ships upon the top of an Hill, where they shall be secured from Wind and Weather, and from an hundred other Accidents, they are else obnoxious to."[149] The fast-talking captain hands the barrister a sheet of paper calling for the establishment of a new club called "*the Improvers of* England" with a budget for "a pennyworth of Cheese, Bread, Beer and Mustard."[150]

The barrister sees through Captain Y's banter, exclaiming, "I say you have out stripp'd all the Poets that ever wrote."[151] Poetry here connotes quixotic imagination detached from material constraint. To "out strip" poetry would be to exceed all bounds of credibility. Captain Y surpasses the impracticality of poets, and shares with them the medium of writing. *Coffee-house Dialogue* exposes and makes farcical the tactics Yarranton employed to make *England's Improvement* an actionable reform instrument. Where Yarranton characterizes himself as a dutiful subject of Charles II, the dialogue reminds readers of his rank in Cromwell's army. Where Yarranton alleged to speak with plain candor, Captain Y relies on insinuations, "a little push, a wink, a nod, a smile, or Finger held up to the Nose," suggesting that *England's Improvement* mystified its contents to circumvent conflict.[152] Where Yarranton touted the logical continuity between his proposals, the lawyer fails to see how Captain Y's club proposal "is pertinent to our former Discourse."[153] The barrister proceeds to degrade the credentialed engineer and savvy consensus builder into an aged buffoon, who vacantly charges his sharper conversant of being a "young man [who] cannot see so far as I do."[154]

This travesty so upset Yarranton and his supporters that it provoked two anonymous rebuttals, *England's Improvements Justified* and *The Coffee-House Dialogue Examined and Refuted*, both published in 1680. The first work, *England's Improvements Justified*, pledges to make "Captain Y. vindicated" by revealing the jealousies that drove his detractors: "Malice and Envy are the inseparable Companions of a Diabollical Nature; and that contagion is never more apparent, than by its dreadful symptoms, where it throws out its sulphureous stink-pots of calumnies and slanders, blasting the reputations of the best of men, lessening and levelling at the most Heroick Actions, and endeavoring to make the greatest designs for the weal-publick frustrate and abortive."[155] In *England's Improvement*, Yarranton confessed to fearing the "arrows of obloquy and envy." The author of this tract, by contrast, goes on the offensive by condemning anyone who rages indiscriminately against "Heroick Actions" and "the greatest designs for the weal-publick." *The Coffee-House Dialogue Examined and Refuted*, meanwhile, criticizes the attempted satire of *Coffee-House Dialogue*, claiming that Captain Y's "palpable absurdities" bore no resemblance to Yarranton's actual proposals.[156]

Yarranton did manage to find some sympathetic readers. A laudatory review of *England's Improvement* appeared in a 1676 issue of the *Philosophical Transactions of the Royal Society*, which asserted that "if the best of this Authors ingenuous Proposals may be fortified by good Laws, and those Laws duly executed, we may hope, that the Trade of *England* may, in a short time, recover, and prosper, as it doth among the Wealthiest of Forraigners; for the great relief of our vast number of Indigents, and to free this Kingdom from the shame and burthen of idle Beggars, and of sturdy Vagrants."[157] The reviewer praises Yarranton's superlative genius, and even plays back his logical organization, passive voice syntax, and figuration of shared interest ("we may hope"). But rankled apologias and hopeful reviews could not stint further assault on Yarranton's reputation, including a fresh libel, *A Continuation of the Coffee-House Dialogue* (1680), that resumed mocking the hapless Captain Y.

That *England's Improvement* continued to be debated as a work of speculative writing—rather than a source of realized action—implies that the pamphlet failed to create material change in its Restoration world. Rhetorical projection, no matter how resourceful or painstaking, was not the same as completing a project. Neither Yarranton's logging operations nor his river navigations materialized on his terms. England continued to import linens and iron long after 1677 and did not adapt a land registry until the nineteenth century. The granary banks were never built. A national bank arrived only after the Dutch stadtholder William of Orange invaded Britain and became one of its joint monarchs. *England's Improvement* also miscalculated the commercial trajectory of the Netherlands, which declined during the 1700s under the weight of factionalism and war with France, Spain, and England. The Dutch, it turned out, *could* be beat with fighting.

The 1680s exposed Andrew Yarranton to further personal attacks, including new allegations he had conspired with Presbyterian insurgents in 1662. His last publication, *A Full Discovery of the First Presbyterian Sham Plot* (1681), warily refutes old charges of treason. Yarranton hazards in this work to call his accusers papal agents, an incendiary charge in the years preceding the Duke of York's coronation. Then, in the midst of slanderous exchange and fomenting partisan discord, Yarranton was found dead: he was beaten and thrown into a bath tub, according to biographer John Aubrey.[158] Yarranton's apparent murder brings disturbing closure to a strange and prolific public life. His ideas would never form the basis of English economic policy or voice the "unanimous Prayer of the Nation in General."[159] His vision of a better England would, however, continue to circulate. *England's Improvement* was posthumously reprinted in 1681 (along with its advertised "second part") and again in 1698. Yarranton's proposal remains legible today to the extent that its printed pamphlet survives in archives.

Improvement projects originated as a kind of writing that sought to realize itself through action. The next chapter demonstrates how such writing became public through the technology of print. Understanding which projects became influential in early modern Britain, and which ideas of improvement remain accessible today, entails examining the material operations that turned proposals into objects. The world of print located projects at a physical vestibule between the rhetorical flights of proposing and the bodily labor of undertaking. Projection's paper chase, I will show, played a crucial role in making improvement thinkable in a period when paper was often all that hopeful schemes produced.

Chapter 2

Company in Paper

Aaron Hill's Beech Oil Bust

Daniel Defoe opens his *Essay upon Projects* (1697) by grousing that Britain "swarms with such a multitude of Projectors," each issuing "Innumerable Conceptions which dye in the bringing forth, and (like Abortions of the Brain) only come into the Air, and dissolve."[1] Defoe bemoans the pestilential volume of projects (the countless output of an authorial swarm) and their infinitesimal lifespan (dying from creation). His *Essay* ridicules Britain's transitory culture of scheming while contributing to it new proposals for highway repair, banking, and poor relief. A critic and sponsor of new enterprise, Defoe dubbed his era the "Projecting Age" to mark its vigorous exchange of ephemeral plans.[2]

But for projects to exist in ways that Defoe could attack, they required matter. They needed to circulate outside projectors' brains in media that would not simply melt into air. During the seventeenth and eighteenth centuries, this form was usually paper. While some schemes surely circulated by word of mouth, the challenge of credibly explaining new enterprise compelled most projectors to exploit the opportunities for descriptive nuance and narrative breadth afforded by print. In the 1600s and 1700s, projects materialized as sheets that were folded into pamphlets, bound into books, curled into scrolls, posted as broadsides, and cut into cards, bills, and tickets. The impression of ink on paper made visionary proposals into graspable objects that could be read, copied, scribbled on, and discarded. Print rendered projection a tangible event even though—and precisely because—so many schemes failed to leave the page.

Print also made a "Projecting Age" available to us belated readers, who access this period through the papers it left behind. Maximillian Novak associates the late seventeenth century with a "swarm of proposals . . . (usually in pamphlet form)."[3] Catherine Skeen locates a "print whirl of broadsides, pamphlets, and tracts" in eighteenth-century Britain and Ireland.[4] Novak and Skeen foreground the seeming innumerability of projects over the physical properties of individual schemes. For Novak, the "swarm" image takes precedence over the object, "pamphlet," which he couches in a parenthetical subclause. Skeen foregrounds the rapid motion of "whirl" over the print forms she lists. Nouns like "swarm" and "whirl" construe projection as a kinetic spectacle incorporating barely discrete objects. Metaphors of transience and accumulation also organize Carole Fabricant's description of a long eighteenth century "littered with the corpses of failed or abortive projects."[5] The project in this mortuary trope is explicitly a dead letter, a pile of defunct instructions. The broadsides and codices that once pronounced the future become in her language relics of expired ambition. Fabricant reduces projects to lifeless debris, the corporal residuum left by Defoe's long-dead swarm.

Representing old proposals as the mere husks of future thought strips projection of its sensuous existence in paper objects and discounts the effects of human handling that schemes received through publication. This chapter defies such foreclosures by showing how proposals became actionable through their printing. I claim that print was an enabling medium of projection rather than its incidental byproduct. Drawing on Raymond Williams's observation that the "strongest barrier to the recognition of human cultural activity is [the] immediate and regular conversion of experience into finished products," I treat printed proposals not as strewn rubbish, but as evidence of a "forming and formative process" that converted mental ambitions into disseminable plans.[6] Print created a vestibule between thinking enterprise and doing it. It was the mechanical process that made projects a kind of work legible to readers as well as a "complex craft carried out by fallible and inconsistent human beings."[7] Applying D. F. McKenzie's observation that the creation of a print work engenders stories "apart from that recounted by its text," this chapter maps the relation of scheming and dreaming to print craft, identifying the central actors, transactions, and networks that made projection a physical, legible phenomenon.[8]

Research into early modern book production has established what Michael Suarez calls the "worldliness of print," while loosening hard and fast divisions between the realms of text and object, rhetoric and document.[9] Christina Lupton distills an extensive tradition of bibliographical scholarship in her claim that the "material and social reality" of writing mediates the "multifaceted present and future of the text as object."[10] This question of textual futurity pertains especially to projects, writing whose very purpose was to construct the here-to-come. As expression that seeks to forge the conditions of its own "present and future," project writing obliges academic discussions of mediation to account for how intended but unrealized action could influence the circulation of writing as "something aware of itself in the present."[11] In Chapter 1, we saw how even the unheeded counsel of *England's Improvement* left its impress in a pamphlet printed by Robert Everingham and sold in Thomas Parkhurst's Cheapside bookshop under the sign of the Bible and Three Crowns. These details tell the story of how one project became a document that outlived the social and economic problems it sought to redress—an object narrative apart from but essential to Yarranton's tale of national improvement.

Investigating project print culture reveals how the commitment of proposals to paper influenced their reception and enactment. However, this culture resists comprehensive mapping and detailed inventory. Sustained attention to early modern enterprise reveals that projectors seldom confined their ideas to constant rhetorical forms ("the proposal") or stable material units ("the pamphlet"), but instead made use of whatever media they could harness to grab readers' attention. Broadside manifestos hawked in St. Paul's Churchyard campaigned for parliamentary statutes to curtail paper credit and charter fisheries. Advertisements in the *Daily Courant* directed readers to manuals for improving their lands, fortunes, and souls. Each of these items advances a project, but none entirely encompasses it. It was not a unified work that created the experience of a project for British readers so much as an orchestration of signs that flashed intermittently within different public venues. Reconstructing old enterprise therefore entails sifting its traces from a variety of archival sources and across numerous genres.

Where the first chapter analyzed the language of projection by taking apart *England's Improvement* word for word, this one traces the materialization of a project sheet by sheet. My focus is a sequence of documents related to the attempted invention of a new eighteenth-century commodity: beech oil. In 1714, the British poet and industrialist Aaron Hill proposed to extract oil from the nuts of beech trees for use as lubricant, food, medicine, and fuel. This appeared to be a promising idea at a time when England imported costly olive oil from France, Spain, and Italy, and beech forests canopied much of the realm. Hill's enterprise initially caught fire but then fizzled two years later, one of many entrepreneurial setbacks in an era renowned for agricultural revolution. What makes the oil venture especially intriguing is that so many of its papers survive today—a seemingly low attrition likely due to Hill's status as a semicanonical poet and playwright. Seldom is it possible to complete such a thorough forensic examination of an eighteenth-century project on the basis of its archival remains. Furthermore, while all projectors paid attention to how their writing circulated, Hill was exceptionally aware of participating in a world of print. His self-published beech oil propaganda mentions books, slips, sheets, and rolls. Years later, he outlined a project for milling cheap white paper. Hill's star-crossed adventures in oil retail foreground collisions between a rhetorically savvy projector and the world of nonsignifying matter he sought—and later fought—to control.

This chapter shows how an eighteenth-century business invented a new consumer good through its fabrication of documents. Where Pamela Smith and Benjamin Schmidt have rightly cautioned scholars against an "instinctive convergence on print media to the exclusion of other sources," my study of Hill reveals how project documents were not simply neutral vessels of rhetoric, but the product of human processes that sometimes became intertwined with nonstationery acts of production, like oil pressing.[12] Hill stressed the physical weight of his printed writings in order to legitimate his business and bolster his prediction that beech oil would became a staple of British diets. I trace the rise, collapse, and legal aftermath of his venture through its constitutive "print media," which sometimes incorporated substances besides paper and ink, and which invited uses other than reading. This chapter embarks on a paper chase of sorts that reveals ultimately how the paper behind Hill's projections chased futures that could not be had.

Aaron Hill's career as literary miscellanist and frustrated visionary is well studied. His beech writing in particular has received attention in biographies by Dorothy Brewster and Christine Gerrard.[13] But where Brewster and Gerrard explore the oil enterprise to illuminate Hill as a biographical subject, my chapter places the oil company at the center of its story to show how his writing contributed to the formation and dissolution of a joint-stock company. This defunct enterprise can help us specify the incremental differences between proposal documents that merely foretold industrial endeavor, and those that, to varying degrees, brought industry into being. Finally, I argue that in the aftermath of failed projects, printed proposals can also begin to explain the emergence of new pejorative terms, like "bubble," as an anxious response to the unregulated proliferation of projects on paper.

Patent Promotions

The paper trail begins with Aaron Hill's 1713 petition to patent his discovery of "how from the Fruit, or Triangular Seed of the Beech Tree, may be express'd a

sweet, pure, and wholesome Oil."[14] The beech project obviously did not orig-
inate with Hill's attempt to patent it, but his petition is the earliest written
evidence of the venture. Though projectors routinely sought state support in
the form of charters, grants, and tariffs, relatively few pursued patents owing
to the costly application process and difficulty of enforcing registered claims.[15]
Hill's venture would compete for investment with several other patent projects
from 1713 and 1714, including devices for drying malt and hops, drawing water
out of mines, and grinding dye woods, and Henry Mill's "machine for transcribing letters."[16] Petitions for these inventions and others were evaluated by
the attorney general not for merit but rather compliance with the 1624 Statute
of Monopolies. This law limited to fourteen years the period when the "true
and first Inventor" of an enterprise would enjoy the privilege of "sole working
or making of any manner of new Manufacutres within this Realme."[17] So enduring was disgust over Charles I's sale of commercial privileges to subsidize
his "Personal Rule" that even a century later patentees felt obliged to disclaim
the example of Caroline courtiers, who monopolized the sale of salt, soap,
starch, glass, coal, and iron to personal fortune and consumer agony.[18] Since
1624 it had been the task of the attorney general to safeguard the realm by
denying state sanction to exploitative schemes.

Hill distances himself from the stigma of patent profiteers by describing
beech oil as a vital yet harmless discovery. Where Charles I's cronies inflated
the prices of domestic staples, Hill presents beech oil as a cheap, homegrown
substitute for olive oil imported from the Catholic kingdoms of southern Europe. In so doing, he promoted a new idea of the patent projector not as a
parasitical insider but as a public-minded entrepreneur. Hill argued that by
extracting oil from the beech mast that blanketed Britain's countryside only to
be "eaten up by Hogs," his company could eliminate a crippling trade depen-
dency at a limited cost to pannaging commoners and their pigs. This proposed
substitution of foreign goods for domestic ones through industrial imitation,
a process Maxine Berg calls "the invention of commodities," would entail
"nothing but the Charge of shaking from the Trees," and transporting the mast
to London, where engines would "Grind and Press Three Hundred and Twenty
Tun within the year."[19]

Hill's petition apparently satisfied reviewers, who granted him a patent on
October 23, 1713. Patent bestowal meant that a clerk in the Chancery tran-
scribed in Latin an account of beech oil and its uses onto parchment sheets
that were stitched together to form continuous rolls, kept in the Court of
Chancery.[20] The text of the enrolled patent took the form of a letter from the

attorney general to Queen Anne professing beech oil's radiant ingenuity and commercial promise. Technical specification, the requirement that a patent application describe an invention in concrete detail, would not become compulsory until the 1770s.[21] This meant that Hill was free to pontificate vaguely on the social merits of beech oil without explaining how he would go about harvesting beech mast, cracking nuts, and storing their oil.

Between 1710 and 1718, 36 percent of patent applications either lapsed or were rejected, an unprecedentedly high failure rate.[22] This fact gave Hill modest standing to elevate his discovery over other schemes—to distinguish beech oil from projection's degraded fray just as Yarranton and Defoe tried to do with their respective schemes. In an era when patents could mean "whatever their holder could promote them as meaning," Hill eagerly publicized his award to investors and customers, targeting those involved with the oil-intensive manufacture of woolen textiles, soap, and rope.[23] The original patent, confined to cumbersome court scrolls, was an unfit promotional vehicle. Therefore, Hill copied its flattering language into a portable "Abstract of the Letters Patent," an essayistic summary of the patent that he would insert into pamphlets and newspaper notices. This abstract identifies Hill as the inventor of beech oil and stipulates that "no others" could claim its "Profit, Benefit, Commodity and Advantage."[24] This text lends official support to Hill's undertaking while also projecting Britain itself as a functional civil society capable of securing the "Profit, Benefit, Commodity and Advantage" of its inventors: "KNOW YE, That We, being willing to give Encouragement to all Arts and Inventions, which may be of such Publick Use and Benefit, of Our Especial Grace, certain Knowledge, and meer Motion, Have Given and Granted, and by these Presents, for Us, Our Heirs, and Successors, Do Give and Grant, unto the said Aaron Hill, his Executors, Administrators, and Assigns, Especial License, full Power, sole Priviledge and Authority . . . [to] have and enjoy the whole Profit, Benefit, Commodity, and Advantage, from Time to Time, Coming, Growing, Accruing and Arising, by Reason of the said Invention."[25] The patent supports Hill's promise of a vigorous beech trade by demonstrating the power of the crown to foster, define, and regulate innovation. The attorney general turns private ingenuity to "Publick Use and benefit" through the authority of "these Our Letters Patents, or the Inrollment thereof," instantiating state power through stationery practice.[26] Hill derives legitimacy from the abstract, which also reaffirms the role of the patent office as Britain's clearinghouse for commercial invention.

News of Hill's patent appeared four days later in the October 27 issue of the *Post-Boy*, one of several London-based periodicals founded after the lapse of the Licensing Act. Published thrice weekly between 1695 and 1728, the single-sheet *Post-Boy* catered to the city's growing appetite for news on trade and diplomacy. The patent notice appeared alongside reports from the Spanish royal court; an account of the Prussian envoy's travels through Holland; records of ship arrivals at Dublin, London, and Harwich; and advertisements for gowns and picture cards: "A Patent is pass'd the Seals, for granting to Aaron Hill, Esq; the sole Priviledge of a new Invention to make *Oil* from the Fruit of the Common Forrest Tree the *Beech*, which Invention, we hear, the Author affirms, will not only serve the Nation with an Eating-Oil as good as that from *Florence* and *Genoa*; but also supply the *Soap* and *Wollen* Manufactures, and all other Demands of Her Majesty's Subjects, without the Importation of *Forreign Oil*, to the particular Advantage of the *Wooded* Estates of this Kingdom, and general Employment of our *Poor* in one of the worst Seasons of the Year."[27] The notice begins by mentioning "Seals," pieces of wax embossed with the royal insignia. "Passing the seals" meant that a Chancery employee affixed a wax emblem of crown support to Hill's patent prior to its enrollment at Chancery. This literal stamp of approval validated Hill's claim that a domestic substitute for "*Forreign Oil*" would conserve wealth, raise land values, and employ idle people. The grammatical subject of this announcement is the first-person plural "we," a pronoun reflecting the *Post-Boy*'s gathering of multiple authorial voices under a single editorial organ, and perhaps also the writer's desire to identify with the public who would judge Hill's project through share purchase and oil consumption. The conflation of news writers and readers into a hopeful "we" anticipates the notice's concluding identification with the object form of the first-person plural noun, "us": "a little Time will shew us, whether a Pretension to so important a Discovery in Trade will be attended by the Consequences which so rais'd in Expectation makes us hope for."[28] The author qualifies Hill's optimism, harboring "hope" that the beech oil enterprise could succeed by making a physical demonstration of its worth. At the same time, this "us" demotes Hill's "discovery in trade" to "Pretension," evoking the speculative nature of similar projects that failed, their patents and promising rhetorics notwithstanding. The ambiguous "us" hopes and defers hopefulness by classifying beech oil as a commercial "discovery" whose merits would manifest over time. Until this unspecified date, beech oil remains "Pretension," capable either of gratifying or upsetting its stakeholders. The need to make beech oil appear as more than pretense would drive Hill to write pamphlets and newspaper advertisements with the intention of placing the products of an as-yet intangible future in the hands of readers: to "shew" readers through means other than words.

Folds and Readers

Hill's own writing about beech oil was less circumspect than the patent announcement. In December 1713, he took out the following notice in the *Post-Boy* to promote a new pamphlet proposing the establishment of a share-held corporation. The topic of the beech oil project's first newspaper advertisement was neither beech nor oil, but a paper tract: "*Given Gratis*, at the Oil Annuity Office against the Upper-End of *Mountague-House* in *Great Russel-street, Bloomsbury*, a Book, Entitled, †*† An Impartial Account of the Nature, Benefit, and Design of a new Discovery and Undertaking, to make OIL from the Fruit of the BEECH-TREE; by Authority of Her Majesty's Royal Letters-Patents, under the Great-Seal of Great-Britain. With Answers to All that can possibly be said against it. And Proposals for raising a Stock of 20000 l. upon Annuities for 14 Years, at 50 *per Cent. per Ann.* upon a good and solid Security."[29] The text invites readers to Hill's home (grandly rechristened as "The Oil Annuity Office") with the promise of free literature, *An Impartial Account*.[30] Hill chose to distribute his prospectus "gratis" from a private residence at a time when many pamphleteers arranged for the sale of their proposals in open-air markets, like St. Paul's Churchyard. Project writing regularly competed for eighteenth-century readers alongside "poems, plays, novels, periodicals, histories, travelogues, and more" according to Skeen.[31] George Wittkowsky speculates that readers of Swift's mock project *A Modest Proposal* (1729) would have been "accustomed to the sight of 'humble petitions' and 'modest proposals,' displayed on the book-stalls of London, Edinburgh, and Dublin, dealing with economic problems."[32] By contrast, Hill used gratis print as a loss leader, a strategy for baiting investors reminiscent of seventeenth-century projectors' "calculated use of print in search of profit as the printed page became complicit in the luring in of the consumer."[33]

Still, even as Hill gave away printed literature, he was careful to do so economically. *An Impartial Account* was printed on three sheets of paper folded three times each and bound together into a pamphlet. This type of book, known as an octavo, made fiscal sense for packaging a free manifesto because it could fit more text on fewer sheets than the larger quarto and folio formats when using sheets and type point of the same size. Pamphleteers and their publishers sought to limit sheet counts in the early 1700s, when paper accounted for 50–75 percent of book production costs, a problem exacerbated by Britain's lack of a white paper manufacturer.[34] Of the four beech oil pamphlets that Hill published, all were octavo, a trait they shared with other project proposals, including Carew Reynell's *True English Interest*, Defoe's *Essay upon Projects*, Charles Davenant's *An Essay upon Ways and Means of Supplying the War*, and later, Swift's project pastiche *A Modest Proposal*. Project writing by no means appeared only in octavo (Yarranton's *England's Improvement* was a quarto, and Nicholas Barbon's 1690 *Discourse of Trade* assumed the even smaller duodecimo format). But Hill's exclusive use of octavo for the beech oil pamphlets reflects a conscious weighing of costs against a desire for grander modes of presentation.

Hill's need to conserve paper and reduce costs also influenced the length of his pamphlets. Because each sheet in octavo makes eight leaves (sixteen pages), an octavo pamphlet must have a leaf count divisible by eight (page count divisible by sixteen), otherwise there would be blank pages left over— pages that thrifty printers would need to sew into other works (or other copies of the same work) to avoid wasting paper. *An Impartial Account* contained exactly thirty-two pages. This suggests that Hill had the final document form of his writing in mind during composition, and that his project writing answered physical requirements. These requirements were by no means rigid. It was the job of print shop compositors to make whatever adjustments were needed to parcel text efficiently. Still, the notion that the length of Hill's pamphlets was the product of negotiations between author and printer is bolstered by the fact that all the beech pamphlets match octavo specifications (Table 1).

The only pamphlet with a page count not divisible by sixteen was *Proposals for Raising a Stock*, which used exactly one and one-half sheets. Such works of twenty-four pages (twelve leaves) could be made through a procedure known as half-sheet imposition, which made two octavo pamphlets from three sheets of paper by cutting one sheet, with identical content on each half, down the middle, using four leaves in one pamphlet and four in another.[35] That all the beech oil pamphlets were octavos does not mean that print format straightjacketed Hill's writing; whether sheet counts factored at all into his

Table 1. Formats and Sheet Counts of Aaron Hill's Beech Oil Pamphlets

Title	Year	Format	Leaves	Pages	Sheets
An Impartial Account	1714	8°	16	32	2
Proposals for Raising a Stock	1714	8°	12	24	1½
Account of the Rise and Progress	1715	8°	56	112	7
An Impartial State of the Case	1716	8°	8	16	1

composition process remains a matter of speculation. My point, rather, is that these pamphlets were not infinitely customizable containers sized to accommodate boundless effusions of language. To the contrary, cheap print formats both created and limited the rhetorical possibilities of project proposals.

Hill hammered out the details of *Impartial Account*'s publication in partnership with several actors from the London book trade. He had worked previously with a number of different stationers in the preparation of poems, speeches, and histories, including Thomas Bickerton, William Keble, John Mayo, and Bernard Lintot. But in 1714, Hill turned to an entirely new printer, "J. Gardyner," to press and bind his first beech oil pamphlet. Records from the Electronic Short Title Catalogue suggest that "J" or John Gardyner was an active though unprolific printer during the first two decades of the eighteenth century. Of the eight works attributed to his press between 1700 and 1720, notable pieces include Nahum Tate's *Funeral Poems* (1700), John Pomfret's *A Prospect of Death* (1703), and parallel English and Italian librettos of *Dorinda* (1712). Why Hill employed Gardyner on this job is uncertain; perhaps it was Gardyner's connections to the Tory news purveyor John Nutt, though the availability of his presses and price of print runs were almost certainly factors as well.[36]

Impartial Account's imprint does not name a publisher, the party who "selects, organizes and above all, finances, the manufacture of books."[37] Given *Account*'s free distribution at the Annuity Office, and the fact that a later beech oil pamphlet identifies the "patentee" as publisher, it seems probable that Hill discharged this role himself. Self-publishing was common among English projectors who either could not find publishers for their proposals or elected to pay for printing themselves.[38] In return for absorbing production costs, Hill retained editorial control over his writing (except for the control ceded to the compositor in all printing), as well as the standing to negotiate with printers over the cost and scheduling of production runs. The resulting pamphlet would be the first product of the beech oil enterprise, an undertaking that invested first in paper in order to later capitalize trees. Knowing firsthand the cost of the medium that carried his words, Hill would waste no time enlisting the substance of his pamphlet as a persuasive resource.

Publishing Seeds

An Impartial Account opens with a copy of the patent abstract, the report that commended beech oil as a prodigious national discovery, on the four leaves following the title page. Hill foregrounds this official correspondence to ease his own argumentative burden at a time when new business proposals met with skepticism and projectors were typecast either as dilettante speculators or as overconnected monopolists. Hill speaks in his own voice for the first time on page 7, where he criticizes the doctrinaire cynicism of Britons who opposed all forms of new enterprise: "Every New *Proposal* must expect to meet with Opposition, from the *Envious*, and the *Ignorant*. And, as all untrodden Steps in Trade, are naturally subject to general Incredulity, and an undistinguishing Untowardness of Apprehension: It will be necessary to undeceive the World by barely doing Justice to the Undertaking."[39] *An Impartial Account* expects indiscriminate spite for taking "untrodden Steps in Trade." Hill therefore tries to shield his venture from envy and ignorance, to do "Justice to the Undertaking," by outfitting beech oil with a badge of state endorsement, his own cogent rhetoric, and the respectable codex form. Like Yarranton, who sought shelter from "the Arrows of Obloquy and Envy, that are usually shot at the Projector," Hill defends the beech oil business against critics whom he anticipates. This preemptive vindication leverages the materiality of Hill's pamphlet to verify the substance of his ideas: another tract refers to itself as a "book" multiple times, and with more exacting tactility, "the Book in your Hands."[40] That Hill equates his octavo pamphlet with a "book," a term usually reserved for longer print works, perhaps reflects the same aspirations of grandeur that led him to proclaim his house an "Annuity Office" before any mast was harvested or profits reaped. By labeling his pamphlet a "book," Hill furnishes himself with a solid explanatory instrument to "undeceive the World."

The alternative to print, for Hill, was speech. *Impartial Account* opposes its "sheets" to the "Noise" of detractors, comparing the permanence of writing to the fleetingness of talk. Where Defoe sneered that projects are "blown up by the air of great words," Hill contends that it is antiprojectors who are actually most vacuous: "these Busie-bodies, these Tongue-Champions, who, like a Drum, owe all their noise to their being hollow."[41] *An Impartial Account* distinguishes itself from this empty cacophony by seeming to declaim silent truths in prose made matter. Hill's diction exhibits what Joad Raymond calls "bibliographic self-consciousness," an awareness of how "physical construction and distribution shaped the social and rhetorical performances of pamphlets."[42] Hill highlights how his writing "circulated as paper, print, and commodity," in Christina Lupton's phrase, to frame *Impartial Account* as the culmination of purposeful action, while characterizing his critics as chatty reactionaries.[43] In his second beech oil pamphlet, *Proposals for Raising a Stock* (1714), Hill addresses these naysayers directly: "Light Heads are always Merrily dispos'd, and *Grave* ones often ready enough to laugh at any Thing, which looks like *Project*: I have more Reason than most Men to know this Truth, for scarce a Day passes in which I have not Pleasure to hear my self heartily Rail'd at in the *Coffee-Houses*, by People, who, all the while they are endeavoring my Hurt, have no Malicious *Intention*, and are equally Strangers to my *Person*, and *Discovery*."[44] Hill considers laughter a serious threat to his enterprise. So confused is London's coffeehouse banter that even spirited teasing can dampen the prospects of new enterprise by making it risible. Lounging in coffeehouses, vital nodes for sharing news and conducting business, merry Londoners manage to scandalize projects without factual knowledge or "Malicious Intention."[45] Against this heedless racket, the pamphlet, which probably circulated within those same boisterous venues, renders beech oil's virtues "clear and visible as the Light of Heaven" in an ocular register that shines through raillery.[46] Hill's 1715 pamphlet, *An Account of the Rise and Progress of the Beech-Oil Invention*, subjects its verbose critics to visual inspection to "expose to Scorn and Impudence and Folly . . . those idle Cavils and Objections which are made against it."[47]

Hill used the heft of print works to legitimate his venture, declaring in a later pamphlet that "the Business we are now upon, is no *Project*, 'tis a *Discovery*."[48] The presence of a "book," Hill believed, raised beech oil from dubious "Pretension" into a matter of natural fact. "Many, doubtless, have heard Talk of this Discovery before the Book comes to their Hands," Hill reflects, "and most of them were possibly possessed of an Opinion, that 'twas nothing but a Project."[49] By grasping that book, readers can feel the difference between a substantive "Discovery" and an illusory "Project": "A Project is a Notion, which, having no real or visible Existence, the Issue subsists at best upon a precarious Probability. But a Discovery is a Secret in Nature, or in Art, which having long lain hid, is brought to light by some fortunate Accident, pretends to nothing, but what Experience justifies, and carries its Demonstration along with it."[50] The bibliographically self-aware Hill makes beech oil "real" and "visible" through the medium of paper. He implies that the pamphlet's physicality testifies to beech oil's commercial prospects, an opportunity that "long lain hid," until lately "brought to light." Unlike the project, which contrives that which is not really there, "discovery" implies the existence of something concrete that carries "its Demonstration along with it." Hill's "demonstration" derives authority from its pamphlet mode, the testimony of the patent abstract, and the fact that oil droplets indeed filled the seeds of British beech trees. Empirical experience, Hill argues, is the test of whether an idea actually inheres in nature or is merely conjured from words: "People in Coffee-houses, or elsewhere, pretending to speak ill of the Invention, or advise against it; make This your Test of their Intention and their Honesty; Tell them, that Reason, and not Noise, shou'd be the End of Talking."[51] Hill encourages his readers to employ reason, a faculty derived of sensory experience, to judge the beech oil enterprise instead of relying on coffeehouse scuttlebutt. He insists that rational exploration should be the "end," both the goal and cessation "of talking," an individual search for truth in nature inspired (but not deterministically governed) by his own pamphlet's propositions.

Impartial Account then issues its readers a specific challenge: to stop reading about beech oil and begin making it themselves. The pamphlet's last page refers to "small Parcels" of mast "fastn'd to the Books," and offers directions for breaking the nuts and releasing their oil: "Pull of the outward Husk, then break the Kernel to Peices, take the smallest Bit you can find, no bigger than a Pins Head, lay it upon the Nail of your left Thumb, and squeeze it hard with the Nail of your right Thumb. By this means the Oil will come out upon both your Nails, and by the Quantity which Issues from so small a Bit, you will no longer wonder that a Bushel shou'd produce Two Gallons."[52] Hill invites readers to judge his venture by handling some mast, pressing its oil, tasting a few drops, and watching them burn with a bright blaze in candle flame. This extension of print technology to incorporate plant matter literalizes projection's goal of turning rhetoric into action, in this case, by enabling the reader to press and consume a tiny amount of oil. Instead of heeding "idle Rumours," or even taking Hill's pamphlet at its printed word, prospective investors could perform their own experiments, make deductions, and "no longer wonder."[53] Where *Impartial Account* opens with the testimony of the attorney general, it closes by inviting readers to verify beech oil's saturating plenitude firsthand through an exercise that Hill hoped would set apart his discovery from mere projects. These instructions invite readers to become discoverers themselves through a stationery contrivance that transforms *Account* into seed packaging, a wrapper irreducible to its words.[54]

Projection's Archives

Hill commits his ideas to "books," works thought to impart practical knowledge while advancing reputable discourses of trade and horticulture. *Impartial*

Account fashions itself as one work "among others," to use Yarranton's phrase for imagining the interconnectedness of late Stuart improvement tracts. Hill quotes, excerpts, and alludes to other writings in order to make his oil enterprise seem conversant with recent developments in British commerce and natural philosophy. These techniques of intertextuality—bibliographical consciousness of *other* works—locate external evidence to fortify Hill's claims. For example, *Account* cites the London Custom House's bills of entry to predict that beech oil would enjoy phenomenal sales "so prodigious indeed is the Demand for Oil, that tis a difficult matter to guess high enough for the Consumption of the whole Kingdom. It appears, by the Bills of Entry at the *Custom-House*, that, from *May* to *August*, this present Year was Imported, at *London*, Nineteen Hundred Tun of Oil. At this Rate, *London* alone, Imports above Seven Thousand Tun of Oil a-Year."[55] The bills of entry record the number and tonnage of goods legally imported and exported through London's ports each day. Hill could have calculated these figures by consulting the official manuscript bills at the Custom House offices, on the north bank of the Thames. Indeed, the prepositional phrase "at the *Custom-house*" implies that he went to the trouble of doing just this. But it probably would have been more convenient to simply purchase a summary of the bills, which were printed on newssheets and distributed throughout the city on non–holy days.[56] Whether or not Hill actually conducted research in the Custom House archives, he appears to have successfully retrieved pertinent records of trade, suggesting access to archives and facility with their contents.

Hill distills the custom records down to a single number: nineteen hundred tons, the officially recorded volume of oil imported through London between May and August 1714. The scarcity of extant bills makes it difficult to verify Hill's computations against their putative source, and by extension, to ascertain what role oil played within Britain's overall mercantile landscape.[57] There is no discussion of vegetable oil in Charles Davenant's *An Account of the Trade Between Great-Britain, France, Holland, Spain, Portugal, Italy, Africa, Newfoundland* (1715), which singles out linens, wine, brandy, silk, paper, and animal skins as Britain's most costly French imports.[58] However, Davenant touches on oil consumption implicitly through his analysis of the lubricant-devouring woolens industry, which accounted for 57 percent of English exports in 1700.[59] The widespread patenting of inventions for expressing the essence of rapeseed, sunflowers, and other oleos plants further implies a commercial demand for homegrown oil.[60] Hill dramatizes this deficit by manipulating the raw numbers he found in the entry books. He uses the figure of nineteen hundred tons to estimate annual oil consumption in the metropolis ("above Seven Thousand Tun") and then goes on to extrapolate the total amount of oil consumed by the entire country every year: "*Bristol*, also brings in, at least an equal Quantity to supply the Woollen Manufactures of the *West*; Every Twenty Pound of Wool requiring Five Pounds of Oil, before it can be made pliable, and fit to work upon. The *Northern* Ports, for the same Use, require the same *Supply*; so that it must be a very moderate Calculation, to allow to other the Out-Ports as much *altogether*, as to *London*, and *Bristol*; And this will make the yearly Importation of Oil, about Eight and Twenty Thousand Tun."[61] The "very moderate Calculation" that Britain imports twenty-eight thousand tons of oil per year is conservative according to Hill, who ultimately abandons numerical estimation to surmise that homegrown oil would find an inexhaustible domestic customer base. Analyzing customs data to forecast demand was a basic commercial practice in eighteenth-century Britain, and this was exactly Hill's point: to present himself as a conforming man of business and savvy discoverer of trade secrets rather than a fantastical projector peddling groundless schemes. *Impartial Account* attests to the exigency of beech oil by characterizing Hill as a knowledgeable analyst able to satisfy readerly expectations of empirical rigor in an investment prospectus.

The evidence Hill pressed into service could be narrative and testimonial as well as statistical. *An Impartial Account* reproduces several pieces of correspondence, including a letter from one W. Cecil, a Parisian noble who claims that France contains abundant beech forests that could be harvested should England suffer a bad crop.[62] In another pamphlet, *Account of the Rise and Progress of the Beech-Oil Invention*, Hill copies a letter from King James I to his lord lieutenants calling for the establishment of an English silk industry through the plantation of mulberry trees. The king's subjects were unmoved by their monarch, a fact Hill recounts bitterly: "And what do you think was the Effect of all [James's] Reasons? Why scarce a Man thought decently of his Attempt: Not a seed was sown; Not a Tree was planted; But the merry Creatures laugh'd immoderately at their good old Sovereign's being turn'd *Projector*, while they universally neglected and despised the Excellence of his Intention."[63] Hill invokes James I's letter to decry Britain's long-standing bias against new invention. In so doing, he links himself to an innovative sovereign who was laughed off as a projector, suggesting that they both shared myopic enemies and the same raw material: trees. This historical digression furthermore connects beech oil to a century of improvement efforts: *An Impartial Account* sympathizes with the first Stuart monarch, James, while brandishing the

authenticating seal of the last one, Anne. Where antiprojectors were quick to
invoke the scandal of early modern patent monopolies, Hill dwells on frustrated invention from the same era to remind readers that while Britain had
fallen for deceitful schemes in the past, its subjects had also squandered legitimate opportunities to make progress.

Hill delivers a history of his detractors while intervening in contemporary
debates over the use of English forests. *Proposals for Raising a Stock* (1714), for
instance, quotes at length from John Evelyn's *Sylva; or, A Discourse of Forest-
Trees and the Propagation of Timber in His Majesties Dominions* (1664). Commissioned by the Royal Society, this volume remarks that beech seeds yield
"sweet Oil, which the Poor People eat most willingly."[64] According to Evelyn
as quoted by Hill, the mast itself has "even supported Men with Bread."[65] By
copying passages from a book that "few Gentlemans Studies have been without, for these last Forty Years," Hill uses an acclaimed work of natural science
to verify beech oil's edibility.[66] This citation also suggests that Hill conceived
of his readers as "gentlemen" who could afford massive folios like *Sylva*, as well
as dedicated "studies." The residential study, according to Hill, was the ideal
setting in which to read about beech oil. This private and privileged space, he
believed, would encourage careful reading and knowledgeable investment, in
contrast to the discordant coffeehouse.

The image of a "gentleman's study" further implies an ideal collection of
books that could be read alongside *Proposals*, including monumental works
like *Sylva*. Hill implies that his writing warrants distinguished literary company by quoting Evelyn, and then later by directing readers to other relevant
sources through in-text citation: he specifically references "Sir Hugh Platt in
Jewel-House of Art, and Nature, Page 189," and "Lawson's Natural History of
Carolina, Page 94," to display his searching erudition.[67] Hill flaunts his debts
to the fields of botany and geography by inviting readers to track references to
the precision of page number. These citations embed *Proposals* within a community of knowledge-producing documents, modeling in a piece of investor
propaganda the citational structures of objective scholarship.

Hill's interest in academic discourses did not keep him from exploiting
more quotidian modes of print. In January 1714, he took out newspaper advertisements in the *Post-Boy*, the *Daily Courant*, and the *Englishman* to publicize
two print works: the free pamphlet *An Impartial Account*, with its bundle of
seeds, and the Beech Oil Company subscription books, now open at the Annuity Office. An announcement later that month informed readers that the
subscription books were closing, the enterprise having raised £13,000 of stock,

in spite of "ridiculous reports, and mistaken Notions which have with so much malicious Industry, been spread abroad to discourage the Undertaking."[68] That beech oil provoked rapid investment and malicious response confirmed Hill's expectations that his proposal would stir controversy, that some readers would censure his ideas while others grasped its underlying value.

Hill answered his critics through a second pamphlet, *Proposals for Raising a Stock of One Hundred Pounds; For Laying Up Great Quantities of Beech-Mast for Two Years*, published in April 1714. This work recalls the lucrative yet turbulent month of January when "in Ten Days Time, the whole Sum was subscrib'd" notwithstanding a "Thousand *Silly* Stories" attacking the enterprise.[69] If any of these "stories" were printed, none survives. Judging from Hill's response, it appears that his detractors faulted beech oil for being a capital-hungry scheme, a charge that drew on a tradition of antiprojection exemplified by works like *Angliae Tutamen; or, The Safety of England* (1695), which attacked projectors who "support their Necessities . . . without any regard to the Good of the Company in which they are engag'd."[70] To forestall accusations of graft, Hill announced that he would relinquish control of the Beech Oil Company to an elected board of managers who would keep all stock "entirely out of the Power of the Patentee, and subject to the Direction and Management of the Subscribers Themselves."[71] By putting a board between himself and investment capital, Hill hoped to appease critics. The more immediate effect, however, was to complicate the enterprise's management while multiplying its outlets of communication.

The Beech Oil Company's growth from a one-man project to a publicly subscribed corporation generated new documents, including shareholder memoranda and meeting announcements, which appeared in periodicals like the *Post-Boy. Proposals*, for instance, promises to give investors "Ten Days Notice in the Gazette" before the meeting to elect directors.[72] Newspapers provided a timelier mode for broadcasting messages than pamphlets, which could not be published with the thrice-weekly frequency that the company required to keep annuitants abreast of company news. Disseminating these "internal" messages through public media also had the advantage of promoting Hill's venture, giving nonshareholders a glimpse into the exciting affairs of Britain's growing beech oil industry. Hill's advertisements directed new investors to free literature at the Oil Annuity Office. Gratis pamphlets sent investors back to the newspapers for recurring updates.

Until the summer of 1714, the Beech Oil Company existed only through its members, pamphlets, records, the investment capital it had accrued, and its

Bloomsbury headquarters. Then, a June announcement in the *London Gazette* proclaimed, "Agents are now fix'd in all proper Places of this Kingdom; and the ten Northern Counties."[73] Hill alleged that men in his employ had located leasable beech groves across Britain, and were now ready to hire workmen to harvest mast. The sudden invocation of action—of the project's obtaining life outside the page—suggests that the "social and material reality" of the company now extended beyond writing. Print, in its myriad shapes and forms, now mediated between Hill's futuristic proposal rhetoric and the acts of labor that would apply his vision to the world.

Hill's Poem and Harley's Trees

Hill solicited investors through newsprint while courting a noble patron in verse. In 1714, he composed *The Dedication of the Beech-Tree*, a blank-verse panegyric addressed to Robert Harley, Earl of Oxford and High Treasurer under Queen Anne. This poem emblematizes Harley's capable leadership through the image of the beech tree, consecrating him lord of the "*oily* Harvests."[74] What privileges Hill hoped to obtain from his tribute are uncertain: he may have intended the poem to support his beech business by securing Harley's financial support, though Hill might also have used his versifying talents to earn the esteem of a powerful politician.[75] Christine Gerrard observes that the Tory Earl of Oxford "was scarcely an auspicious choice" for favor seeking in April 1714, three months before Anne fired him from the treasury.[76] Following Anne's death that August, Whig politicians, empowered by the Hanoverian succession, stripped Harley of his remaining offices, had him impeached, and then imprisoned for two years in the Tower of London.

Hill chose a bad time to air his devotion. But even despite Harley's decline, *Dedication* still emitted a praise song that might be heard widely, publicizing the beech discovery among consumers of Tory panegyric, a highbrow audience anticipated by the work's lavish material attributes. Where Hill issued his *Impartial Account* and *Proposals* in octavo, *Dedication* was printed in folio. British publishers often reserved this spacious format for serious works of art, scholarship, cartography, and theology (including sacred texts). The folio's large pages left ample space to display pentameter lines attractively, leaving wide margins and white space between lines. *Dedication*'s format befitted its task of commemorating Harley while designating beech oil a product worthy of elaborate, even ornamental presentation.

Hill gave away his cramped octavo pamphlets at the Annuity Office. *Dedication*, by contrast, was sold by the Tory publisher John Morphew. Hill had already purchased advertisements in Morphew's *Examiner*, so it is unsurprising that he would arrange for his poem to occupy retail space in Morphew's shop near Stationers' Hall. Here *Dedication* could have jostled for attention alongside titles in natural philosophy, literature, and politics, including Case Billingsley's *The Longitudes at Sea*, Daniel Defoe's *A Letter to the Dissenters*, Delarivier Manley's *L'Atlantis*, and Jonathan Swift's *The Publick Spirit of the Whigs*, all works sold by Morphew in 1714. That *Dedication* was sold (both wholesale and retail) distinguished it from Hill's gratis pamphlets, which were given away to spur investment. Hill's new poem sought to burnish a Tory hero's reputation, please readers of the same partisan persuasion, and put forward the beech tree as a fit synecdoche for British horticulture and industry.

Dedication portrays Britain as the blessed recipient of a mild climate and fertile soil. As the outgrowth of Britain's propitious geography, beech trees would, Hill claimed, render vital service to the kingdom's globe-ranging imperial ambitions. He predicts that this nut-bearing plant will one day displace the nonnative olive, "Oleus Plant, the Pride of Sunnier Climes," as a symbol of Britain's commercial and cultural supremacy:

> The humblest Forest of our favour'd Land,
> Grew proud beneath this Bounty of his Hand,
> Confess'd the *Secret* he vouchsaf'd to teach,
> Disdain'd the *Olive*, and enthron'd the *Beech*.[77]

Dedication associates providential gratitude with a Tory worldview personified by Harley, whom Hill credits with perceiving how the kingdom's arboreal resources would raise its collective welfare. The historical basis for this praise is uncertain, though it may have had something to do with Harley's appointment as warden of the beech-filled Sherwood Forest in 1712, a position he lost with his other offices in 1714. Under Harley's stewardship, even the kingdom's "humblest forest" purportedly yielded matter that, when gathered and distilled, could supplant a foreign luxury good. Modeling a sound mercantilist preference for domestic goods over imported ones, the Earl of Oxford instructs Anne's subjects to render the once-dominant olive "disdain'd," and the humble beech "enthron'd":

> *France* shall no more her courted *Vineyards* boast,
> But look with *Envy* on our Southern Coast,

Which *now* enrich'd with matchless *Oil* and *Corn*,
Unequall'd *Vintages* shall *soon* adorn.[78]

Hill's poetic alchemy transforms a vegetative deficit (Britain's lack of olives and grapes) into an impetus for innovation (the discovery of beech oil). *Dedication* predicts that Hill's business will strengthen Harley's realm by supplying a new exportable good that would balance trade deficits and exert British influence over Continental consumers, the same claims of economic independence made by the patent abstract. Once Britain develops its own oil source, France can only gaze jealously across the channel to the fertile woodlands and ripened grain fields of its former customer. In these couplets, the "matchless" and "unequall'd' produce of domestic groves and tillage eclipses France's metonymic vineyards, foretelling an era when rural England supplies oil to the world.

These visionary topographies dimmed with Harley's fall from power. Hill's untimely panegyric was soon followed by another mishap. In June 1714, the following notice appeared in the *Post-Man and Historical Account*: "Ten Share Tickets in the beech Oyl Company, NO, 4222, 4223, 4224, 4225, 4226, 4227, 4228, 4229, 4230, 4231: were taken out at the Office in St. Paul's Church yard on Thursday the 16th instant, and deliv'd there, by mistake of the Clerk, to the wrong Person. The Person that has them, is desired to bring or send them forthwith to the Office, they being of no use to any but the Owner, a stop being put to them. Note: if they are not brought or sent speedily, both the Tickets and the Person that brings them will be stop, wherever they are brought, as they must be, and Tallied, before any can receive them."[79] To incorporate the Beech Oil Company, Hill issued tickets, pieces of paper that conferred on their holders a share in the business's profits and an opportunity to direct it through election to the board of managers. Losing the tickets, conceivably, could mean forfeiting this stake. Hill sought to quash the unsettling notion that misdelivered tickets could disenfranchise annuitants (and vest unintended parties) by claiming that he put a "stop" on shares numbered 4222 through 4231. Despite this precaution, Hill still wanted the nullified tickets returned, so much that he took the trouble to publicize this embarrassing incident. The newspaper notice reveals Hill's struggle to control the documents that organized his project. Hill feared that his venture could lose credibility not owing to a failure of persuasive rhetoric, but rather through the misplacement of objects, an accident reflecting the worlds of contingency through which proposals circulated.

Despite Harley's waning influence, occasional human error, and the steady

drumbeat of libel and reproach, Hill would amass £120,000 of stock by the
end of 1714, and turn it over to the newly elected board of directors (of which
he was a member). That winter, Hill proclaimed that "this Company is already
in a pretty considerable Forwardness."[80] While company agents scoured British
forests for beech groves and oil markets, the board voted to lease a warehouse
in Vauxhall along the Thames for the unloading and processing of mast ship-
ments. Hill designed and built machinery for separating beechnuts from their
burred mast. Newspaper advertisements suggest that the company began collecting mast and shipping it down the Thames that fall.

Prior to these events, Hill composed a new "book," *Account of the Rise and
Progress of the Beech-Oil Invention*, containing "seven Sheets of Paper," and to
be "given away *gratis*, at the Sign of the Golden Key, a Woollen Draper's, in St.
Paul's Church-yard; where Shares continue to be sold daily."[81] Hill tallies the
sheets in his pamphlet to emphasize the work's length, which contained 112
octavo leaves. The notice also indicates that the Beech Oil Company had
moved its operations from Hill's home into a draper's shop near St. Paul's.
Relocating to a site of cloth production and wholesaling enabled Hill to associate beech oil with the textile trade it sought to infiltrate, suggesting cooper-
ation between an upstart patent company and an established British industry.
Relocating near the epicenter of London's book trade at St. Paul's had the additional convenience of placing Hill close to the majority of the city's printers,
publishers, and booksellers, whose services he would seek frequently in subsequent months.

Despites its optimistic overtones, Hill's notice also betrays frustration.
Though he would continue to give away *An Impartial Account* at the Annuity
Office, Hill implores potential readers "not to send for it, unless you resolve to
read it presently, and with due Attention; it being a very wonderful thing, that
many People, upon whom this Book has been already thrown away, have kept
it in their Hands three Weeks or a Month, and either not read it all, or run it
over so carelessly, that they know nothing of the Matter."[82] Gratis print was not
free, especially in the case of the most recent and lengthy pamphlet. This is
why Hill scolds readers who mistreat his print works, knowing as he did the
cost of making pamphlets down to the single sheet. The "wonderful thing" of
a pamphlet should be read immediately and with due care, he urged, so as not
to waste the labor and materials expended in its creation. Where the Harleyian
beech tree symbolized a limitless profusion of oil and the global extension of
British political influence, this reprimand bespeaks the hardships associated
with making and marketing the first batch of a good. Hill constructs worlds

of poetic infinitude that belie his constant grappling with constraints stemming from cost, distance, and shareholder conflict. *Dedication* presents as pre-
destined a project that struggled to conceive of its own success in the face of
ceaseless obstacles.

Railing in Print

The year 1715 would prove disastrous for the Beech Oil Company. A paltry
mast harvest disheartened shareholders and called into question Hill's talents
and credibility. The cost of employing "vast Numbers of Workmen" left the
company unable to make a payment due to its annuitants.[83] Christine Gerrard
observes that the September Jacobite Rising "can have done little to enhance
public faith" in Hill, who fawned over Harley and marketed his business in
Tory periodicals.[84] What's more, newspaper advertisements from that spring
indicate that the company now faced competition from rival oil ventures. A
May 24 notice printed in the *Post-Boy* announces that "Four Gentlemen have
the Knowledge of a certain English Vegetable, whose Seed yields plentifully, an
Oil, as sweet, pure, and wholesome to eat, as the best Foreign Oil; will keep
much longer and better (some of it having stood a whole Year in a Window,
where all the last and this Summers Sun has lain, and not in the least changed),
and such Quantities of it can be yearly made, as will supply the Nation for all
the Occasions of Soapmakers, Clothiers, and other Trades, as well as for Eating, and be afforded cheaper than beech or Rape Oil."[85] Hill secured "the sole
Privilege of a new Invention" through his patent, but he could not prevent
others from using protectionist rhetoric to hawk their own solutions to Britain's oil shortage. What crop the "Four Gentlemen" discovered is unstated,
making it all the more intriguing. Radishes seem plausible, given that this root
produced oil-rich seeds and became an object of commercial speculation in the
early 1700s. The notice tantalizes readers by revealing that the vegetable in
question is already "very commonly and profitably Eaten by People of all Degrees in the Kingdom," that its essence is more wholesome and durable than
"Foreign Oil," and that it could be made "cheaper than beech or Rape Oil."
The advertisement supplants beech with a mystery crop, relegating Hill's invention to the status of rape (canola), another oil crop supposedly surpassed
by cheaper alternatives. Where beech oil was at first dismissed for its untested
novelty, it now faced the equally damning charge of obsolescence.[86]

Beech oil's critics, whom Hill had hitherto imagined as loud-mouthed gossips, were now entering their complaints in the realm of print. Another newspaper advertisement, published in the September 30 issue of the *Post-Boy* took explicit aim at the Beech Oil Company and its cost projections: "Whereas a Project hath been formed by Pretences made to purchase Beech-Mast at the Price of 1 s. per Bushel, or a lesser Price, which may deceive a great Number of People by inducing them to believe it may be purchased and gathered at so Cheap a Rate; This Notice is given to prevent the further Success of such evil Intentions, that James Tanner, Esq; Mr. James Parlow, and Mr. Abraham Thomas, of Hatchet-lane in Windsor-Forest, are willing to pay 2s. 6d. per Bushel this plentiful Year, for any Quantity of found and ripe Beech-Mast."[87] The notice refers to Hill and his partners as "Pretences," a portmanteau combining the figure of the "prentice," an inexperienced craftsman, and "pretense," an untested notion of self-worth. Tanner, Parlow, and Thomas challenge Hill's assumption that mast could be had at minimal cost by offering to buy quantities of beech seed at a rate one shilling and sixpence per bushel more than the beech company was willing to pay. It is unclear whether the three men wanted to do anything beyond thwarting the "evil Intentions" of Hill's company (or whether they even thought they could buy mast at that rate). Tanner, Parlow, and Thomas appear to position themselves as public guardians concerned that a "great Number of People"—including potential shareholders, customers, and woodland property holders—were being deceived into thinking that beech seeds could be "purchased and gathered at so Cheap a Rate." By hammering away at Hill's foundational premise that valuable oil could be made from near-worthless tree matter, the advertisement purports to expose the faulty reasoning behind a well-known enterprise.

Hill's opponents often spoke through publications like the *Post-Boy*, a periodical that simultaneously ran notices touting the myriad applications of beech oil. The print media that Hill exploited for publicity and praised for its truth-bearing capabilities could also be weaponized against him. Even Hill's own pamphlets became targets of vandalism. The British Library's copy of *Account of the Rise and Progress of the Beech-Oil Invention* contains marginalia refuting several of Hill's claims regarding beech seeds and their availability. Using a pen to bracket statements as "true," "false," and "intirely false," the anonymous reader-scribe pours over *Account*'s text, ironically showing a degree of assiduity that Hill requested of readers when he announced that this work would be given away gratis.[88] Of course, the purpose of this fact-checking was to discredit Hill, presumably for the benefit of whatever future readers would come to encounter his ideas in that copy. The very pages that Hill leveraged to assert the weight of his discovery now bore a skeptical inscription questioning their contents.

Plagued by luckless circumstances and out-maneuvered on the page, the beech oil enterprise also faced a crisis of capital, like so many "pretension"-laden projects before it. In response to the poor harvest, political instability, and criticism in newsprint, Hill took the radical step of allowing subscribers to withdraw their entire investments. This offer stipulated that divesting annuitants would receive the total amount of their original investment plus 25 percent of the principal. Hill intended for this magnanimous display to comfort shareholders and foster faith in the company's long-term financial health. It backfired when almost everyone accepted the buyout. This left the company depleted of stock just as oil production began to lurch forward.

Forging Evidence

Hill's need for new sources of funding inspired his longest piece of beech writing, *Account of the Rise and Progress of the Beech-Oil Invention*. This 112-page pamphlet recounts "all the Steps which have been taken in that Affair, from the First Discovery, to the present Time."[89] Hill again promises readers to "make you a Present of the following Discourse; that is, I give you the Book *gratis*."[90] The new *Account of the Rise* opens with an extended tirade against those Britons whose habitual animus toward all forms of speculative enterprise had made "this word *Project* . . . downright scandalous."[91] Like *An Impartial Account*, *Account of the Rise* shields its proposals from degraded project terminology and disparages skeptics incapable of crediting worthwhile discovery. The goal of (re)financing the Beech Oil Company would provoke Hill's most passionate attack against England's hostile reception of new ideas.

But *Account of the Rise* contained more than polemic. It is the first piece of writing in which Hill divulges how he first stumbled on the idea of retailing beech oil—how the discovery was discovered. This anecdote takes place in Naples in 1700, where Hill, then fifteen years old, was trekking across southern Europe en route to Turkey. While in southern Italy, he fell sick with fever and was treated with a concoction of almond oil.[92] Upon his recovery, Hill passed by a grove of beech trees. He plucked off some of the mast, chewed it, and noticed that the seeds tasted like the almonds that had cured his fever. Hill ordered an apothecary to grind up a few pieces of mast, express their oil, and seal it in a jar. He then watched the jar for the length of a year and observed that the beech oil never rotted. Upon returning home to England in 1712, Hill realized that southern England contained vast acres of unused beech forest and settled on his scheme to harvest these woods for their durable, medicinal oil.

This pleasingly compact vignette recasts adolescent experience as the impetus behind innovation: the beech oil project contributes a moment of personal insight to the collective work of national improvement. Composed in 1715, after the beech oil enterprise had sprawled into an embattled joint-stock company, the memoir straightforwardly recasts the enterprise as a genuine effort to capitalize on an undervalued resource. Hill undertakes a biographical exploration of the venture's origins in order to reinstill readers with its spirit of inaugural optimism unmediated by complaints and competitors. This streamlined narrative vouches for the altruistic motivations behind his business by returning readers to its moment of innocent discovery. Hill then exhibits a range of papers that underscore just how sophisticated the operation had since become.

We have seen how Hill drew on archival sources, like the Custom House bills of entry, to legitimate his business. The beech pamphlets were also capable of fabricating entirely new documents to showcase the Beech Oil Company's intricate record-keeping practices. One page of *Impartial Account* simulates a ledger illustrating the volume of oil that could be pressed and bottled per pound of investment. This "Account of the whole Charge of making 220 Tun of Oil" factors each of the venture's costs, including land rental fees, wages, the price of tools, and shipping expenses to calculate that an investment of £2,500 would yield 320 tons of oil, at a unit cost of £7.8 per ton. The only limit to oil production, according to this ledger, would be the amount of capital raised over the fourteen-year duration of the patent. (Hill anticipated increased competition and lower profits once his protection expired.) Where Hill found evidence of a widespread appetite for beech oil in the custom bills, his table attests the company's ability to meet this need, on the supposition that each bushel of mast yields two gallons of oil "far better than most Jarr-Oil, commonly sold by Wholesale for Ten Shillings *per* Gallon."[93]

Besides numerical evidence, Hill's pamphlets also reproduce administrative forms used to vest shareholders. Among these forms is the receipt that subscribers obtained after depositing the first 25 percent of their investment. Printed across two facing pages, the receipt leaves blank spaces for Hill (or one of the directors) to write by hand the amount of money placed in the subscription, the total value of the share, and the name of the investor. Once fully vested, a subscriber could submit this receipt to the Oil Office and exchange it for a "Warrant, Indented, Cypher'd, and Seal'd with the Seal of the said Office."[94] The existence of these forms demonstrates that Hill's business had established procedures for receiving subscriptions and that it one day expected to return dividends. Hill's stationery contrivance makes these internal processes publicly visible; *Impartial Account* commends the professionalism and permanence of the Beech Oil Company by touting its efficient processing of paper.

Account of the Rise in 1715 would exhibit an even larger collection of documents. Among these incorporated forms were instructions addressed to one Jacob Westley on how to "obtain proper Information, for establishing a Staple of Beech-Oil, for the Supply of the Cloathing Trade in the County of Worcester."[95] Hill also included letters from regional agents who reckoned high demand for beech oil among drapers, soap makers, and merchants in northern England as apparent proof that "Beech-Oil can never want a Market."[96] *Account of the Rise* even includes copies of a beech-surveying guide addressed to one William Cross in preparation for a "Journey for Procuration of Beech-Mast, through the Counties of Dorset, Somerset, and Wilts."[97] This guide includes some rather matter-of-fact advice on the importance of speaking to "all Innkeepers, Travellers, Country-men" and entering notes in "a Paper-Book, by way of Journal," as well as some more inventive argumentative strategies for convincing landholders to hire poor parishioners to harvest mast on their property.[98] This collage of documents purports to expose the inner workings of the Beech Oil Company, characterizing it as an ongoing operation rather than a futuristic enterprise. Hill argues for the viability of his project by appearing to test its propositions against external evidence. In reality, this evidence is strategically curated so as to convince the reader to accept Hill at his word.

One of the pamphlet's most striking, perhaps scandalizing features was its directory of annuitants, a list of men and women who purchased stock during the first and second offerings.[99] This "schedule" names forty-two subscribers and sums their investments, ranging from John Mennel's purchase of £3,455 in stock (entitling him to £24,185 in annuities over the fourteen-year life of the patent) to Dorothy Louch's contribution of £10 (commanding £70 over that same period). Hill had once referred to "eminent Merchants, Gentlemen of great Estates, and even Noblemen" whose names could be "seen by the Books at the Office" in a *Post-Boy* notice.[100] *Account of the Rise* discloses those names, identifying a community of beech investors that readers could join, albeit belatedly: that most of the listed subscribers had by this point withdrawn their investments did not deter Hill from exploiting their reputations.

Hill touted the Beech Oil Company's "progress" even though its investors were abandoning him en masse. Only after ninety-five pages does *Account of the Rise* address the decision of its shareholders to cut ties with the venture. Hill dismisses his investors' skittishness as a consequence of one anomalous bad harvest and the wonted impatience of eighteenth-century speculators (likely the same hurriedness that led readers to rifle through *An Impartial Account* without "due Attention"). It was bad weather and fickle investors that made the beech oil business shrink "into a very narrow Compass," according to Hill, and not an inherent flaw in his design or error in execution.[101] Frustrated but undaunted, Hill continued to believe the company required only a fresh infusion of capital to rebound and grow.

But Hill never raised the money to save his business. Newspaper advertisements from 1716 paint a bleak portrait of the company's final days. An April notice in the *Post-Man and Historical Account* urges all remaining subscribers to meet "about a matter of great importance, to prevent the total loss of their money," suggesting that the company verged on dissolution such that quick action was necessary.[102] By this time, the Annuity Office had moved again, from the draper's shop near St. Paul's to Essex Street in the Strand, where new investors were, as ever, cheerily invited to register their names in the "numerical book" of subscriptions.[103] Given the company's sudden loss of cash, the board's decision to relocate may have been a measure of fiscal necessity, a spatial displacement reflecting the disarticulation between Hill's boundless ambition and the project's diminished resources.

The move to Essex Street coincided with the company's decision to liquidate its remaining beech oil reserves. Where Hill originally hoped to supply soap makers and wool drapers across rural Britain, the transportation of oil from Vauxhall required funds that the company now lacked. The directors resorted to dumping its remaining oil reserves in whatever London markets it could find. Advertisements that ran in the *Daily Courant* on May 12, 15, 23, 24, 25, and 28 announced that the company would sell oil at 10 shillings per gallon from its new Annuity Office near the Strand. Those who wanted oil to "eat with Sallads, and for other delicate Uses" could purchase one-gallon stone jars. Purchasers desiring larger quantities were invited to "apply themselves to the said Directors at [Essex Street] every Wednesday in the Forenoon."[104]

A better bargain was available to buyers in "Coffee-houses and other Places in and about the Cities of London and Westminster, where beech oil could be had at 2 s. a quart."[105] In his first pamphlet, Hill demeaned coffeehouses as hives of obtrusive chatter. But the board of managers now approached these spaces as potentially lucrative sales venues. The notice suggests that selling oil within coffeehouses could help "defeat the evil Intentions and Confederacy of People," confronting the venture's loudest detractors with samples of a finished commodity. Perhaps Hill took some satisfaction in placing his invention in the hands of Londoners who doubted the company would ever materialize beyond its printed promises. But the gimmick also bespeaks the operation's mounting desperation. By late September, beech oil appears to have been available only at the Essex Street office and Vauxhall warehouse, suggesting that the company no longer had the means or reason to transport its product.

Two beech oil announcements ran in September issues of the *Daily Courant*. One notifies company shareholders that a meeting would take place on September 26 to elect a new board of managers. The other addresses any customers "willing to contract for a Quantity" of oil. These advertisements would run in tandem throughout the month. A November 10 notice marked the last time that Aaron Hill's beech oil business would promote itself through a London periodical. This did not mean, however, that beech oil vanished from the public record. To the contrary, Hill's venture would obtain a strange and prolific documentary afterlife through its postmortem mockery.

Oil Bubbles

Hill published his final beech pamphlet in 1716. The purpose of *An Impartial State of the Case Between the Patentee, Annuitants, and Sharers, in the Beech-Oil Company* was not to sell oil, but rather, as the title page proclaimed, to vindicate its author to "the General Satisfaction of all the concern'd Parties," namely the annuitants who blamed Hill for the loss of their money.[106] Unlike earlier proposals that foretold vast profits and a nation's gratitude, *An Impartial State* baldly concedes that "Disappointments of the *Beech-Oil Company* this Year have made abundance of the Sharers peevish."[107] Hill knew that several of his former investors were now pursuing suits at the Court of Chancery to recover their subscriptions, funds that he maintains were spent on legitimate operational costs. Hill directs aggrieved shareholders to consult "the publick Accounts, and *Minute-Books* of the *Office*," as proof that the business ran legitimately, if not always profitably: "So that it plainly appears, that, out of *twenty five thousand Guineas*, I have *given away*, in two Articles only, *twenty three thousand seven hundred and fifty Pounds*, for the Publick Advantage. And I can easily prove that the little Remainder has been short of making Good the Charges I have been at, for their Service: By which means I am not one Farthing a Gainer by the *Company*, notwithstanding the Clamour and Malice of some Unthinking Adventurers: And for the Truth of All This, I appeal to their own *Office-Books*."[108] The same books that Hill used to promote his business he would now call on to exonerate himself from charges of embezzlement. *An Impartial State* alleges to show Hill's innocence "plainly" by transforming company records into the exculpatory evidence of a failed but above-board enterprise. "Truth" again resides in books for Hill, even when those books trace an ultimately disappointing story.

Despite Hill's efforts to defend the company and clear his name, beech oil was soon travestied as a disreputable venture born of a dangerously speculative age. One especially caustic jeremiad, Thomas Baston's *Thoughts on a Trade, and Public Spirit* (1716), portrayed Hill as a diabolical "Oil Projector" guilty of penning "several learn'd Treatises on this Subject, and very modestly calls every Man a *Fool* or *Knave* that has not a mind to let him finger their Money; but till his last Cheat is blown up, as all the rest have been, perhaps we may not have a new one."[109] Baston accuses Hill of authoring pseudoscholarly "learn'd Treatises" to raise the price of company stock before "'tis known whether the Project has any intrinsick Value in it."[110] By calling out *Impartial Account*'s conspicuous attempts to enter discourses of science and geography, *Thoughts* intensifies the reservations of the writer who initially reported on Hill's patent in the *Post-Boy* of 1713, and who worried that the project might never become more than "Pretension." But unlike this author, Baston is able to disparage Hill's project with the conviction of hindsight by placing beech oil in the company of laughable adventures in mining and munitions: "*First*, The Projector finds out some fair-fac'd Project, such as getting Silver out of the Mountains in *Wales*, *Salt Petre* from *Bun-Hill*, or *Tom-Turds-fields*, *Oyl* from *Beech-mast*, and many such like."[111] It is not beech oil itself that Baston finds contemptible so much as the rhetorical and print strategies Hill employed to convince readers that commercial value could be extracted from waste matter. Most aggravating to Baston was Hill's habit of labeling anyone an enemy of invention who "has not a mind to let him finger their Money."[112] Where Hill promoted beech oil as a singular discovery, Baston lumps his scheme in with every other "*villanous* Project to cheat the Publick."[113] Baston demeans Hill's enterprise as the "Off-Spring" of the era's heedless lust for profit and esteem, one idea belonging to an indistinct multitude—the same metaphor that critics like Skeen, Novak, and Fabricant would reactivate centuries later.

Anxiety over projects on paper increased exponentially in 1720 with the crash of the South Sea Company and the popularization of a new catchword for expansive yet hollow enterprise: bubble. The Scottish economist Adam Anderson cited beech oil as one example of a bubble, a company that expanded rapidly through investor enthusiasm before common sense reduced the business to "proper size and value."[114] Beech was one of several "oil bubbles"; there were also schemes to commodify the essence of poppies, sunflowers, hemp, and radishes. Writing several decades after the collapse of the Beech Oil Company, Anderson suggests that Hill's propaganda best serves as a "warning to posterity" on the glittering hazards of Britain's Projecting Age.[115] Just as the metaphorical bubble possesses substance only in its circumference film, so do the ventures Anderson caricatures obtain matter only in the printed sheets of their promotional literature. Adapting Defoe's metaphor of projects "blown up by great words," Anderson reduces to popped nothingness an enterprise that actually took serious strides toward materializing itself through labor practices, finished products, and, however momentarily, consumer purchases.

Hill never answered Baston or Anderson, nor did he write anything to mitigate the disgrace of his company's dissolution. When a band of annuitants sought to revive the beech oil patent in 1720, Hill appears not to have taken part.[116] He would, however, continue to defend projection as a vital and generative activity, an especially unpopular chore following the South Sea Crash. In 1721, Hill composed a one-act tragedy, *The Fatal Extravagance*, performed at Lincoln's Inn-Fields. This short drama depicts the strife that engulfs a family following their disastrous investment in the South Sea Company, "this last, worst, Adventure, of lost Hope, / Which has, at once, dissolv'd a Wealth so vast!"[117] The play's villain, however, is not a projector of colonial fortune, but rather a predatory creditor, Bargrave, who lends money to Woodley, a friend of the protagonist, Bellmour. Bellmour seeks to avenge Woodley's imprisonment for debt by confronting Bargrave:

Who, but thy self, spread all those Snares about me,
Which, first, entangling, next o'erthrew my Virtue?
Who stain'd the Native Whiteness of my Soul,
and Spotted it with Follies?[118]

It is the rapacious financier, Hill suggests, that profits from bubbles, and not the public-minded projector, who enterprises heroically against the "dark Doubtfulness of deep *Futurity*."[119] Bargrave dodges Bellmour's accusations of entrapment, but the two enemies soon take up swords. Their violent duel perhaps dramatizes the litigious combat that pitted Hill against his former annuitants. Bellmour runs Bargrave through with his blade but later kills himself for fear of legal retribution and losing his lover, Louisa. *The Fatal Extravagance* avenges the projector but also fates him for tragic demise to underscore how systems of lending and capital investment ultimately confound those who toil to modernize Britain.

Unlike his tragic stand-in, Hill would survive the Beech Oil Company's failure. Indeed, by December 1716, he was back to proposing new projects for homemade chinaware, rice farms, river breech repair, and even the milling of white paper. The last undertaking made paper its medium and theme, a projection to cheapen the conditions of writing and thus perpetuate the promotion of future endeavor. This project, like most of Hill's others, failed to exist beyond its proposal ink.

Piecing together the Beech Oil Company from its print remnants yields anything but a unified narrative. To the contrary, this research illuminates the tendency of projects to fray into innumerable loose ends. The mediating effects of paper formats and stationery relationships even call into question what counted as project writing in this period. That Hill's scheme collapsed scandalously means that he would coauthor its eulogy with his venture's critics, further complicating beech oil's beleaguered legacy—the history of its once future promise. Print, in this context, bears evidence of partly realized projection. Where the ideas expressed in Andrew Yarranton's *England's Improvement* remained within the domain of rhetoric and imagination, Hill's managed to move matter in the world. The Beech Oil Company went far enough toward fulfilling its goals that it invites counterfactual conjecture: What if rainy weather had not hindered mast gathering? What if Harley had remained in a position to champion the company? What if Hill's annuitants had kept faith in his vision? These questions imagine the circumstances under which projects could succeed, in which print objects proved capable of spurring and sustaining the actions they prescribed. This action and its tenuous archival status form the subject of my next chapter.

Chapter 3

Projects Beyond Words

Undertaking Fen Drainage

I have argued that projects consist of written plans for action and the possibility of action itself. Chapters 1 and 2 focused on those plans, specifically their rhetorical construction of possibility and circulation among readers. This chapter turns to the action of projects, when enterprise left the realm of prospective language to remake the actual world. The transformation of proposal text into human task was called "undertaking" in seventeenth- and eighteenth-century Britain, as well as "enactment," "execution," and "performance." These terms describe an activation of potential that distinguished the project from other forms of writing as a vehicle for imagining and compelling societal change through incremental endeavor. Projectors sought to bring about—not just describe—the practices, events, and institutions they conceived through the written word. Undertaking encompasses this bringing about, the processes meant to carry a project from conception to completion.

The successful execution of new enterprise typically required some combination of money, labor, land, political will, and expertise. Some projects faced opposition. Others required ready markets, royal favor, or parliamentary permission. Undertaking is the juncture at which projects made demands on society's resources in order to span the ontological gap between language and the "doing of language," between "the world of signs and the world of things."[1] Undertaking is therefore also the moment at which most projects burned up. Andrew Yarranton extolled Dutch land banking but could not will a single parish to institute it. Aaron Hill rhapsodized on the mercantilist virtues of beech oil but could not increase mast yields or quell Jacobite rebellion. Hill's scheme did succeed in getting off the ground, momentarily, to command labor, organize correspondence networks, and create sales opportunities, though the Beech Oil Company ultimately wound up on the scrapheap of history. Hill's project failed to the extent that its undertaking never bore out the promises that spurred it. The world refused to conform to the vision of his proposal.

Today the words "project" and "undertaking" are synonyms, but during the long eighteenth century, the latter term usually meant the carrying out of the former. Robinson Crusoe implies this distinction when he contemplates "Projects *and* Undertakings beyond my reach."[2] Defoe chose Crusoe's words carefully. Two decades earlier, in his *Essay upon Projects*, he prefaced a scheme to renovate England's decrepit highways by asserting, "I am not Proposing this as an Undertaker, or setting a Price to the Publick, for which I will perform it *like one of the Projectors I speak of;* but laying open a Project for the Performance."[3] He adds, "I do not doubt but 'twou'd be easy at any time to procure Persons at their own Charge to perform it for any single County, as a Pattern and Experiment for the whole Kingdom."[4] Defoe claims to circulate a blueprint for others to execute. He distinguishes between the remunerative "undertaking" of road renovation and the disinterested labors of proposal authorship, styling himself as a benevolent sponsor of public works rather than someone who stood to profit from their implementation.[5]

Defoe distances himself from the unseemly figure of the projector by refusing to undertake his own scheme, suggesting that performance was a controversial and potentially discrediting stage of projection. Another tract from the 1690s, Mary Astell's *Serious Proposal to the Ladies* (1694), similarly distinguishes between "wiser heads" who could "improve and perfect" her prose, and "kind hands" who could "perform and compleat" her plans to build a monastery to moralize and instruct English women. Without performance, *Serious Proposal* would constitute "a few hours thrown away, and a little labour in vain," a diverting read rather than an actionable plan.[6] Astell solicits hands rather than heads to raise in stone the ideals of female intellectual sovereignty that her pamphlet envisioned through rhetoric. It is this call for action that makes *Proposal* a proposal, a distinct endeavor rather than mere meditation.

Undertaking could transform projects from discursive exercises into history-making events. But for us belated readers of eighteenth-century culture who approach old proposals as objects in archives, that event proves elusive. Some projects, like those of Astell and Defoe, had no undertaking to speak of. Other enterprises, like Hill's, left behind caches of proposals, patents, newspaper advertisements, and court records. But even this evidence of a project's

partial implementation leaves much unilluminated: the fatigue of mast pick-
ers, the pace of oil auctions, and the gathering gloom of shareholder meetings
all belong to the experience of Hill's project and yet seem to have generated no
written remains. Undertaking is projection's end—its goal and terminus—and
yet this culminating action is forgettable because it usually takes place outside
signification. On the occasions when undertakings enter language, either as
anticipated by proposals or recounted in histories, they do so like any old
performance: in "haphazard, partial, and inevitably distorted ways."[7] Claire
Sponsler uses this phrase to describe the deterioration of Morris Dance when
recounted through writing, though her words could also apply to the orchestrations of bodies, facilities, and machines that extracted nut oil and surveyed
cloisters. Language, it seems, cannot fully capture the project in progress. No
text can deliver the undertaking.

Sponsler confronts the ephemerality of historical experience by identifying
its nonlinguistic modes of transmission and storage. Dance, she observes, persists through personal memory and bodily reenactment, channels "outside of
representation."[8] Another performance scholar, Diana Taylor, describes a "non-
archival system of transfer" to explain the endurance of performance beyond
language.[9] School construction and road mending may not count as performance in the sense of being self-conscious artistic productions—what Richard
Schechner calls "showing doing."[10] But these actions do qualify as "performance" defined as the discharging of a task: similar to today, an inhabitant of
the eighteenth century could perform work toward a goal as well as drama for
an audience.[11] And just as the physical embodiment of drama exceeds the lines
of a play text, so too does undertaking as the execution of a task obtain a material life irreducible to blueprints. For Defoe, Astell, Sponsler, and Taylor,
"performance" grasps the capacity of projected action to exist independently
of the words scripting it.

Performance theory prods us to see the toil and expertise that propelled
eighteenth-century projects into existence, but did not itself became archivable
evidence. In most cases, neither these practices nor their authors are accessible
to us today. What's more, performance specialists have shown little inclination
to recover their methods. While modern playhouses continue to stage works
like Wycherley's *Country Wife*, often with detailed attention to the sets, cos-
tumes, and casting of his drama's original performance, no one to my knowledge has ever reenacted the paving of a Stuart-era highway or the cutting of a
Georgian canal. All that remains of such implementations is writing in print
and manuscript, extant diagrams and maps, and archeological traces in the

reworked soil. This means that our search for the project beyond words must at least begin within the same archives around which scholars like Taylor and Sponsler have charted methodological bypasses. Working under these constraints, performance studies is useful insofar as it suggests constructive approaches to reading the evidence we have—specifically, toward reassembling old projects in their moment of enactment. And that is the goal of this chapter: to use a project's extant print remnants to infer the experiences of its undertaking, and thereby test the limits of what we can know about old endeavor through reading.

The specific project that I am attempting to reanimate was among early modern Britain's most costly, controversial, and transformative: the drainage of the Great Fen. The reclamation of England's water-logged eastern coast constituted an all-consuming fantasy among projectors, from patent seekers of the Tudor era to joint-stock speculators in the 1700s to nineteenth-century civil engineers like Thomas Telford. The conversion of flooded plains into arable tillage invited improvers to reimagine land and the societies atop it; like the God of Genesis, they could part waters and conjure worlds. Drainage schemes promised to save "drowned" land and reincorporate fenland peasants into England's mainstream public life and agricultural economy. Drainage was a project that bred subsequent projects of cultivation and social control. It consolidated land ownership in the hands of a few wealthy adventurers while rendering commoners disposable to superseding regimes of grain and animal husbandry.

Fen drainage forms a particularly instructive case study in the implementation of enterprise because, unlike so many other schemes from the period, it eventually worked—or at least worked well enough and long enough for its architects to claim success. In contrast to beech oil, drainage passed entirely through the undertaking stage to impose a heretofore unknown set of economic and political conditions on life in the East of England. The once partly submerged Anglian coastland is today one of Britain's most fertile and productive growing regions. Indeed, the reality that drainage succeeded in creating can appear so long-standing and given that its indebtedness to early modern projects is easily missed, its fraught undertaking and tenuous maintenance either massaged into progress narratives or forgotten altogether.

This chapter works against such closure by detailing the workings of one especially pivotal drainage venture, known as the Bedford Level, which was first attempted in the early Stuart era, revamped during the Interregnum, and subsequently revived, celebrated, elegized, protested, and sabotaged during the late 1600s and early 1700s. Engineered by Cornelius Vermuyden and financed by the Bedford Level Adventurers, this particular effort only partially fulfilled its mission of converting five hundred square miles of wetland into year-round tillage. However, its reconfiguration of the fens formed the setting and starting point for subsequent reclamation projects, the implementation of new technologies, and the development of administrative bodies that eventually secured the region from seasonal flood. Some of the channels and embankments built at Vermuyden's behest remain visible today, indeed contribute to keeping the former fenlands dry. This chapter describes the human actions that fashioned drainage's preservative infrastructure by reading through and against the Bedford Level's extensive proposal literature. It simultaneously shows how authors of the period wrestled with the extratextual experience of enacting a project— even made conspicuous the distance between written instructions and embodied action—within petitions, libels, and historical accounts by William Dugdale (1662), Samuel Fortrey (1685), and Thomas Badeslade (1725) that continue to influence the stories we tell about fenland today.

Such reading reveals that the term "undertaking" held many meanings in this period. In some texts, drainage's performance entailed strictly manual labors like digging trenches, piling embankments, and barrowing off peatish soil. Other authors found the action of drainage projects in the supervision of this toil, the liquidation of assets to pay wages, the lobbying of members of Parliament, and the armed protection of work sites against riot. Having already examined Yarranton's fundraising propaganda and Hill's struggles to incorporate a business, this chapter bears down on the manual work behind drainage projects. I begin with a historical overview that traces how the notion of undertaking evolved between the General Drainage Act of 1600 and the 1650 effort to revive the Bedford Level. I next show how Vermuyden translated a controversial yet widely shared vision of eastern England as an untapped economic resource into technical plans for organizing the work, and how rival drainers critiqued the feasibility of his approach. Vermuyden's plans called for labor— "kind hands" and many of them, to borrow Astell's term—whose sights and sounds I illustrate in the context of the Bedford Level's shifting terrain. Finally, this toil furnished the region with a system of earthworks that was supposed to secure dry ground in perpetuity, but often failed, requiring new forms of work while igniting fresh conflict.

This chapter shows how a project's vision of improvement boiled down to work plans that summoned labor and required constant maintenance. What this investigation of drainage's undertaking contributes to my overall study of projection is a long look at the final stage of a project from the vantage not only of its architects and financiers, but also of its laborers. This view makes clear that project implementations were never seamless translations of words into work, but rather took the form of collisions between the rhetorical contemplation of future possibility and an intransigent reality. The undertaking was no victory march. It instead highlighted the fissures between abstract knowledge and mechanical application that doomed most projects to failure, many risibly so. The difficulty of undertaking explains why even the technological triumph of drainage, what H. C. Darby calls "one of the mighty themes in the story of Britain," enfolded a great many moments of failure when shovels hit ground and things went wrong.[12]

Where existing accounts of fen history often dwell on the "before" and "after" of drainage, my study of drainage's undertaking focuses squarely on the process itself. Much attention has gone to the dazzling metaphors and rich imagery of improvers and their opponents, as well as the social and ecological fallout of reclamation schemes, particularly through careful and evocative readings of a handful of much-quoted passages. My focus on implementation takes a new angle on some familiar writings by inferring from their less-canvassed corners how exactly drainage lurched from superlative fantasy to hard-fought reality. Reframing fenland improvement within the world of early modern projection draws into relief what should be an obvious fact: that "drain" was not itself a transitive verb, something that one could simply do to land, but rather constituted the result of many distinct yet concerted actions. Distinguishing between these labors that projectors sought to synchronize within their narratives of collective action affords an opportunity to tell new stories about projects and fens both.

Undertakers and Adventurers

Premodern fenland contained about twelve hundred square miles of salt marsh, moors, meres, creeks, and rivers emanating from a North Sea estuary called the Wash.[13] Much of the region's population lived on a ring of coastal silt that supported cereal cultivation and the ancient port towns of Boston, Spalding, Wisbech, and King's Lynn. Beyond the silts stretched sparsely populated peatlands that flooded regularly and could be underwater for months at a time in winter. Deluges resulted from heavy rainfall and poor outflow where the Rivers Witham, Glenn, Welland, Nene, and Ouse entered the Wash. These waterways tumbled down from the uplands at great speed but slackened on the flat peats, where they meandered the rest of the way to the sea. The wind, tides, and sand of the North Sea could repulse these feeble currents, causing rivers to back up and spill over the surrounding mores.

Flooding thwarted large-scale agriculture and permanent settlement beyond a few upland hills or "islands," like the cathedral town of Ely. Most of those who occupied the peats made their living by grazing sheep and cattle, though many supplemented their pastoral incomes by fishing, fowling, cultivating subsistence crops, harvesting sedge and reed, and transporting goods by boat through the maze of shallow creeks. Efforts to convert portions of the fens into grain tillage may date as far back as the Roman conquest, when soldiers dug the eight-mile Car Dyke across Lincolnshire as a catchwater drain and perhaps also a canal.[14] Medieval fen parishes tried to mitigate flooding by scouring rivers of their accumulated silt so that they would flow faster, and by requiring property owners to maintain embankments. Some of these arrangements were formalized in the thirteenth century through the establishment of royally appointed sewer commissions charged with coordinating the "precarious balance of water management" between parishes and monasteries.[15]

But it was not until the reign of Queen Elizabeth that the state mandated a general drainage of the entire region. In 1600 Parliament passed "An Act for the Recovering of Many Hundred Thousand Acres of Marshes, and Other Grounds Subject Commonly to Surrounding, Within the Isle of Ely, and in the Counties of Cambridge, Huntingdon, Northampton, Lincoln, Norfolk, Suffolk, Essex, Kent, and the County Palatine of Durham," which proclaimed that "wastes, commons, marshes, and fenny grounds . . . may be recovered by skilful and able undertakers, whereby great and inestimable benefit would arise to her majesty."[16] This law opened the fens to projectors who could convince officials that they commanded the knowledge and labor needed to drain them. Parliament had no money with which to pay these prospective drainers up front and so pledged them parcels of salvaged land so long as those plots remained dry. This offer of real property attracted from England and abroad a series of entrepreneurs, engineers, and energetic amateurs who saw in the Anglian wetlands an unprecedented convergence of improvement mandates and profit possibilities.

By advocating a course of action to achieve future benefits, the framers of the 1600 Drainage Act partook in projection. Their edict made a persuasive case for the national benefits of drainage, while legislating economic incentives meant to expedite the work. What the state left up to its respondents were the particular methods, numbers of skilled and unskilled laborers, and technologies of maintenance required to realize this vision. Like Defoe's *Essay*, Parliament proposed enterprise for others to perform. This delegation of agency gave rise to two figures who "dominated affairs in the Fenland during the seventeenth century": the "adventurer," who furnished fenland improvers with upfront capital and expected to make a return on investment through the acquisition of drained property, and the "undertaker," who was responsible for carrying out an agreed-on plan of drainage by recruiting workers, appointing surveyors and overseers, and managing the enterprise in a timely, cost-conscious fashion.[17] From the start, drainage projects materialized through a volatile combination of speculation and earthmoving: they advanced (and regressed) through the wagers of financiers and the toil of workmen.

Undertaking was controversial work in all its forms, as Defoe recognized in his road repair proposal. The framers of the General Drainage Act may have presented reclamation as a public service to crown and country, but many who inhabited the fens saw drainage as an assault on commoning rights and an affront to the sewer commissions. Despite a proviso that "this assignment shall hinder no man's liberty," the law authorized undertakers to seize wastes as well as portions of noble estates as the prize for improving them.[18] In this contentious atmosphere, drainage projects often began with confident proposals and rapid implementations only to devolve into fiascos. The Somerset judge Sir John Popham attempted to drain fenland near Upwell in 1605, but the scheme was dropped in 1608 after Popham died and the banks failed, leaving an unfinished channel remnant called Popham's Eau.[19] The Dutchman Cornelius Vermuyden received permission to drain a section of Yorkshire crownlands called Hatfield Chase in 1627, though this effort faltered under heavy rain and local protest, including petitions from the villages of Fishlake, Sykehouse, and Snaith claiming that undertakers had salvaged wetlands only at the cost of inundating dry ground downriver.[20] Such episodes lent the impression that drainage was at once a tyrannical confiscation of land and an impossible quest. The return of floods in Yorkshire and elsewhere confirmed, for one pamphleteer, that drainage was as unjust as a monopoly, but as fanciful as "the Philosophers stone."[21]

Among the first fenland improvers to claim success at general drainage was a consortium of local property owners known as the Bedford Level Adventurers. At a 1630 meeting of sewer commissioners held in King's Lynn, Charles I granted Francis Russell, Earl of Bedford, the right to drain a section of the Great Fen that seeped across Lincoln, Northampton, Norfolk, Suffolk, Cambridge, and Huntington. This region soon become known as the Bedford Level in tribute to the earl who would spend a fortune trying to drain it. Bedford signed on with thirteen coadventurers to make the level into summer ground (land that would be dry pasture in summer but prone to winter flooding) through the dredging of nine drains, new artificial waterways that would expedite the flow of upland water to the sea. Among these cuts, the longest was a channel between the villages of Earith and Salter's Lode, known as the Bedford River, which gave the tortuous River Ouse a straight line to King's Lynn and the Wash. Bedford's surveyors declared the Bedford Level complete in 1637, but it soon reflooded and was deemed "incomplete and defective" by royal inspectors in 1638.[22]

Fed up with privately financed attempts at general drainage, Charles I declared himself "undertaker" on July 18, 1638, in return for the lion's share of land targeted for salvage. Charles appointed Cornelius Vermuyden, who had been knighted in 1629 for his drainage efforts at Hatfield Chase, to oversee the works. An "expert man in the Art of banking and drayning," Vermuyden seemed to epitomize the competent specialist that the 1600 act solicited, his spotty record and controversial reputation notwithstanding.[23] Perceiving that drainage would affect not only fen dwellers but also the navigable waterways that connected inland cities like Cambridge and Peterborough to the sea, the king required Vermuyden to circulate his proposal for public comment. Vermuyden submitted his plan to Charles in 1638 and published a quarto version of it four years later in London under the title *A Discourse Touching the Drayning the Great Fennes*. This piece of project writing lumps together the administrative labors required to initiate drainage with the physical toil of emptying a fen: for Vermuyden, the "composing of an Agreement" and the difficulty of "the Worke" both belong to the process of undertaking.[24] He refers to an array of executive authorities as "undertaker," from James I, who sought to take charge of drainage himself in 1620, to the Earl of Bedford, who "performed" drainage insomuch as he paid others to work.[25] When *Discourse* characterizes fen reclamation as a "performance," the performers are "divers persons of quality who made a purse," financiers rather than the workmen who realized their investments.[26] Vermuyden does not mention laborers in his proposal, though it is clear that his ambitious plan to cut channels, combine rivers, and erect sluices would require thousands of bodies, effective overseers, and competent surveyors.

Vermuyden conceived of his attempt to renovate the Bedford Level as an "undertaking," of which the *Discourse* was only a limited prospectus. Seventeenth-century historians of the region often preferred "undertaking" to the more notional and inflammatory term "project." Samuel Fortrey's *History or Narrative of the Great Level* (1685), for instance, opens with a notice from the bookseller proclaiming that the work would change the minds of those "that have had a prejudice against the Undertaking."[27] Thomas Badeslade calls general drainage "an Undertaking glorious in it self; but unhappily, by taking wrong Measures . . . put those very Lands . . . into a worse Condition than they were in before."[28] Both Fortrey's and Badeslade's language characterize drainage as an ongoing process in 1685 and 1725 respectively, a present event and live source of controversy. Badeslade pries apart the enterprise by opposing its "glorious" intentions to the "wrong Measures" that sold out this promise. Evaluating those measures against the intentions they expressed (and perhaps betrayed) draws us one step closer to the actual ground, from the grand visions of fenland improvers to the directions they issued for actually doing the work.

Vision to Method

Early modern drainage advocates devised elaborate metaphors to express what fen was and should be. A much-cited 1629 pamphlet by one H.C. characterizes the fens as a noxious swamp, and fenlanders as pastoral generalists who scraped by on subsistence labors. The fens he regards as "putred and muddy, yea full of loathsome vermine," as well as a refuge for outlaws, and backwater of religious nonconformity.[29] Drainage, H.C. argued, would repatriate these alienated subjects who lacked means "to baptize a Child or to administer the Communion."[30] It would modernize the regional economy and extend the charity and oversight of the Anglican Church. Undrowning the fens would even restore a "goodly Garden of a Kingdom" subsumed by tidal muck. H.C. imaginatively excavates an entire society from the fens to frame drainage as the restoration of a sunken topography to its former prominence.[31] Given such striking imagery, it comes as a letdown when H.C. turns to consider "Riuers, Draynes, Goates, Sluces, Bankes, and such like costly workes of Sewers" that would materialize this artificial Eden, and promptly declares his pamphlet "no place fit to discover the manner of the Workes."[32] H.C. proposes drainage as a godly mission but then refuses to describe the chores and machinery that would effect this transformation.

By contrast, the "manner of the Workes" was exactly what Vermuyden's 1642 *Discourse* set out to anatomize. For all the colorful analogies and

hyperbolic imagery woven throughout drainage propaganda like H.C.'s, undertakers had to compose clear, literal-minded plans that could withstand the
scrutiny of privy councils, sewage commissioners, and even competing adventurers. Compelling rhetoric could not compensate for a lack of experience in
"making Drains, Sluices, Banks, Scours, &c." or an absence of "speculative
Knowledge relating to Rain, Tides, Laws of Motion, Out-falls, &c." according
to Badeslade.[33] It was the methodological dimension of drainage—its marriage
of "making" to "knowledge"—that undertakers debated most vociferously
rather than the social ramifications of their work. Drainers, by their nature,
tended to share the vision of fenland improvement laid out in the 1600 act,
and affirmed in the Lynn Law of 1630, but "differ much in their way," observed
Vermuyden, who grasped the disparities among different approaches to
reclamation.[34]

   Discourse claims to divulge the methodological "particulars" of Vermuyden's plan to improve four hundred thousand acres of fenland. In charting
his course for drainage, Vermuyden was entering (or given his experience at
Hatfield Chase, reentering) a raging debate over the cheapest and safest methods for reclaiming eastern England. One school of thought, advocated by the
Dutch engineer Jan Barents Westerdyke, held that the best way to drain fens
was to dredge existing rivers and raise their banks. The scooping out of silt
would increase the velocity of water and with it the river's capacity to carry
outflows. Higher banks would protect against seasonal floods. The basic idea
was that a thorough scrubbing of weeds and silt was what these channels
needed to send upland water out to sea.[35]

   Vermuyden felt that this "Ordinary Way of Drayning" was too costly. He
calculated that the fenland's existing serpentine rivers would require eighty
thousand rods of embankment, "the yearely reparation whereof would be . . .
very great."[36] Vermuyden proposed instead to dig new riverbeds that would
give the region's natural waterways straighter, shorter routes to the sea.[37]
Shorter rivers meant less riverbank, and therefore fewer miles of costly embankments. Just as the 1600 drainage act prioritized "disburdening her High-
ness of many chargeable banks and works of sewers," Vermuyden offers his
own scheme to "avoyd nere the moity of the Bankes."[38] What protective ridges
and walls his project did require would be spaced apart widely to provide beds
that could accommodate flooding. *Discourse* claimed that this method elimi-
nated the need for scouring, as his new rivers would send water outward at a
great enough speed to prevent sedimentation.

   "I shall endeavour to contrive the workes that way," proclaimed Vermuyden, whose aggressive approach to water management was soon attacked by other drainers as simplistic and infeasible.[39] Edmund Scotten questioned Vermuyden's "pursuance of his designe," predicting that the Dutchman would "not be able to performe" it.[40] Scotten claimed that Vermuyden's artificial channels would merely shift around excess water while cutting off the flow of natural rivers, thereby jeopardizing their outfalls at the Wash. Scotten accused Vermuyden furthermore of misunderstanding the nature of fen topography. He faulted *Discourse* for proposing to rechannel existing rivers that already possessed sturdy clay banks through moorish grounds that were prone to land-slips. This charge emphasizes the indifference of Vermuyden's plans to the land he proposed to improve. Scotten argues that the project's performance will reveal the fatal imprecision of its design.

Scotten also sneered at *Discourse*'s brevity, dismissing the paltry thirty-two-page pamphlet as an unserious attempt to describe the scores of technical decisions that general drainage required. Rather, like the Catholic clergy, Vermuyden aimed to "keepe men as ignorant as they can, that they may the more easily deceive them, and leade them whether they list."[41] Scotten felt that *Discourse* lacked the rigor needed to guide a successful undertaking, and that its author skimped on details deliberately. On these same grounds, another drainer, Andrews Burrell, called *Discourse* a "*mysticall designe*" in one work, and claimed in another that Vermuydem sought to "dazle the Kings apprehension of the worke."[42] Burrell contrasts Vermuyden's verbal dexterity with his history of maladroit "worke," specifically belittling his "Art of Sluce making," a presumably stinging piece of libel meant to show how slick rhetoric could bely shoddy craftsmanship.[43] Vermuyden could impress in prose, he suggests, but not "make" anything of value.[44] Burrell concludes his attack by adumbrating his own scheme for draining the Bedford Level, supplying those details missing from Vermuyden's *Discourse*. This plan tabulates the endeavor's cost at 180,000 pounds and records individual expenses stemming from drain making and officer salaries down to miscellaneous "Nailes omitted."[45] This scrupulous—thereby actionable—counterproposal illustrates by contrast the diligence supposedly lacking from Vermuyden's plans.

Scotten and Burrell portray Vermuyden's drainage plan as nebulous and delusional at a time when more tested approaches existed: namely, digging a small number of straight cuts in conjunction with desilting and embanking natural riverbeds. We have seen already how critics sought to discredit English projectors by questioning their character. But unlike the writings that would libel Andrew Yarranton as a cantankerous republican and Aaron Hill as a greedy bubble broker, Scotten and Burrell challenge Vermuyden's ability to "effect the thing," as William Dodson put it."[46] At issue was not only the quality of *Discourse*, but Vermuyden's capacity to enact his language. This "thing" entailed claiming wetlands from the will of the waters, and also preserving navigation to inland cities, respecting property boundaries and commoning rights, and keeping already-dry land above floods. Under the terms of the Lynn Law, successful drainage needed to transform the fenlands without disturbing what already seemed to work in the region. No one questioned Vermuyden's ability to tell a good story that balanced the need for change and conservation. At issue was "the certainty of doing it," to again draw on Dodson's rhetoric of actualization.[47] Critics of *Discourse* established performance as the only meaningful criteria for assessing Vermuyden's worth as a drainer. Only shovels and time could supply proof of sound projection.

Vermuyden's "doing" of Bedford Level began in 1642 but came to an abrupt halt when England plunged into civil war and the fens became contested territory between royal and parliamentary forces. Drainage infrastructure grew derelict and vulnerable to attack from commoners who opposed reclamation during this turbulent period. By the time workmen returned to the Bedford Level in 1650, their mandate bore the seal of a republican government that had just abolished the monarchy. Obviously, there was much that Vermuyden's *Discourse* could not have predicted when it was first presented to the king in 1638. Therefore, as the Adventurers endeavored to plant some version of his vision in the soil of a new commonwealth, that proposal would serve as a less and less reliable guide to the project it inaugurated.

Method to Work

The Commonwealth Parliament rebooted drainage in 1649, four months after executing Vermuyden's former champion, Charles I. The "Act for the Draining the Great Level of the Fens" (later called the Pretended Act) gave William, son of the deceased Earl of Bedford, six years to convert the existing level into "winter ground" that would remain dry in all seasons. On January 25, 1650, Vermuyden became Director of the Works.[48] The undertaking he oversaw resembled the *Discourse*'s approach to reclamation insofar as it called for the creation of new channels. However, the Bedford Level Adventurers also faced challenges that Vermuyden could not have anticipated in 1638, such as the requirement that they rehabilitate existing drainage works left to decay "by reason of some late interruptions."[49] Besides repairing old edifices, they were tasked with creating a new bypass channel for the Ouse, the Hundred Foot Drain or "New Bedford River," that was to run alongside the "Old Bedford River" of 1637, and raise embankments surrounding both courses to form a receptacle for flooding. New sluices were to be erected at Erith and Denver, where the New Bedford River departed and rejoined the Ouse respectively. Neither the Hundred Foot Drain, nor the washlands, nor the sluices are mentioned in *Discourse*. As Margaret Knittl surmises, "what Bedford's workmen did was seriously at odds with Vermuyden's ideas."[50]

Plans alone cannot tell us what "Bedford's workmen did," though other forms of evidence provide a glimpse into the event of drainage. For instance, a 1657 journal entry by William Dugdale observed "no less than 11000 men sometimes imployed at worke, at a time building the New Bedford Level."[51] Darby excerpts the reflections of a seventeenth-century traveler near Wisbech who watched "a little Army of Artificers, venting, contriving, and acting outlandish devises," and counted six hundred men at work making a river navigable between Frosdick Slough and Deeping, at the northern edge of the level.[52] We can infer still greater detail about this scene from the Pretended Act itself, which granted workers free passage through fenland properties for themselves and their "horses, carts and carriages."[53] This provision reflects the constant need to haul men, tools, and building materials to the banks of old rivers and channels under construction.

Against the clamor of tools and carts, a witness to drainage would have heard a multilingual weave of Dutch, French, and English words spoken among workmen and overseers. Many of Vermuyden's laborers came from abroad, and we know that he had employed "numerous Dutchmen and Flemings" in Hatfield Chase.[54] The antiquarian George Stovin notes that many "Dutchmen and French Protestants with their famalays" came to "participate in this Levil."[55] Dutch mercenaries worked alongside Huguenot refugees, who "fled out of their native Country for fear of the Inquisition, only to enjoy the free exercise of their Religion here."[56] The fens also received the conscripted labor of Scotsmen taken prisoner at the Battle of Dunbar, who, Keith Lindley notes, wore "distinctive smocks in order to distinguish them from English workmen and make escape more difficult."[57] Dutch seaman captured during the first Anglo-Dutch War were also deposited in the fens. One wonders how Vermuyden, naturalized as an English subject in 1624, felt overseeing his former countrymen, now toiling as prisoners of war in a foreign realm.

These workmen executed a variety of tasks, the two most important of which were building up embankments and cutting new rivers.[58] Embanking must have seemed a Sisyphean task. Work crews using hand shovels scooped up soil into mounds alongside channels in the hopes that these piles would hold back floods. Solid clay was the preferred material, though embankers often had to settle for peatish soil, because stronger materials were "not near at hand; that they must all be fetch'd at a great Distance, and at a great Expence."[59] Depending on the thickness of peat, laborers may have required turving spades to slice through the surface layer of decomposing vegetation to obtain bankable matter. Initially heavy and damp, moor soil dried out and shrunk when exposed to air. This meant that many a peat bank "lost its tufness," crumbled away, and yielded to flooding rivers.[60] Breaches were frequent and dangerous. Scotten wearily recounts the jury-rigged efforts of weary property owners who shoved "Earth, Brush, Faggots, and Fodder, sheaves" into failing embankments to preserve them against floods.[61]

Vermuyden recognized the vulnerability of embankments and therefore sought to limit their use by trenching new courses to the sea. These man-made channels followed straight lines and the land's limited gradient, cutting through moor and marsh, as well as pastures, cultivated estates, and highways—mentions of bridge construction recur throughout the company's papers. Nicholas James explains how the builders of the New Bedford River forged across "21 miles of former marsh too wet, at first, to support anything heavier than the labourers themselves."[62] They contended with the same summer heat, humidity, and gnats that famously pestered travelers such as Samuel Pepys, John Evelyn, Celia Fiennes, and Daniel Defoe. Drainage workers also faced the threats of violence against their works and themselves from fenland residents hostile to Vermuyden's enterprise. The finished New Bedford River reflected a colossal expenditure of bodily labor, though as James notes, given the use of wooden shovels, the effort left "no trace of the thousands of workers attested at that time."[63]

How exactly new rivers got dug was a mystery according to Walter Blith, the Commonwealth husbandry writer, who commented that "no man as I ever yet saw or heard, hath published any thing at all to any such purpose as to dismystery."[64] Accordingly, Blith dedicated a section of his *English Improver Improved* (1652) to "pull off the vizor of those apprehensions" purportedly concealing this process.[65] He concedes from the outset that composing this laborious choreography would test his powers of description and pledged therefore to "indeavour to draw it into as plain a Map or Platform, as the roughness and confusedness of the work, or my weaknesses will admit."[66] Blith's tortured modesty registers the dissonance between an act of labor, as performed in the fens, and the ability of his prose to convey a sense of drainage in execution. The tension between language and action, at the heart of Vermuyden's proposal and those of his detractors, also colors Blith's self-doubting prose.

Nonetheless, *England's Improver* instructs the reader how to dig a small cut of the sort that could drain a boggy plot, or serve as a division ditch between two adjoining properties—not reclaim a fen in its entirety, but remedy a piece of land that presented fenlike conditions. The task first entails identifying a descent in the land that a channel could follow, cutting parallel lines to mark the channel banks, and then digging straight down through turf and undersoil to create the bed. A later drainage writer, Charles Labelye, adds that these channels required "sufficient Slope to their Sides to hinder the Lands from falling or calving into them."[67] Blith's manual includes a woodcut depicting "Tools or Instruments" that "shall make the work more facile and delightfull," including a trenching gouge, parring spade, and trenching wheel plough, alongside an action scene of a laborer armed with trenching spade cutting "its' trench & the Water Following."[68] Blith even gives directions for fashioning these tools from scratch using iron and willow branches, should his readers not have finished implements on hand. *England's Improver* pairs word and image to depict in miniature a task that would engage thousands of workers on the Bedford Level.

Beyond embankments and channels, the third major component of Vermuyden's drainage network was the Denver Sluice, which protected the outflow of the Ouse as it approached King's Lynn. A seventeenth-century sluice was part edifice, part machine. It consisted of a stone or wooden span anchored to the opposite banks of a river. Depending on its length, this span included a certain number of arches or "tunnels," through which a controlled amount of water could pass. In the case of the sluice at Denver, doors would open and shut to repel inbound current from the North Sea and speed the outflow of upland rainfall at low tide. Sluices needed solid banks, ideally made of clay, so that freshwater floods or tidal surges would not dislodge them. Vermuyden built the Denver Sluice from stone, though other drainers used whatever materials were available locally. Dodson, for instance, proposed brick sluices at Ely and Saltors Load, oak planks in Norfolk, and deal timber at King's Lynn.[69] Sluice construction brought specialized labor to the fens in the form of masons and woodworkers. Their presence reminds us that the project of fen drainage required not only menial shovel work, but practical knowledge of architecture and mechanical engineering.

Vermuyden's workers made quick progress. Parliament had set October 10, 1656, as a deadline for completing all embankments, cuts, and sluices, and it ordered undertakers to labor "without cessation or intermission, until the work be done, unseasonable times and extremity of weather only excepted."[70] Vermuyden's laborers kept well ahead of schedule. Their overseers knew that as long as the works remained unfinished, floods threatened to swallow up reclaimed land. In this vein, Blith warned that land reclamation was "not to be trifled withall, it must be the speedy and powerful carrying on at once."[71] He concluded, "a little season lost, may lose the cost and works of a whole Summer. . . . Works may run further backward in a week, than they were brought forward in a month."[72] The fickle will of upland water, statutory deadlines, and the poor quality of banking materials likely made for hurried working conditions on the level. The need to carry on "at once" reflected everyone's fear of seeing labor and material washed away.

Given these pressures, it was incumbent on undertakers to recruit "ingenious and laborious workmen" and "carefull" overseers to prosecute the work efficiently.[73] Observed Blith, "he is a rare man that can sort all his works so into each workmans hand."[74] Just as Vermuyden's *Discourse* translated the vision of fenland improvement into practical methods, and methods into work practices, a good overseer could distribute tasks among properly equipped laborers. Those allocating and managing work would have needed to account for differences of skill, strength, language, and motivation, especially among Scottish and Dutch conscripts, who were imaginably less than eager to toil in the service of the English Commonwealth, and sometimes even sought escape.

At the very bottom of the company hierarchy, able-bodied workmen would have required stoic patience in the face of harsh labor conditions and uncertain compensation. The Bedford Level Adventurers derived operating capital from the security of not-yet salvaged land, intermittent payments from estate owners whose properties were adjudged improved by drainage, and a limited ability to levy taxes. This often left little cash on hand to pay workers. In 1651, five hundred laborers petitioned for the payment of five thousand pounds that had fallen into arrears.[75] Burrell accused Vermuyden of paying wages "in Bullockes, Sheepe, Beere, Cloth, and other commodities" at inflated prices, falsifying exchange rates to cheat workers of their due.[76] Stovin records that workmen were also responsible for "having houses to Build for themselves" in the midst of the level.[77] Burrell's and Stovin's accounts suggest that while drainage employed thousands of unskilled workers, it frequently left those laborers without means to support themselves.

Despite these hardships, Vermuyden's drainage of the Bedford Level was adjudged complete by sewer commissioners on March 25, 1653, forty-three months ahead of the mandated deadline. The printer to William Bedford's *A Particular of the Ninety Five Thousand Acres* (1653) declared "the Work hath been so effectually prosecuted . . . the Work is compleated."[78] March 25 was declared a day of Thanksgiving, and the cathedral bells at Ely rang out across a new, man-made landscape of orthogonal drains and vertical banks. The Adventurers officially took possession of ninety-five thousand acres as payment. The immense task of reclaiming the Bedford Level at last seemed to have been achieved. But this sense of accomplishment proved fleeting. It would not take long for the region's inhabitants and commissioners to realize that Bedford Level suffered from major defects stemming both from its design and execution. The return of floodwaters in the mid-1600s confirmed that drainage's undertaking was far from done.

Work to Works

Church bells punctuated Vermuyden's quest to reclaim the Great Fen. His project appeared to conclude at the moment that drainage could be turned over from armies of laborers to the earthworks and edifices they built. Undertaking, in a sense, would be perpetual, though it no longer required toil beyond the everyday operation and upkeep of infrastructure. At least that was the plan. An anonymous poem appended to Fortrey's *History or Narrative of the Great Level* (1685) revels in this fantasy. "True and Natural Description" describes how oceans are "tam'd," rivers "govern'd," and lands "reclaim'd." This vision dwells specifically on the machinery that would manage this new terrain:

Waters with banks confin'd, as in a Gaol.
Till kinder Sluces let them go on Bail;
Stream curb'd with Dammes like Bridles, taught t'obey.[79]

Tropes of incarceration and equestrianism empower banks and sluices to control "unruly" water. In substituting earthworks for workers, the poet takes a figural cue from Vermuyden, whose own metaphorical reasoning pronounces, "*Welland* and the *Sheire-drayne* will be turned to be good servants in stead of ill Masters to those Countries."[80] Drainage for both the poet and Vermuyden entails the subjugation of water to human authority. But for the former author, drainage could now be seen as the aftermath of heroic labor: no longer a prospective undertaking but a monumental inheritance: "Your Banks shall stand / Like the immortal Pyramide, and your Land / Forget it e're was Sea."[81]

This speech hails drainage's capacity to make land "forget" its submersion and thereafter invite new forms of settlement. Turning to the future, the poet predicts that drainage would foster a wondrous society resembling the garden kingdom H.C. foresaw half a century earlier:

> When Cities shall be built, and Houses tall,
> As the proud Oak, which you their Founders call,
> Fair Orchards Planted, and the Myrtle Grove,
> Adorn'd, as if it were the Scene of Love.
> Gardens with Flowers of such auspicious hew,
> You'ld swear, that *Eden* in the Desert grew.[82]

Drained land populates spontaneously. Cities "shall be built" and orchards "planted," creating a vertiginous theater for romance and return to edenic innocence. Heroic couplets lend progressive order and metrical inevitability to fenland development. The pastoral imagery of arbors and gardens signals not only an end to wetland "desert," but the conclusion of work itself. Drainage restores Eden and thereby constitutes the last labor of mankind, who by "the sweat of his brow" and vehicle of projection has returned himself to a prelabor paradise.

In reality, the Bedford Level continued to devour labor through burdensome maintenance tasks. Perceiving the tendency of drainage infrastructure to decay, the framers of the 1630 Lynn Law specified that the "work of draining being once performed and finished, may be for ever after maintained."[83] Similarly, a 1663 act that superseded the Pretended Act of 1649 stressed that Bedford Level drainage "cannot be preserved without a perpetual constant care, great charge and orderly government."[84] Despite this statutory call for vigilance, by the time Charles Labelye toured the south section of the Bedford Level in 1745, he found "the Banks in general (few excepted) in a very bad Condition, most of them full of Breaches, or considerably wounded, or lashed by the last Floods; and in many Places, especially on the South Side of the

River *Ouse*, there is hardly so much as the Appearance of any Bank left for several Miles together."[85] So much for carceral earthworks and postlabor Edens. Vermuyden recognized that the Bedford Level would require periodic upkeep but underestimated the cost of this commitment. Maintenance, it turned out, was not a postscript to drainage, but an ongoing struggle against rain, tide, and wind to protect salvaged land from the will of the waters. The disintegration of Bedford Level compelled adventurers, undertakers, legislators, and monarchs to rethink man's intervention in the fen, and his capacity to shape landscape to lasting effect.[86]

Embankments were a major point of failure. Ones made of peat soil were especially prone to erosion, though all water-abutting earthworks had to contend with rats that made "their holes in the banks close to the water when it is at the shallowest in infinite number, and feeding vpon the frie of fish, doe multiply like fishes."[87] Fenlanders drove cattle on the top of embankments, taking advantage of their straight, unobstructed courses, but breaking them down in the process.[88] Cattle transport posed such a problem that the Lynn Law forbade any passage on the banks except for towing boats. Writing in 1666, Dodson warned that the annual charges assessed by "Countrey men which get all the money for Repairing every Year" could eventually "exceed the Profit."[89] He suggests that embankments were so prone to landslips that local laborers counted on their erosion as a source of employment.[90]

Tidal sands built up against sluice doors, sealing them shut. In 1725, Thomas Badeslade found the Denver Sluice stuck in the closed position, meaning that it sequestered upland water in the path of the New Bedford River.[91] Plant life flourished on the beds of new channels, catching silt and clogging outflow. As early as the 1630s, Vermuyden bemoaned that the fenlands were "growne full of Hassacks, Sedge, and Reede, and the Rivers full of Weeds," observing how even newly made drains near Deeping Fen were "already almost growne up with all kind of Water weeds."[92] Plant growth in slowmoving drains necessitated the regular employment of workmen called roders, who walked upstream using long rakes to rip through the skein of stems.

But the Bedford Level faced a more dire threat than weeds or rats. By expediting the outflow of fenland rivers, Vermuyden removed moisture from the surrounding soil. The withdrawal of water had the unintended effect of exposing peat bands to the air, causing them to dry and crumble, then blow away. This phenomenon, known as wastage, caused the lands to sink, and as drained fen fell below the surface of surrounding waterways, it became increasingly susceptible to floods. In this sense, fen drainage became self-defeating.

Vermuyden employed pumps on the Bedford Level after concluding, according to Darby, that the "only solution was to pump the water from dyke to
drain and from drain to river, and so to sea."[93] These pumps, powered by
horses, men, and later wind, accelerated the desaturation of peat, and thereby,
its descent. Darby notes that wastage "removed the gentle gradient that allowed rivers to flow downhill."[94] By the 1690s, the fens were below sea level
and required wind pumps to send water out to sea, which of course caused the
level to fall faster.

Drainers dealt with the gradual but persistent problem of erosion at the
same time they faced the prospect of sudden, catastrophic flooding. C. N. Cole
reports that the Old Bedford River failed its first test spectacularly when it
opened in 1637.[95] The Denver Sluice "blew up" in 1713 following a string of
calamitous events. First, a rain-swollen New Bedford River emptied so much
water into the Ouse that it rose high enough to prevent the sluice doors from
opening. As the river rose with the incoming tides it exerted such upstream
pressure on the sluice that the entire edifice burst, leaving the mouth of the
New Bedford River strewn with unnavigable ruins. Perhaps no sight better
epitomizes the eventual failure of Bedford's vision than this debris, which
evoked the futility of Commonwealth-era drainage while creating an obstacle
that future projectors would be forced to incorporate within their plans.[96]

Finally, fenlanders opposed to drainage found that they could undermine
the project through simple measures like throwing dirt in division ditches by
night or sinking hemp in newly cut drains, as commoners on the Isle of Ax-
holme did during Vermuyden's draining of Hatfield Chase.[97] More daring sab-
oteurs could arm themselves and capture control of sluices, causing them to
open at high tide and close at low—reflooding fenlands through the instruments of their drainage. The General Drainage Act of 1663 specified punish-
ments for anyone who "shall cut, throw down, or destroy any of the said works
made or to be made" and classified as a felon anyone who did this work "ma-
liciously."[98] This edict reflects the extent to which the performance of drainage
encompassed not only control over land but mastery of its inhabitants.

The Bedford Level again became a focal point for projection as it became
evident that Vermuyden's methods had achieved only partial success. In 1665,
the Royal Society's Georgical Committee published a questionnaire in the
Philosophical Transactions seeking information on agricultural and pasturage
practices throughout England. One of the survey items asked "what are the
best waies of Drayning Marshes, Boggs, fenns, & c.?"[99] This open-ended query
suggests that drainage remained a problem of technical knowledge—of

identifying and implementing the right "waies"—after the Restoration, a challenge that no one had conclusively solved. This included Vermuyden, whose son of the same name was elected a fellow of the Royal Society in 1663. During the reign of Charles II it remained uncertain whether fen could, let alone should, become farm. The undertaking of Bedford Level had seemed to discredit one set of methods (and one projector) without pointing the way toward permanently workable solutions.

Fen and Farm

Not until the invention of steam-driven pumps in the nineteenth century could fens be kept consistently dry, if still prone to flooding in case of extreme precipitation. But like the windmills that preceded them, steam pumps also caused wastage, and so the land continued to sink. Steam power has yielded to diesel and electric, but the work of drainage remains ongoing today in the fenlands, much of which now sit below sea level. Pumping stations and sea walls guard Anglia's fertile farmland from the North Sea. If this machinery were to cease functioning, the lands would return to their soaked premodern state.[100] Vermuyden's undertaking remains ongoing, even if he is no longer at the helm. The Bedford Level Adventurers set into motion a series of actions that his *Discourse* could only partly anticipate, and which history has only incompletely preserved.

Approaching drainage through its constitutive actions results in a different story of the fens than the one told by its improvement literature. Undertaking presents a mass of details, perspectives, and hardships that the project form smoothes away in its attempt to create a compelling, obtainable future. Where the blueprints of drainage foresee reclamation as a steady, schedulable progression, undertaking surfaces delays and regressions. Where proposals anticipate the modernization of southeast England through the reordering of elements, undertaking involves more mud, rats, and noise than certainty. The performances that made early modern projects real also required their authors to relinquish control and adjust their visions, as the material world asserted itself against human prescription. To "effect the thing," in Dodson's words, proved harder than to write it.

That Bedford's undertaking remained incomplete did not keep it from inspiring and instigating future authors. Fen drainage's raising of land from water certainly fired the imagination of Blith, who enthused that salvaged soil

would be "capable of the impress of any Husbandry whatsoever."[101] The creation of tillage had resounding effects on the region's inhabitants. Dugdale
reports that the Bedford Level transformed itinerant beggars into agrarian
wage earners: "That before this drayning, the Country thereabouts was full of
wandring Beggars; but very few afterwards; being set on work in weeding of
Corn, burning of ground, thrashing, ditching, Harvest work and other Husbandry: All wages of Labourers, by reason of this great use of them, being then
doubled."[102] Anti-drainers asserted that these wages came at the cost of self-
sufficient livelihoods, a view summarized in Keith Lindley's observation that
Anglia's fenmen lived "tolerably well compared with the peasantry of other
agricultural regions."[103]

Accounts like Dugdale's cause the mundane labors of ditch digging and
bank piling to recede behind the master narrative of drainage's economic transformation of England's coast. The subordination of process to outcome appears in literary works of the eighteenth century that commemorate the
undertaker's ordering of water, land, and people without attending too closely
to the details or contingencies of this achievement. John Dyer's *The Fleece*
(1757) commemorates the Bedford Level Adventurers over a hundred years
after their first attempts at general drainage. "Moors, bogs, and weeping fens,
may learn to smile," he sings, casting drainage as the cultivation of affect in
soil.[104] Dyer shudders to think what the fens once were: a "dreary pathless
waste," a disorienting wilderness where "the coughing stock / Was wont with
hairy fleces to deform." This forlorn landscape lasted until "Russel" (either
Francis or William)

> drain'd the rushy fen,
> Confin'd the waves, bid groves and gardens bloom,
> And through his new creation led the Ouze,
> And gentle Camus, silver-winding streams:
> Godlike beneficence; from chaos drear
> To raise the garden and the shady grove.[105]

The Bedford River Complex of the south level becomes a "new creation" that
transforms the River Ouse into a "silver-winding stream," a figment of poetic
imagination rather than physical landscape. With "Godlike beneficence," Bedford draws paradise from "chaos drear," a cosmological vision that salutes the
magnitude of drainage's project while turning into amorphous divinity the
labors and mechanisms of its enactment. Drainage is poeticized: stripped of its

routines, technology, methods, and conflict, and returned to the pristine vision articulated by its earliest exponents.

Dyer finds in the Bedford Level a case study in human fortitude and the pasturage to feed his wooly sheep. The erosion of embankments and weeding up of channels could not erase the impression that drainage was indeed opening land to new uses, from cattle grazing to grain crops. Drainers generated tillable acres at a time when poets like Dyer were exploring the economic resources and social potential lodged within the kingdom's rural land. In *The Fleece*, drainage's laborious undertaking, recast as divine origination, set the stage for new forms of idealized labor. Enter the agrarian swain, who in the lines of georgic poetry would become one of the most visible agents of English improvement.

Chapter 4

Inheriting the Future

Georgic's Projecting Strain

Projectors taxed their talents, fortunes, and reputations to propose new endeavor. Andrew Yarranton allegorized the plight of rural debtors to campaign for land banking. Aaron Hill courted Tory investors by penning a folio of heroic verse. Drainage propagandists evoked Genesis to accuse fen dwellers of idleness and heterodoxy, and to legitimate their own salvific schemes. Their plans attempted to make that which was unreal seem real, or at least realizable, whether by portraying marsh as sunken tillage or commoners as a ready source of labor. Project writing established patterns of syntax and metaphor that laminated imaginary futures over an imperfect present, inviting readers to compare what was and what could be. These brazen acts of rhetorical invention would inspire and incense early modern poets, playwrights, and novelists, who depicted projects in order to catalyze plots, enliven scenery, barb jokes, and brand characters. Such authors made impossible schemes a narrative set piece, and the projector, a stock buffoon. However, the literary reprocessing of project writing's tendencies extended beyond caricature. As I will show, the depiction and formal imitation of proposals would shape not only the fate of individual schemes, but the credibility of improvement itself as the promise of discrete enterprise.

I opened this book by suggesting that projects left much of their evidence in capital-L Literature, self-consciously aesthetic writings that reported on plans for action, the future possibilities they opened, and the trouble left in their wake. The next two chapters track diverging responses to the Age of Projects that became two of the eighteenth century's most pervasive and memorable modes of expression: georgic poetry and satirical fiction. My aim is to plot the reception of projects through the innovation of form, demonstrating how poets and satirists internalized projection's stylistic qualities, argumentative logics, and conceptions of time. I show how writing that responded to the world-making pretensions of projects often wound up partaking in their imagination of action, and formulating their own strategies for depicting the future in its uncertain potential. By incorporating the projector's persuasive labors within freestanding literary creations, authors not only exposed but restaged the proposal's exchange of observable fact for subjunctive futurity. In a period when it could be hard to distinguish between project literature and literature about projects, indeed when the confessed schemers Daniel Defoe and Jonathan Swift became scribal luminaries, scores of cast-off schemes received new life—or least a second viewing—in works of imaginative writing. How projects persisted within and pushed back against the literature that sought to mock, cherish, eulogize, and defuse them is the inquiry of my final chapters.

This chapter examines writing on the possibilities of land. It had been the mission of seventeenth-century improvers from Cornelius Vermuyden to Carew Reynell to enrich and populate Britain's countryside. Enclosure, fen reclamation, new roads and bridges, navigable rivers, and granaries and textile factories were all meant to capitalize rural acreage and stabilize the communities that grew atop it. By the 1700s, English poets were beginning to describe these envisioned landscapes as an already-achieved topographical fact. Their verses transpose the bustling, intensively cultivated world that projectors foresaw into present reality. We have seen, for instance, how John Dyer credited the ruinous drainage ventures of William and Francis Russell with creating pasture for his shepherd and wool for British looms. *The Fleece* (1757) was one of dozens of poems that reveled in images of golden tillage, blushing orchards, barge-filled rivers, and busy swains: a landscape that projectors portrayed as the hypothetical output of their schemes. Poets found the culmination of projects in the here and now, even when history seemed to refuse such presentation.

Poems of the land varied in length, stanzic organization, and modes of address, and they proliferated across several overlapping generic categories: landscape, loco-descriptive, topographical, bucolic, pastoral, prospect. Many works celebrated the industry of rural laborers in the spirit of *The Georgics* (29 B.C.), Virgil's four-book didactic poem detailing the chores of plowing land, raising fruit and vines, caring for chattel, and tending beehives. Eighteenth-century English poets revived georgic in the vernacular through poems addressing contemporary modes of husbandry. Some works, like John Philips's

Cyder (1708) and James Grainger's *Sugar Cane* (1764), modeled themselves on Virgil's example by dispensing precepts on the manual arts of orcharding and plantation management through multibook works. Others, like John Gay's *Trivia; or, The Art of Walking the Streets of London* (1716), satirized didactic poetry in the vein of Virgil, and his Greek predecessor Hesiod, by applying an instructive mode of address to self-evident actions like walking. Still other works, like Alexander Pope's *Windsor-Forest* (1713) and James Thomson's *The Seasons* (1730), offer little actionable advice but endeavor instead to showcase georgical themes of virtue through toil and a benevolent Pax Romana/Britannica within their sweeping tours of the countryside.

The question of why a georgical revival took place in eighteenth-century Britain has long stirred debate. Many point to Dryden's mammoth translation project *The Works of Virgil* (1697), which popularized the entire rota, and most especially *The Georgics*, which he proclaimed "the best poem by the best poet." Historical events like the Acts of Union (1707) and the Treaty of Utrecht (1713) prompted Britons to imagine themselves as a unified and powerful people inhabiting a second Augustan Age of domestic peace and imperial expansion.[1] Anthony Low conceives of georgic's eighteenth-century efflorescence as a belated response to seismic epistemological shifts that rocked the kingdom a century earlier, including the rise of Baconian natural philosophy and a courtly reappraisal of labor no longer as the base sentence of man's fall but an honorable and edifying pursuit. Low goes so far to posit a seventeenth-century "georgic revolution" coupling radical changes in public sentiment to a "fruitful combination of poetic vision and new science."[2] Resisting such efforts to construe georgic as a mere "way of life" rather than a poetic mode characterized by personification, periphrases, allusion, and digression, Courtney Weiss Smith has recently asked what made verse (rather than prose) the eighteenth century's medium par excellence for describing husbandry in its "minute workings and its broadest moral and religious implications."[3] A sound explanation of georgic, she claims, must account for both the cultural themes that georgic poets advanced, and the "structural patternings" that became their mode's signature feature.

How British poets recast Virgil's poem to suit what Samuel Baker calls a "modern age of science and commerce" is therefore a question of history *and* form: of science and politics, metaphor and prosody.[4] Joseph Addison famously sought to reconcile georgic's linguistic attributes to its cultural context when he characterized the mode as "some part of the Science of Husbandry put into a pleasing Dress, and set off with all the Beauties and Embellishments

of Poetry."[5] Addison designates georgic a product of metaphrasis, the beautification of "Science . . . into . . . Poetry." He argues that Virgil's achievement
was to purify and embellish the technical minutiae of farming, singing what
before had only been spoken through a process of formal gentrification pleasingly apposite to husbandry's own conversion of soil, seeds, water, and manure
into edible goods. Modern critics have attributed the same methods to Virgil's
British imitators by suggesting that poets like Philips took their didactic conceit from *The Georgics*, stylistic cues from English bards like Milton, and factual content from husbandry manuals, improvement treatises, write-ups of
experiments, the correspondence of the Hartlib Circle, and the output of the
Royal Society's Georgical Committee.[6]

By pinpointing georgic's appropriation of classical and contemporary lit-
eratures, metaphrastic readings attempt to unwind the intertextual knots that
tend to frustrate synchronic interpretation. However, understanding exactly
how British print culture made early modern "georgic revolution" a viable
theme for eighteenth-century poetry also requires examination of the original
works that poets consulted, and ostensibly elevated. This is no easy task. Georgic's hereditary lines are obscured both by the sheer volume of materials credited with stimulating the mode, and by the implementation of categories like
"science," "husbandry," "rural," and "didactic" that label but hardly assist interpretation of precursor works. Such analysis is challenged further by the
limiting assumption that these writings will one day blossom into poetry, that
they are merely the raw ingredients of later artistic achievement, what Kurt
Heinzelman reduces to miscellaneous surplus outside "the sign of 'the literary.'"[7] In presupposing poetry as the end result of a refinement process, we risk
overlooking the world-shaping ambitions and verbal creativity of the materials
that georgic sources while discounting the divisive stakes of teaching early
modern Britons what to do with land.

This chapter argues that projection was a crucial precondition for georgic
poetry, its staging and resolution of discord, its conception of a quarriable past
and pliant future, and its imagination of rural land as wealth in potential.
Sifting through the prose "put into poetry" reveals that the project served as an
indispensable vehicle for advancing seventeenth-century programs of agricultural improvement, a distinct form of writing that georgic poets wrangled to
control in their verses, and an ideological heritage that organized georgic poetics alongside more widely acknowledged epistemic influences like commerce,
partisanship, patriotism, and imperialism. Georgic poems, I contend, undertook projection in the general sense that they superimposed on reality idealized

visions of Britain's heartland through the same forms of future-making rhetoric we have traced within the proposal form. They also delved deeply into the bodily knowledge and physical toils that propelled some schemes toward reality. Reading poems alongside proposals shows how Pope, Smart, Dyer, and Grainger derived more than didactic content from husbandry projectors. They found in project writing procedures for constructing a future that renders Britain's countryside a territory of global consequence, and a working knowledge of how particular projects touched the land.

Less stirringly, georgic poems also absorb the stench of prospective failure that clung to husbandry projects. Kevis Goodman observes how georgic's program of historical mediation forges a "glittering verbal tekhnē" at the same time it provokes "unpleasurable feeling" and "sensory discomfort."[8] I claim that georgic derives its combination of bad feeling and dazzling diction partly from improvement literature's rhetorical struggle to rouse readers to action, particularly in communities where custom prevailed and innovation was feared. Where Low portrays georgical revival as a celebration of Britain's march toward science, empire, capitalism, and modernity, the mode's versification of defunct schemes points to a desultory present in which the culmination of British history suggests no clear way forward. The appearance of projects, by name or allusion, in *Cyder*, *Windsor-Forest*, and elsewhere illuminates landscapes brimming not only with evidence of modernization, but also with the ruins of missed opportunity, even as this cautionary debris is itself reworked by poets to chart new courses of action. The discursive category "project," I will show, signals a more unruly inheritance than does Addison's "science of husbandry," and a less predictable story of generic adaptation than accounts positing that georgic merely recycled the precepts of husbandry tracts. Georgic poems could not assimilate farming manuals by lending them local color and an iambic beat: they struggled mightily to square the collapse of old plans with their own confident pronouncements, a struggle evidenced in the mode's digressive form and omnivorous content.

Acknowledging how projects galvanized and haunted georgic poetry suggests new explanations for several of the mode's attributes. Georgic's much-noted struggle to negotiate accuracy and aesthetic—artisanal fidelity and artistic license—appears to replay the projector's use and disavowal of the persuasive rhetorics enabling him to claim expertise. By the same token, georgic's digressiveness, its attempt to impart knowledge "through a By-way" in Addison's phrase, seems to mimic the proposal's tendency to deploy narrative, imagery, verse, and epistolary prefaces as an alternative to perforce argument.[9]

The orchestration of mutually dependent schemes that held together Yarranton's sprawling tract *England's Improvement by Sea and Land* also orders the idealized landscapes of poets, who made congruous experimental forms of cultivation, state-sponsored public works, expanding markets, and bustling ports. But an awareness of projection offers more than an opportunity to revisit familiar aspects of the mode. What tracing this relationship makes visible is how georgic poets went about composing verses to facilitate time travel and prophecy, and how future making itself became an eighteenth-century poetic theme and practice.

I begin by showing how Addison's "science of husbandry" qualified as a field of projection in the eyes of its seventeenth-century undertakers and critics. Farming constituted a speculative enterprise in and of itself, as well as the activity that made possible ventures in the manufacture of clothing, leather, oil, beer, rope, and many more staples. My intent is not merely to retrace what Andrew McRae calls "the consolidation of a coherent textual tradition in support of agrarian projects," but to show how these writings were received *as* projects in the seventeenth century, that is, as potentially controversial interventions into rural life.[10] Surveying this age of agricultural projects sets the stage for my readings of three poems in the georgic vein. I first analyze John Philips's *Cyder* (1708) to map the intercepts between an early example of Virgilian georgic in English and an exchange of orcharding proposals in seventeenth-century Herefordshire, focusing on one exemplary project-manual by the clergyman John Beale. I next survey the man-made topographies of *Windsor-Forest* (1713). Where Pope's landscape has traditionally been read in light of its mythological resonance and Stuart symbolism, I show how his poem also responds to the fact that the woods of Surrey and Berkshire hosted scores of improvement schemes dating back before the Restoration. Many of these projects conceived of the forest as an underutilized waste, a view that Pope seems both to countenance and reject. Having analyzed georgic's response to the didacticism and geography of projection, I conclude by turning to the explicit antiproject sentiments contained within James Thomson's *The Seasons* (1730). Often read for its salutary depiction of agrarian labor, Thomson's work also represents time as an inexorable force that negates human efforts to capitalize land. *The Seasons*, I argue, both celebrates and denies improvement's possibility by scrutinizing what "men project."[11]

Though this chapter concentrates on three early georgics composed between 1708 and 1730, the legacy of projects would also influence later georgics, including Christopher Smart's *Hop-Garden* (1752), John Dyer's *The Fleece*

(1757), James Grainger's *Sugar Cane* (1764), and Richard Jago's *Edge-Hill* (1767). By focusing on *Cyder*, *Windsor-Forest*, and *The Seasons*, my goal is to foreground several representative moments from georgic's long-standing attempt to reconcile the controversial history of seventeenth-century improvement with its own program of idealizing Britain's rural interior. This struggle, between tradition and innovation, certainty and speculation, would leave its impress not only on the georgic mode, but on all eighteenth-century British writings that depicted the working of land.

The Age of Agricultural Projects

Low attributes "georgic revolution" to natural philosophy's elevation of husbandry into noble ritual, and the spread of new farming techniques that raised the value of British soil. On the latter count, he lists "essential innovations" such as crop rotation, fertilizer development, and meadow flooding that "came into common practice between 1550 and 1650," and appeared capable of securing perennial abundance.[12] This claim presupposes both a consensus view of what counted as "innovation" among early modern agrarians, as well as the existence of handbooks and treatises that could translate novel ideas into "common" labor forms. "Continuing practice," notes Joan Thirsk, would have relied on "gentlemen instructing, or bullying, their stewards and bailiffs and . . . prevailing upon their tenants" to turn experimental approaches into routine agricultural practice.[13] Given the contentious, even coercive character of land improvement, it is unsurprising that large-scale initiatives like fen drainage were dismissed as "mere projects" by those who opposed them. But even modestly scaled undertakings, including the mere task of disseminating knowledge, could provoke controversy because this enterprise empowered readers to rework land they controlled. In the seventeenth century, even humdrum guides to soil and animal care could be construed as projects in the second person that applied the "science of husbandry" to reforming the country one plot at a time. As the Commonwealth planter and projector Ralph Austen put it, "a Cisterne of water is but a multitude of drops."[14]

Husbandry pamphleteers understood that the expertise they imparted could uproot time-honored customs—that any disseminated precept might pave the way for wider-ranging social and economic change. This is why many of the figures whom eighteenth-century georgic would laud took pains to distance themselves from the upheaval and confusion associated with projectors.

Samuel Hartlib submitted his *Legacy* to the vetting of a committee in order to authenticate its lessons at a time when "projectors have cast so many bitter things in the publick Fountain, whereof all have drunk, and their minds are so poysoned."[15] Walter Blith worried that his *English Improver Improved* (1652) would leave him "scandalized as a Projector."[16] Seven decades later, John Houghton lamented that "scarce any one durst offer for improvements, lest he should be called a *projector*."[17] Each of these husbanders feared that by authoring manuals they would be seen in the same light as predatory monopolists, delusional inventors, and vicious stockjobbers. That Hartlib, Blith, and Houghton felt it necessary to rebuke projection writ large underscores their struggle to distinguish informational tracts from speculative proposals.

Indeed, charges of projection can bring to light the tendency of agricultural pamphleteers and natural philosophers to digress from matters of empirical fact and practical recommendations into the proposal mode. For instance, the long-form title of John Evelyn's *Sylva; or, A Discourse on Forest-Trees*, easily the most important late Stuart work on arboreal stewardship, touts the "propagation of timber in His Majesties dominions" as a result of the author's lobbying. Evelyn not only catalogues the attributes and industrial uses of native trees but proposes mandating the plantation of timber nurseries through a parliamentary act for "the Setting but of two or three *Trees* in every *Acre* of Land that shall hereafter be enclosed, under the Forfeiture of Six-pence *per* Tree, for some *publick* and *charitable Work*, to be levy'd on the *Defaulters*."[18] Evelyn further boasts that it was at his "*Instigation*, and by the Direction" that England planted two million trees.[19] The *Sylva* of 1670 validates its own call for legislative action by claiming to have already effected a portion of the work. This self-conscious document of scholarly knowledge projects future woodlands while certifying an earlier edition of the same proposal a success.

Despite the griping apologetics of authors like Blith and Houghton, and the institutional prestige conferred on *Sylva* by its folio format and Royal Society imprint, agricultural writings were often demeaned as projection. The Royal Society, which established an aptly named Georgical Committee in 1664, became a lightning rod for such charges. Society member Robert Boyle had encouraged his colleagues to take up questions of husbandry in 1663, asserting that farming knowledge had yet to advance beyond "the lame and unlearned Observations and Practice of such illiterate Persons as Gardeners, Plow-men, and Milkmaids."[20] When the Georgical Committee did get to work convening meetings, circulating questionnaires, and publishing articles in the *Philosophical Transactions* on the cultivation of mulberry trees, potatoes, melons, and tobacco, these efforts often met with indifference or hostility. Henry Stubbe referred to all the Society's efforts as "but projecting," though he reserved special disdain for the institution's experiments in rural industry.[21] He scoffed that Gresham College's lately touted methods for deriving saltpeter from manure had been common knowledge since "the daies of *Queen Elizabeth*" and predicted that "turning the now comparative *desert World* into a *Paradise*, may not improbablie be expected from late *Agriculture*."[22] Against such complaints, Royal Society apologist Joseph Glanvill differentiated his institution's goal of "making *Knowledge Practical*," from "the little Projects of serving a *Sect*, or *propagating* an *Opinion*; of *spinning* out a *subtile Notion* into a *fine thred*, or forming a *plausible System* of *new Speculations*."[23] A need to legitimate experimental endeavor in the face of such attack, particularly endeavors intervening in debates over land use, would shape how Society Fellows went about conceiving and promoting their work. As Koji Yamamoto has surmised, what bound together the assorted pursuits of the Royal Society besides belief in "notions such as godly reformation" was a need to renounce the "greedy projector."[24]

Early accounts of seventeenth-century agriculture suggest that educating land owners remained controversial work throughout the 1700s. The Scottish economic historian Adam Anderson insinuates that late Stuart agricultural improvers failed to untangle their didactic labors from projection's web. His *Historical and Chronological Deduction of the Origin of Commerce* (1787) describes several "bubbles" from the 1600s and 1700s that "drew in numbers of unwary persons to their undoing."[25] Anderson indexes dozens of land proposals that range from the mundanely conventional ("improvement of glebe and church," "improving tillage and cattle for the corn trade," "gardens") to endeavors practiced in the Netherlands and elsewhere abroad but as yet unsubstantiated at home (the manufacture of textiles from hemp and flax) to controversial industrial pursuits that prioritized certain uses of nature over others (making iron and steel) to high-risk enterprise considered infeasible by many (Hill's beech oil invention, mulberry orcharding to raise silk worms, the cultivation of colonial crops like tobacco and sugar). In assessing risk from the comfort of hindsight, Anderson's chart marks the intersection between Defoe's "Age of Projects" and Low's "Georgical Revolution." Its contents confirm what self-conscious husbandry pamphleteers feared a century earlier: that the popularization of "innovative" strategies for managing land had reduced husbandry to a subfield of projection.

Like Anderson's *Historical and Chronological Deduction*, georgic poems also sought to reconstruct the legacies of seventeenth-century improvement. Unlike Anderson's, these poetic works did so in a more generous, even celebratory spirit. Restoring early modern agriculture to a framework of projection resurfaces the dubious reputation of this enterprise, an experience of doubt often glossed over by progressive epistemes like "New Husbandry" and "Agricultural Revolution." The remains of failed agricultural endeavor persist within eighteenth-century topographical poetry in passages that register possibility and ambition as well as contingency and frustration as the conflicting signatures of projection's cultural legacy. In turning now to *Cyder*, we can see how revisiting old endeavor advances georgic's own project of dredging national history for material to recast Britain's future.

Herefordshire Ruins

In 1708, the Oxfordshire native and former Christ Church student John Philips composed a long poem on the arts of orcharding and cider fermentation. Often regarded as the first English georgic, *Cyder: A Poem. In Two Books* traces the production of its titular beverage, from the plotting of fruit groves to the bottling of juice. Book 1 opens with the following sentence:

> What Soil the Apple loves, what Care is due
> To Orchats, timeliest when to press the Fruits,
> Thy Gift, *Pomona*, in *Miltonian* Verse
> Adventrous I presume to sing; of Verse
> Nor skill'd, nor studious: But my Native Soil
> Invites me, and the Theme as yet unsung.[26]

The invocation of Pomona, Roman goddess of fruitful plenty, recalls the inverted syntax that Virgil used to inventory the topical matter of his *Georgics*. Philips also claims a modern source of literary inspiration, crediting *Cyder's* unrhymed iambic pentameter to the author of *Paradise Lost*. Critics have taken Philips's adaptation of Virgilian grammar and "Miltonian" meter as evidence of a poet perpetuating canonical history by conspicuously "inheriting a set of literary traditions."[27]

This poetics of heredity goes far in illuminating *Cyder*, a classically allusive work by an author who first gained notoriety burlesquing Milton in *The Splendid Shilling* (1701). Literary mimicry cannot, however, explain the third entity that compels the speaker: "my Native Soil." Philips acknowledges that his "nor skill'd, nor studious verses" achieve neither the verbal economy of the *Georgics* nor the cosmic grandeur of *Paradise Lost*. He therefore invokes domestic land to displace these aesthetic standards with a new obtainable criterion: novelty. Philips declares his central theme of cider making "yet unsung." *Cyder* may not be the most correct or sublime poem, but it claims to be the first on its subject, making an unprecedented, if not supremely artful, contribution to British horticultural knowledge. "Native soil" inspires Philips to frame *Cyder* as indebted to tradition but groundbreaking in invention—a new sort of unattempted rhyme.

Cyder's protectionist economics and celebration of Anglo-Scottish Union through the image of "well blended streams" would seem to equate "native soil" with the entirety of Great Britain. However, the poem's action concentrates in the Golden Vale of Herefordshire, a West Midlands region famed for its temperate weather and abundant orchards. Philips's father owned an estate in the parish of Withington, and his grandfather was canon of Hereford Cathedral, where Philips was himself later buried. As Thirsk describes, the county was home to "small circles of energetic gentlemen" who advanced projects for planting, irrigation, road improvement, and canals, transforming a land that Philips knew firsthand into a test bed for public works and agricultural experimentation.[28] This was the region, *Cyder* tells us, where Philip Scudamore's "skilful Hand" invented the redstreak apple, which became a vital stock for the kingdom's cider industry.[29] It was the site where ancient Silurian tribes built a spired city, Ariconium, that rivaled the architectural glories of imperial Rome. It was the birthplace of a beverage that Britons hoped to export "to the utmost bounds of this / Wide Universe."[30] *Cyder*'s Herefordshire is both an actual place, full of familiar landmarks and personages, and an imagined countryside illustrating the future that rural improvement could obtain.

Herefordshire's exemplarity derived partly from the pivotal role that the West Midlands played during the civil wars. Soldiers who survived fighting in the region often gained a taste for cider "and carried its fame further afield."[31] The region's renown owed something also to the efforts of postwar pamphleteers, who depicted Herefordshire as a progressive fruit belt and model society. The region's most prominent publicist was John Beale (1608–83), a county resident who promoted orcharding and cider production through his work as an author, editor, and collaborator. The *Oxford Dictionary of National Biography* tells us that Beale's father experimented with apple grafts on his Yarkhill Estate during the 1620s, and his mother was related to the same Scudamore whose invention of the redstreak *Cyder* toasted a century later.[32] His uncle was the courtier Robert Pye, who served as Auditor of the Exchequer under James I and Charles I, and who, with Scudamore, "helped to establish Herefordshire's reputation in the seventeenth century as an English Pomerania."[33] Beale corresponded with Samuel Hartlib during the Commonwealth and later became a founding member of the Royal Society's Georgical Committee. Ever "experimenting, commenting, and speculating," Beale had a hand in many of the era's most important horticultural publications: he published Ralph Austen's *Treatise on Fruit Trees* (1653), assisted John Evelyn in drafting *Pomona* (1664), coauthored *Nurseries, Orchards, Profitable Gardens and Vineyards Encouraged* (1677) with Anthony Lawrence, and contributed to John Houghton's periodical *A Collection of Letters for the Improvement of Husbandry and Trade* (1681).[34]

But of all Beale's labors, the work that would most influence *Cyder*'s sense of place was his 1657 pamphlet entitled *Herefordshire Orchards, a Pattern for All England*. Like Philips's confessedly "nor skill'd, nor studious verses," Beale's "plain and unpolished" prose account derives its originality from extolling "native soil" rather than rhetorical art.[35] Like other republican-era tracts by Gabriel Plattes and Walter Blith, *Herefordshire Orchards* instructed newly landed readers how to capitalize on the conversion of parks, forests, and estates into arable tillage.[36] But despite addressing citizens of the Protectorate, Beale's tract would outlive the Interregnum historical context that inspired it. The work's reprinting in 1724 and 1739 suggests its lasting appeal, even in the years following Philips's composition of *Cyder*.

Critics have long identified *Herefordshire Orchards* as a sourcebook for *Cyder*'s meditations on the aesthetics and spirituality of fruit cultivation, and its depiction of the Golden Vale as a postlapsarian Eden.[37] Metaphrastic analysis facilitates such connections. Read through this anticipatory light, Beale's tract seems to epitomize the "the Science of Husbandry" that *Cyder* puts "into a pleasing Dress"—a set of reflections that achieved literary posterity through its enshrinement in verse. But this sort of synopsis greatly simplifies Philips's engagement with *Herefordshire Orchards*, which he treated not only as a repository of images and precepts, but as a plan for action dating from a revolutionary era when written tracts shaped how readers conceived of land and its use. Like Evelyn's *Sylva*, which would sponsor timber conservation to secure England's future naval power, *Herefordshire Orchards* delivers informational content not only to educate individual readers in the art of tree care, but to encourage the drafting of policy that would stimulate commerce and nourish subjects. Philips perceived how Beale's ambitions extended far beyond his

ostensible topic of apple groves, which become the backdrop for his grander
ambition of reforming the rural state.

Though *Herefordshire Orchards* presents itself as a mere manual, it employs
argumentative conventions that we have identified within project proposals.
The tract's goal of furnishing England with a "pattern" for prosperity calls on
readers to export across the realm the technical methods and spirit of industry
that spurred Herefordshire's development. Beale extolls the translation of
knowledge into action by connecting his writing to an established lineage of
regional improvers, a "great number of admirable contrivers for the publick
good."[38] He asserts that every village has at least "some excellent Republican"
and lists by initials several residents who raised the value of their lands through
creative feats of husbandry.[39] Beale occasionally thrills to the kinds of overwrought and mysticizing rhetoric that made projectors suspect in this era, such
as when he characterizes efforts to make cider from crab apples as a "fresh
wonder" that was "lately found out," and confides that the "experiment is not
yet known to many of our Country-Men, it being reserved to few as a novell
mystery."[40]

Herefordshire Orchards makes one of its most elaborate arguments for ar-
boricultural innovation by conjuring the county's illustrious past. In this vein,
Beale reserves highest praise for Scudamore, his maternal kinsman, not only
for inventing the redstreak, but for opposing iron mills in his time, thereby
preserving "woods against the day of *Englands* need."[41] Beale salutes also the
farsightedness of Rowland Vaughan, a local manorial lord who designed trench
irrigation systems for English farms, a "much-desired project" that he demonstrated on his own estate along the River Dore.[42] Beale's allusions to timber
debates and Elizabethan canals bespeak more than antiquarian enchantment.
They reveal his interest in creating the political and infrastructural conditions
for Herefordshire's fruit to circulate as goods. It is this comprehensive view of
improvement—cultivation and everything supporting it—that leads Beale to
bemoan the region's poor transportation network: "For Gardens, we have little
encouragement to designe more than is for the necessary use of our own families, except our River *Wye* may be made navigable for transportation. And by
defect of transportation, our store of cider is become a snare to many, who
turne Gods blessings into wantonnesse & drunkenesse."[43] Without a dredged
and locked Wye, Herefordshire gardeners have no reason to harvest more produce than they can consume themselves. This deficit relegates England's pat-
ternable vale to subsistence agriculture. What's worse, impassable rivers leave
Herefordshire with a glut of cider, inciting "wantonesse & drunkenesse"

among local inhabitants. In an era when "growth in the volume of marketed produce went hand in hand with the development of the transport network," *Herefordshire Orchards* proposes extending northward the navigable portion of the Wye, which did not yet reach the town of Hereford.[44] Beale argues that if advances in arboriculture are not accompanied by equally ambitious acts of civil engineering, then fertile soils can go to waste or even corrupt those that work them.

Of course not everyone supported navigations, especially riverfront property owners who feared damage to their estates. By turning to this fractious realm of riparian engineering, the same project on which Yarranton staked his embattled reputation, *Herefordshire Orchards* underscores how apples and pears bear exchange value only so far as their fermented juice can travel. Beale extends this reasoning through his depiction of another kind of commercial conduit, the droves and highways connecting Herefordshire's "rowes of villages" to each other and to the rest of Britain.[45] Perfumed by blossoms and shaded by walnut trees, these roads accentuate the region's orderly beauty in several passages.[46] However, "where Trade thrives not" those same routes become "oppressed with idle and sturdy vagabonds," a dispersion of poverty stemming from the immobility of goods.[47] The roads function as channels of trade and social barometers that make visible the moral and economic precarity of Herefordshire's residents. Beale's point is that idleness, sin, and starvation can all result from plantation if that enterprise is not buttressed by public works. Horticultural knowledge can effect improvement only in concert with related projects.

The need for controversial enterprise within and outside orchards explains Beale's culminating call for a "patriot" to "break through the difficulties of an obstructive people, and force open a way for trade and commerce."[48] This civic hero might be the engineer who eventually executes the Wye navigation or the Protectorate official who champions the undertaking. It might also be Beale himself, whose doubled vision of harvests (exported or wasted) and swains (industrious or idle) stresses the dire consequences of failing to capitalize land in a manner that is comprehensively imagined and undertaken. Herefordshire can become a "pattern" for rural ingenuity only if it upgrades its logistical links and only "if other Countreys would submit to the same patience and industry, as is usuall amongst us."[49] Beale's conditional statement reminds readers that improvement itself could fail if its authors and undertakers do not anticipate future needs. Without a projector patriot, Herefordshire cannot remain a viable model of rural industry and risks wasting the husbander's care.

Philips was similarly haunted by orcharding's contingencies. He dedicates long passages of *Cyder* to pondering the obstacles that frustrated man's quest to make nature "improv'd by Art."[50] His georgic raises the possibility of failure in the opening lines, proclaiming "Adventrous I presume to sing."[51] Philips is "adventrous" in the sense of intrepidly testing an "unsung" theme, and in undertaking the literary venture of composing a long work of verse. Cognizant of *Cyder*'s aesthetic and financial risk, Philips's speaker obsesses over the challenge of formulating sound precepts:

> thoughtful of Thy Gain,
> Not of my Own, I all the live-long Day
> Consume in Meditation deep, recluse
> From human Converse, nor, at shut of Eve,
> Enjoy Repose; but oft at Midnight Lamp
> Ply my brain-racking Studies, if by chance
> Thee I may counsel right; and oft this Care
> Disturbs me slumbring.[52]

Virgil conceived of poetry as a kind of mental labor, wherein hard-fought verses track the plough's slow progress. His *Georgics* also addressed the accidents that could frustrate any piece of agricultural wisdom, no matter how meticulously phrased. But *Cyder* pushes this risk-bound ethic of care to the point of parody: Philips's speaker is anguished beyond all bounds of georgical studiousness in his efforts to gather knowledge from "sage Experience."[53] His "brain-racking Studies" cost him sleep, company, and the lucid equanimity one would expect from a poetic exploration of human industry in an Augustan mode. His insatiable pursuit of public advantage evokes the figure of the projector, who notoriously garnishes proposals within overwrought professions of piety and self-sacrifice. Like Beale, who conceived of *Herefordshire Orchards* as "for the benefit of all men, and particularly for the good of this Nation," Philips burdens his narrator with the two-fold task of explaining arboriculture through pleasing verse, and imagining a nation-state able to reward and sustain orcharding.[54]

Philips's tenacious pursuit of "thy gain" leads *Cyder* to claw value from Herefordshire's least promising topographies, including barren heaths, "unamiable" hilltops, and rocky ledges.[55] Fertile land, the poem suggests, could support multiple forms of agriculture at the same time: "Apples of Price, and plenteous Sheaves of Corn / Oft interlac'd occurr."[56] The practice of planting trees amid crop fields had been debated throughout the seventeenth century.[57] That fruit hung high above wheat stalks held out obvious possibilities of integration. However, tree trunks got in the way of ploughs and cast shade over tillage. Reflecting his home shire's elaborate incorporation of grain, fruit, dairy production, and sheep grazing, *Cyder* champions the interplanting of trees and corn despite its drawbacks. Philips validates an experimental strategy for increasing the value of land by joining two agricultural pursuits within one consonant line. Like the anonymous *Designe for Plentie* (1652), which touted the "double gain" of produce "upon the ground; and . . . upon the trees," *Cyder* makes different kinds of husbandry compatible through a pleasing arrangement of words.[58] The poem suggests that intensifying use of Herefordshire land will broaden the region's economy and enrich its literary representation.

Cyder's speaker displays a projecting spirit both in his sleepless quest to realize Herefordshire's commercial potential and his prosodic intervention into arguments over land use. Like Beale, he also acknowledges the speculative nature of his didactic labors. *Cyder*'s speaker toils "if by chance" his lines might convey something useful to the reader, while conceding that no amount of knowledge can ensure healthy orchards:

> A thousand Accidents the Farmer's Hopes
> Subvert, or checque; uncertain all his Toil,
> 'Till lusty Autumn's luke-warm Days, allay'd
> With gentle Colds, insensibly confirm
> His ripening Labours.[59]

Agriculture emerges here as it own hope-filled, accident-prone enterprise. Only the autumn harvest can validate an orcharder's efforts. Until the fruit falls, the caprices of temperature, rainfall, and insects render "uncertain all his Toil." *Cyder* counterbalances its idiom of possibility and persistent faith in "the Promise of the coming Year" by depicting frustrated planters who improvise against faithless soil and bad weather.[60] Philips purports to dispense authoritative lessons on fruit care at the same time he concedes the possibility that any orchard can become a failed project.

Cyder sensationalizes this prospect of ruin within one of its many narrative digressions. The longest one describes the sudden collapse of an ancient Britannic city, Ariconium, into a bottomless chasm. Ariconium is *Cyder*'s most arresting emblem of ruined investment. In Philips's mythic account, the once proud city finds itself "ingulft / by the wide yawning Earth," its inhabitants and buildings "Crush'd, and o'erwhelmed," and then ultimately drawn down "to the Realms / of endless Night."[61] The destruction reduces everyone and everything that belonged to Ariconium to "one sad Sepulchre."[62] This report of indiscriminate wreckage appears to undermine *Cyder*'s progressive spirit: what, after all, is the point of improving land prone to such cataclysm? Philips suggests that Ariconium's worth remanifests centuries later. The city leaves behind coins, urns, and "huge unwieldy Bones," which the modern swain uncovers while plowing a field.[63] Ariconium survives more extraordinarily in the fertility of the land, whose trees are now "with ruddiest Freight bedeckt," nourished by the remains of Herefordshire's Silurian forefathers.

Rachel Crawford has read the scene as performing an intergenerational transmission of virtue, whereby flourishing plants express Herefordshire's heroic genealogy. Courtney Weiss Smith argues that Ariconium's ruins demonstrate "the soil's absorption of the events of history," the same meaning-filled soil that solicited Philips's song.[64] I argue that the trope of sanguinary fertilizer also gives *Cyder*'s speaker an opportunity to model resourcefulness of the sort that Beale and his fellow fruit pamphleteers evinced in prose: just as this narrator sought to extract use value from every inch of land, so too does the poet derive from the materials of history evidence of Britain's hallowed past to support his vision of the future. Ariconium's obliteration swells the redstreak. Likewise, the Silurians who built the city lend Herefordshire a salutary genius and flattering origin myth. Philips identifies the descendants of those ancient tribes in the forces of Charles I, who lost the civil wars (several battles of which were fought in royalist strongholds throughout the Midlands), but found redemption in the Stuart Restoration and the reign of Queen Anne, who fulfills the long-prophesized unification of Great Britain. Philips uses Virgilian form to mediate catastrophic national history, recuperating ruin into prophesy.

Beale closes *Herefordshire Orchards* by calling on a "patriot" to advance controversial river engineering projects. Philips concludes *Cyder* by saluting Anne Stuart and the "bold designs" of imperialism that he hoped her rule would realize. In a series of prophetic clauses, the poem declares that "the *British Navy* thro the Ocean vast / shall wave her double Cross, t'extreamest Climes"; "the Swains / Shall unmolested reap"; and cider "Shall please all Tasts."[65] According to the *Oxford English Dictionary*, the auxiliary verb "shall" assists in "forming (with present infinitive) the future."[66] The ability of "shall" to "form . . . the future" explains its utility to Philips, who depicts orcharding both as regional custom and practice for raising British influence abroad. The closing stanza's imperial "shall" validates the "shall" of the individual laborer who at the beginning of the poem selects soil to plant a nursery: "hence thy Industry shall gain / Ten-fold Reward." "Shall" indeed discharges georgic's task of "securing the aesthetic and moral links between country, city, and empire."[67] However, Philips's situation of fruit orcharding atop Ariconium's ruins ensures that the connection between country toil and oceanic fleets is never too seamless, nor the arc from past to future without a discomforting "affective residue."[68] *Cyder* adapts from Beale's forbearing work of projection both the strategies for extrapolating the future from discrete action, and a nagging awareness of how accidents could prevent fruitful vales from establishing patterns of improvement.

Windsor Wastes

Philips celebrates the enterprising spirit behind Commonwealth cultivation projects at the same time he details the uncertainty of orchard labor. In *Cyder*, the improver persists heroically against the prospect of his own ruin, and Herefordshire's backdrop of sublime historical debris. Alexander Pope, by contrast, despised projectors. His *Dunciad* condemns them to the court of dullness alongside enthusiasts, politicians, castle builders, chemists, and poets.[69] Likewise, his *Temple of Fame* relegates projectors to the "unnumber'd Multitudes," in the company of "Quacks, and Lawyers not a few."[70] Pope characterized the projector as someone who exploits cheap print to promote worthless schemes, polluting with banality the world he claims to cast anew. His propagation attests a society stagnating through a modish fixation on the here-to-come.

Therefore, *Windsor-Forest* (1713), Pope's georgically inspired meditation on rural life and the Peace of Utrecht, seems an unlikely place to find evidence of projection's achievements. This is a work, after all, that salutes the "humbler joys of home-felt Quiet," damns "mad *Ambition*," and characterizes itself as "unambitious Strains" sung on "careless Days."[71] The poem's setting in a royal game park dating from the Norman era further extends a sense of timeless leisure, distant from the contriving futurists who infested London. Windsor's proximity to Runnymede, where King John signed the Magna Carta, meanwhile establishes a sweeping historical context that diminishes the day-to-day churn of pamphlets and intrigue. The remains of Charles I, interred at the Chapel of St. George, consecrate Windsor as a "place of memory," according to Joseph Roach, where cultural traditions run "as deep as time."[72]

Windsor-Forest's symbolically freighted setting can overshadow the poem's attention to actual land in Berkshire and Surrey, a region targeted by improvers throughout the seventeenth century.[73] Early modern schemes for new industry, agriculture, and public works reconfigured Windsor's literal terrain and mythographic possibilities. Indeed, projects created some of the most labor-sustaining and georgical features of the landscape that Pope illustrated in order to champion Tory values and a naturalistic aesthetics. Of the major projectors addressed in this book, at least three had designs on the forest. Andrew Yarranton envisioned a Thames navigation between Oxford and London that would have bisected the royal retreat and required the construction of flash locks, gates, and flushes, "one near Windsor."[74] Aaron Hill listed Windsor Forest among the "many *private Parks*, within a days Journey of *London*, [that] can show an inexhaustible store of *Beech*," though there is no evidence he actually harvested mast on those grounds.[75]

Where Yarranton and Hill discussed hypothetical projects involving Windsor, Cornelius Vermuyden undertook actual work on forest land. In 1623, James I hired him to drain off the "water which now overspreadeth divers parts of the great park of Windsor."[76] Enlisting "divers poor men," Vermuyden completed the project within a year. Impressed with the Dutchman's work, the king commissioned him two years later to drain an inundated chase in Yorkshire, setting the stage for his eventual work on the Bedford Level. Unlike these later ventures, Vermuyden's Windsor drainage succeeded at separating earth from water. This decisive act of landscaping caught Pope's eye a century later:

> Here earth and water seem to strive again,
> Not *Chaos*-like together crush'd and bruis'd
> But as the world, harmoniously confus'd:
> Where Order in Variety we see,
> And where, tho' all things differ, all agree.[77]

Windsor's postdrainage landscape manifests *concordia discors*, the doctrine holding that disparate elements drawn together can form a beautiful congruence. The drainer's separation of "chaos" into "earth and water" reenacts on a small scale God's inaugural parting of the waters to form a variegated universe. Thanks to Vermuyden's efforts, Windsor has come to resemble the world in miniature, a geography where land and water vie with one another to create a pleasing scene without sacrificing their distinguishing characteristics to "crushed and bruised" marsh. An interwoven but unblended prospect of pleasure grounds, fish ponds, grain fields, streams, and foliage stretch as far as the eye can see. Whether the Binfield-born Pope knew of Vermuyden's activities in Windsor Forest is uncertain. Nonetheless, his experience of harmonious confusion seems to derive partly from the designs of a Dutch engineer and the local workers who executed it.

Windsor-Forest's survey of lawns, glades, walks, waters, "tufted trees and springing corn" seeks pleasure in variety.[78] Even when Pope's setting admits uncultivatable "wild heath" and "sandy wilds" he redeems the former surface by lingering over its vibrantly purple shrubs and supplants the latter with "yellow harvests." The resulting landscape is part fact, part fantasy. There is no reconciling Pope's fairyland, where "blushing flora paints the enamelled ground," with Defoe's *Tour thro' the Whole Island*, which two decades later found the same region "given up to Barreness . . . much of it a Sandy Desert, and one may frequently be put in Mind here of *Arabia Deserta*."[79] Pope embellishes his poem's scenery to validate its panegyric: "Rich Industry sits smiling on the Plains, / And peace and plenty tell, a Stuart reigns."[80] At the same time, his Windsor Forest is not pure allegorical contrivance. To the contrary, like Philips's and Beale's Herefordshire, it bears the impress of historical attempts to improve a "dreary Desart, and a gloomy waste" into a populous site of husbandry.[81] Pope uses the beaming, reclining figure of "Industry" to bring georgic productivity to a Norman hunting retreat without disturbing the scene. This personification enables Windsor Forest to host vigorous projection while feeling unchangingly hallowed.

Designated a royal hunting preserve by William the Conqueror, Windsor Forest remained mostly off-limits to the early modern improvers who were enclosing, reclaiming, seeding, and pasturing other parts of the realm during the 1500s and 1600s. Besides Vermuyden's act of landscape beautification, Samuel Hartlib mentions one scheme by the "Sergeant-Plummer of the late kings" to design a conduit for "bringing the Water from Windsor to White-hall," which he "counteth a most reall publick work."[82] This ambitious piece of engineering never materialized. Local landholders, meanwhile, were restricted to using small parts of the forest for tillage, pasture, and firewood, and only so long as these activities did not disturb the local deer population.[83] Woodmote and Swainmote courts tried those accused of laying waste to the wilderness, which encompassed not only venison but the tree leaves that deer used for food and cover. The royal forester's concern for game forestalled large-scale plans to develop the region while discouraging forest residents from experimenting with new methods of husbandry.

All this changed after the civil wars, when Parliament seized control of the

park and placed it in the hands of sequestrators tasked with employing confiscated lands "for the best advantage of the Commonwealth, and to consider and
present some way for improving, disposing, and well management of the public revenue."[84] A portion of Windsor Great Park was divided into small private
holdings, thereby populating the forest with profit-seeking improvers and establishing an environment conducive to projects. Deriving public advantage
(and private wealth) from Windsor first entailed overcoming the land's infer-
tility. Where Herefordshire was renowned for its fruit-friendly soils, Windsor
Forest was full of scrubby heath, whose beauty thrilled Pope, but was "the
barrenest ground" in Blith's estimation.[85] Richard Weston compared a stretch
of especially poor soil between Ghent and Antwerp to "som part of the Heathie
Land in *Windsor Forest*."[86] He went on to describe how industrious Flemings
managed to transform that unpromising tract into "manie hundreds of Acres
of goodly *Flax*, *Turneps*, and *Clover-grass*," implying that English cultivators
might do the same with Windsor.[87] Windsor's want of nutritious soil fired the
imagination of projectors who saw potential in the land's putative lack. Windsor was, in Hartlib's suggestive phrase, a heathy waste that "might bee Experimented vpon."[88]

Commonwealth citizens would subject Windsor to a variety of uses, including tillage, orchards, pasture, and chalk digging. Evidence of these activities appears in Pope's poem interspersed with its pastoral depictions of coursing,
birding, and fishing. We can detect the encroachment of industry when the
speaker muses that "the Forests wonder'd at th'unusual grain" and describes
"*Pan* with flocks, with fruits *Pomona* crown'd"; and perhaps obliquely, when
the poem illustrates the "chalky Wey," of Wiltshire's River Cole. But in no case
does Pope attribute improvement to Commonwealth sequestrators, Hartliban
experimenters, or the purchasers of confiscated parkland. Rather, he ascribes
these advances to the succession of post-Norman monarchs willing to "hear
the Subjects Cries."[89] Lands that had been "empty Wilds and Woods" under
William the Conqueror spontaneously sprout society under Anne: cottages
rise, flocks gather, and wilds spread with "yellow Harvests."[90] Windsor's newfound prosperity results not from the discrete particulars of a given design or
program of improvement, but rather from the oversight of receptive monarchs.
The landscape mirrors Britain's defeat of tyranny, now relegated to a marine
realm ruled by "Pykes, the Tyrants of the watry Plains," while on land "Fair
Liberty, *Britannia's* Goddess, rears / her chearful Head, and leads the golden
Years."[91] At the root of Windsor's topographical diversity is not republican

projection, but an agnostic spirit of progress compatible with Stuart monarchy, what Robert Irvine calls "that which is unchained by "Liberty.""[92]

By conceiving of Windsor's development as the relinquishment of Norman bondage, Pope delivers a rousing portrait of liberty that elides the Commonwealth era when the forest was most aggressively reimagined and economically diversified. The poem potentially alludes to this industrious period via pun, when the speaker asks the muse to "bear me to sequester'd Scenes" of the sort John Denham surveyed in *Cooper's Hill*, though it seems unlikely that Pope would have found tranquil retreat during the middle seventeenth century's "dreadful Series of Intestine Wars," or in its climactic moment of regicide.[93] The Interregnum, late Stuart era, and reign of William and Mary vanish from Pope's rendition of national history, which combines the civil wars and the War of the Spanish Succession into one continuous era of conflict that ended only when "Anna said —— Let discord cease! / She said, The world obey'd, and all was *Peace!*"[94]

Peaceful "Industry" manifests the prudence and diplomacy of Queen Anne, whose brokering of the Treaty of Utrecht Pope credits with returning British swains to their native fields while extending British power across the Atlantic. This allegorical explanation of improvement is most striking (and dependent on metaphor) when Pope addresses Windsor Forest's greatest commodity: trees. Britain's woodlands were subject to many kinds of uses during the seventeenth century. They were cordoned into preserves; milled into timber; burned into charcoal for the manufacture of brick, tile, and iron; and sometimes preserved for future use, as in the Act for the Sale of Crown Lands in 1649, which forbade the felling of trees within fifteen miles of a navigable river.[95] In 1612, one Church Rooke stressed Windsor's uncultivatibility to justify planting trees there: "if some industrious man would apply himself to make triall thereof in Windsor Forest, or some such like heathie barren ground, his endeauour were worthily to be respected."[96] In 1649, the Sequestration Commission counted 2,604 trees in Windsor Forest, a figure whose precision reflects the thoroughness of surveyors as much as the value of wood.[97]

Windsor's many hardwood oaks—the firmest in the kingdom according to one pamphleteer—and position on the River Thames made the region an important source of fleet timber.[98] By the time Charles II restored Windsor Forest as a deer park in 1660, and evicted its Protectorate overseers, forests had already been transformed, according to Elizabeth Heckendorn Cook, from a "theater of royal charisma into tree farm for the British navy."[99] Just as

Yarranton imagined the Irish County of Wexford as a future shipyard, Pope envisioned Windsor's woods as boats in potential. He characterizes trees as "floating forests" and "future navies," before sending them directly into the Thames:

> Thy Trees, fair *Windsor*! Now shall leave their Woods,
> And half thy Forests rush into my Floods,
> Bear *Britain's* Thunder, and her Cross display
> To the bright Regions of the rising Day.[100]

Windsor-Forest realizes the industrial potential of rural land through the trope of anthropomorphic trees and a timber project that undertakes itself. When Philips described a similar scene of shipbuilding in *Cyder*, it was "sweating peasants" who felled an oak, a strenuous act of lumbering that "stems the vast Main" of ships that bear "tremendous War / To distant Nations."[101] By contrast, Pope's landscape improves without human intercession, though in accordance with prudent design: that only half of Windsor's trees become boats leaves an abundance of woods for hunting, industry, and future naval construction. By converting tree fiber into maritime supremacy, Pope's poem encapsulates the work of a project, though it is endeavor unencumbered by written tracts, political lobbying, displaced commoners, or controversy of any kind: "Industry" and Anne alone endow the woods and wastes of the Thames Valley with the raw materials for a blue-water navy that could pacify the world.

Windsor-Forest dwells on land that is reconceived and sometimes literally reworked by projects in order to project British power on the globe. However, Pope's Stuart allegiances and desire to secure Windsor from meddling projectors prevent him from engaging directly with the seventeenth-century policy interventions that made possible a Britainizable world, including the capitalization of game parks. His poem acknowledges the effects of rural improvement while attempting to hold on to Windsor Forest as an escape from busy, tedious London, where, in the words of his fellow Scriblerian John Gay, "News and Politicks amuse Mankind, / And Schemes of State involve th'uneasie Mind."[102] But Pope cannot escape projection. By turning to the country, he succeeds only in moving from its site of print exchange to its venue of enactment.

Projects Out of Season

Cyder and *Windsor-Forest* describe the impact of projection on British land without ever invoking the controversial language of "projects" and "projectors." Philips's georgic imitation and Pope's georgical lyric address the conflict between change and tradition without naming the instruments by which improvement was conceived, contested, and realized. By contrast, James Thomson's 1730 topographical poem *The Seasons* uses project terminology to challenge the notion that scheming could permanently change the world:

> Revolving Ages sweep the changeful Earth,
> And Empires rise and fall; regardless he
> Of what the never-resting Race of Men
> Project: thrice happy! could he scape their Guile,
> Who mine, from cruel Avarice, his Steps,
> Or with his towry Grandeur swell their State,
> The Pride of Kings! or else his Strength pervert,
> And bid him rage amid the mortal Fray,
> Astonish'd at the Madness of Mankind.[103]

These lines are spoken by an elephant. This "truly wise" creature has spent enough years in mankind's company to grasp what humans cannot: that societies rise and collapse regardless of what "men / project." The natural history of a "changeful Earth" exists beyond the contingencies of projection and brings to ruin all that humanity contrives. Time, in this passage, is not a medium against which proposals can validate themselves, a resource to be allotted, or an obstacle to be surmounted. It instead constitutes a centrifugal force that obliterates all evidence of enterprise. The elephant, himself exploited by projects for glorifying tyrants and waging war, regards scheming as the "madness of mankind," a state of agitation and narcissistic refusal to acknowledge mortality in the face of ineluctable time. The pachydermic long view exposes the projector as someone arrogant enough to believe that personal ambition can outlast revolving ages.

Thomson found another figure for "world-revolving power" in the motions of

> th' unwieldy Planets launch'd along
> Th' illimitable Void! Thus to remain,

Amid the Flux of many thousand Years
That oft has swept the toiling Race of Men,
And all their labour'd Monuments away.[104]

Time again engulfs human endeavor. Here it is the immutable tracks of heav-
enly bodies that outlast "labored monuments." Man, according to Thomson,
cannot alter a universe engineered by the "all-perfect Hand" that "rules the
steady whole." The only projection that matters is that of the divine mechanic,
God, whose cosmos erases civilization's fragile artifice. This portrayal of a solar
system governed by natural force and cyclical time suits Thomson's interest in
seasons, which manifest in light and weather the earth's changing position with
respect to the sun. Season, as a consequence of "changeful Earth" and condition of rural labor, organizes Thomson's four-book exploration of British land
and character through the georgic, pastoral, and metaphysical modes.[105] *The
Seasons* binds "Summer" together with "Winter," which introduces a third
revolutionary trope: the "unceasing Hand" of nature that "Rolls round the
Seasons of the changeful Year."[106] Spring becomes summer becomes fall becomes winter regardless of what Britons do. Where Philips and Pope plot linear
pathways from Britain's past to its future in poems that culminate on the high
seas with oak-hewn fleets globalizing Stuart power, *The Seasons* ends where it
begins: "unbounded Spring encircle All."[107]

The Seasons's orbital configuration of time and rebuke of projection does
not, however, foreclose on the prospect of human improvement. In "Autumn,"
Thomson credits "Industry! rough Power!" with elevating mankind from sloth-
ful savagery into a functioning civilization. The laborer's "Sweat, and Pain"
guided by the "directing hand of Art" procures "the soft civility of life." Here,
time's revolution brings not inevitable destruction, but fruitful harvest.[108] "All
is the Gift of Industry," proclaims the speaker, who details the beneficial labors
of mining, forestry, metalwork, and textile production.[109] Industrious Britons
join together to form "a public; to the general good," versifying the Lockean
development of civil society out of a state of nature through the allocation of
natural resources. In "Winter," Thomson identifies an example of such progress in the nation building of Peter the Great, whose ingenuity and craft
knowledge drew Russia out of "Gothic Darkness" by taming "her Rocks, her
Fens, / Her Floods, her Seas, her ill-submitting Sons."[110] The same poem that
urges readers to content themselves with "private Virtues" that repress the
"ardent Risings of the kindling Soul," and avoid being "snatch'd away by Hope,
/ Thro' the dim Spaces of Futurity," also makes farsighted leadership

prerequisite to becoming a viable culture.[111] Projects may be hopelessly ephemeral, but projection is also that which renders society possible in the first place.

The irreconcilability of futile projects and civilizing industry reflects what John Barrell calls *The Seasons*'s "two quite opposite views of history"; as both the tragic story of innocence lost, and the uplifting tale of human perfection.[112] Projects belong to either history as they can harbor both modernization, in the hands of intrepid Peter, and vain despotism, according to the sage elephant. *The Seasons* acknowledges what Patricia Meyer Spacks calls "obvious accomplishments taking place in English agriculture, manufacturing, and trade," while subscribing to the Great Chain of Being, "belief in which made progress impossible."[113] The poem is "at home with such ironies," according to David Fairer, who explains Thomson's ambiguous treatment of human ambition as the by-product of georgic's retrieval of "repeatable strategies from a world of experience where decay and death have entered."[114] Improvement materializes through "observable and repeatable patterns," in Clare Bucknell's similar phrase, that accommodate "the returning rhythms of seedtime and harvest, instead of moving by progressive linear stages."[115] What emerges from these readings is the idea that successful projects create procedures for adapting to unchanging nature rather than refashioning the world into something altogether new.

This more limited idea of projection—as man's attempt to acclimate himself to a destructive universe—emphasizes the iterative relationship between individuals and their plots of land over the collective enterprises that dug canals, planted colonies, built factories, and erected fisheries. *Seasons* rejects those projects that stipulate one-time undertaking to instead hold up a vision of progress through repetition promulgating what Annabel Patterson calls "a conservative ideology based on the 'georgic' values of hard work (in others), landownership as proof of worth."[116] However, the circulation of what Fairer calls "strategies" and Patterson deems "values" implies the existence of authors who wrote in order to reform existing agricultural practice. From this view, Thomson's rejection of egoistic projects and valorization of autumnal industry mirrors the projector's attempts to identify as modest agrarian improver rather than wily salesman. *The Seasons* rejects projectors by name but assents to their self-conception as patriot industrialists. The establishment of a productive countryside and creation of a national public requires "restless man" in the mold of Tsar Peter, even in a poem that endeavors to make industry serene.

The tension between virtuous progress and ineffectual projects manifests again in "Winter," when Thomson invokes his patron, Spencer Compton, Earl of Wilmington. Compton was a prolific Whig statesman, whose forty-five-year political career included stints as speaker of the House of Commons and prime minister to George II. Thomson praises Compton's character but is ambivalent about his projects:

> Nor art thou skill'd in awful Schemes alone,
> And how to make a mighty People thrive;
> But equal Goodness, sound Integrity,
> A firm unshaken uncorrupted Soul
> Amid a sliding age, and burning strong,
> Not vainly blazing, for thy Country's Weal,
> A steady Spirit, regularly free;
> These, each exalting each, the Statesman light
> Into the Patriot; These, the publick Hope
> And Eye to thee converting, bid the Muse
> Record what Envy dares not Flattery call.[117]

Endowed with "many thought" and the faculty of "bold description," Compton proposes "awful schemes" for raising the conditions of British subjects. These plans for governing society are "awful" insofar as they inspire awe, though the adjective also appears to evoke abject dread. Thomson claims that Compton is skillful in enterprise, but then discloses nothing about the contents of these plans. He goes on to locate Compton's true virtue in his resolute patriotism rather than his parliamentary scheming. Instead of "vainly blazing" like a showy but futile projector, Compton labors steadily, as if by "Sweat, and Pain," for the Hanoverian monarchy, and its crown prince, Frederick, to whom Thomson dedicated *The Seasons*. Thomson's backhanded praise accords with Lord Hervey's less generous characterization of Compton as an unoriginal plodder: "as he was to execute rather than project . . . so he was much fitter for a clerk to a minister."[118] Hervey portrays Compton as a capable public servant rather than a visionary statesman, someone better suited to executing the designs of others rather than hatching his own.

Thomson appears to agree. However, he manages to flatter Compton by making patriotic fervor the sole criterion for evaluating his career. The having of good intentions becomes more important than their expression through actionable plans. The project, for Thomson, remains a presumptuous attempt to build futures against divine nature, to transcend rather than synchronize with the seasonal rhythms of georgic. This is why *The Seasons* rejects projection per se while amplifying its promises and self-understanding through what Thomas Brugis called "other termes of Art."[119] Thomson deploys the controversial terminology of projects in order to distinguish between beneficial industry and an unnatural ambition that violates the progressive limits of the georgic mode.

Poetry's Undertaking

No fan of georgic, Samuel Johnson nonetheless believed that didactic poetry performed an important therapeutic function for dispirited British subjects. In his 1744 biography of Richard Savage, he differentiates the work of verse from that of political projection. When confronted by poverty, Johnson explains, the politician will seek "a Remedy for these Miseries, rather than encourage an escape from them."[120] By contrast, the poet "is employed in a more pleasing Undertaking than that of proposing Laws, which, however just or expedient, will never be made, or endeavoring to reduce to rational Schemes of Government Societies which were formed by Chance, and are conducted by the private Passions of those who preside in them. He guides the unhappy Fugitive from Want and Persecution, to Plenty, Quiet, and Security, and seats him in Scenes of peaceful Solitude, and undisturbed Repose."[121] Johnson's poet imagines a way out of a world that political projects can never satisfactorily reconstitute. Like Thomson, he doubts that "rational Schemes" can order a society made tumultuous by risk, violence, and the "private Passions" of corrupt leaders. Therefore, verse emerges as an alternative mode for thinking through possibility, one that delivers a vicarious experience of "Plenty, Quiet, and Security" that legislators can never realize. Johnson's elevation of fanciful escapism over impractical reform captures the disparate aspirations of his subject, Savage, an orphan, poet, patriot, and spurned patronage seeker whose aristocratic entitlement exceeded his station and means.

But the difference between proposing and depicting reform does not hold in English georgics, which fashion themselves as viable contributions to trade knowledge and public works (*Cyder*), configure land to express partisan affiliation (*Windsor-Forest*), and brood over the seeming fixity of prevailing economic realities (*The Seasons*). These verses do not retreat from the fraught politics of improvement but instead confront its promises, inventory its remains, and cull its rhetoric to identify afresh the conditions of Britain's future glory. "Poetry invested in the georgic mode obsessively tests its mediating power," observes Goodman, who perceives how mediation can dredge up re-sidual "excess and dissonance."[122] Ariconium's rubble, Windsor's ghosts, and Thomson's figure of all-devouring time are the dissonant remnants of a pro-jecting age that georgic tries to recuperate, though often at the cost of compro-mising what would seem to be its signature progressive spirit.

Not all eighteenth-century authors brought such constructive attitudes to the legacies of attempted improvement. Much writing from the early 1700s took projects as evidence of everything that was wrong with society. Authors known as antiprojectors employed satire to infiltrate the persuasive logic of proposals in works that both discredited and perpetuated the idea of discrete enterprise. *Their* mediation of projection is the topic of my final chapter.

Chapter 5

Swift's Solar Gourds and the
Antiproject Tradition

By incorporating projection's persuasive rhetorics, histories of enactment, and imaginations of space, poems like *Cyder* and *Windsor-Forest* exemplify Michael McKeon's understanding of literary genre as a "conceptual framework for the mediation (if not the 'solution') of intractable problems."[1] Georgic claims to address the same challenges that husbandry manuals taught cultivators to withstand and then depicts surmounted hardship to affirm British agriculture's capacity to enhance rural life. What georgic ultimately teaches readers is not how to become a better orcharder or shepherd, but rather how the existence of such knowledge relies upon improvers plotting to realize domestic soil's wealth in potential.

Projection's legacies seeped also into the eighteenth-century novel, which cut many of its protagonists from the pattern of the progressive, risk-taking individual. Schemers abound, for instance, in the fictions of Daniel Defoe, whose heroes endeavor to secure wealth and reputation, establish conjugal ties, and escape desert islands, rain forest predators, and death sentences. Defoe casts projectors as wayward heroes within plots that highlight the need for reform enterprise of the sort he advocated through pamphlets. The wily and indigent Moll Flanders fulfills her "Project for *Virginia*" but likely would have benefited from the female academies, bankruptcy protections, and provisions for widows that Defoe proposed in his *Essay upon Projects*.[2] Captain Singleton, likewise, may never have turned pirate had George II disrupted buccaneer operations throughout Africa, as Defoe advised him to do in his *Plan of the English Commerce*.[3] Defoe's *Journal of the Plague Year* dramatizes the emergence of a modern, self-governing capital from the vantage of a Whitechapel saddler who "could propose many Schemes" to forestall future epidemic.[4] Projects are not always good—Roxana yields to her benefactor's "Project of coming to-Bed to me," which she calls a "dear Bargain," while Crusoe finds himself ship-wrecked after his head filled with "Projects and Undertakings."[5] But in most instances, Defoe's novels endorse a venturesome spirit that complements his economic blueprints. Problems that appear insurmountable in his fictions be-come solvable through projects.

The relationship of literature to enterprise was seldom as felicitous outside Defoe's oeuvre. Scores of imaginative works cast doubt on speculative endeavor by mocking projectors, refuting proposals, and sabotaging their conventions through imitation. Whether transparently hostile or artfully parasitic, antiproj-ect sentiment inspired early modern literary performances ranging from court masques and broadside libels to spurious genealogies and patchwork fiction. These writings instilled in projectors an expectation of censure from the mo-ment they conceived new endeavor. Antiprojection was both an outcome and precondition of scheming for a better world in seventeenth- and eighteenth-century Britain: the term encompassed both the scandalizing charge of projec-tion and its fearful anticipation.[6]

Antiprojection often manifested through satire. The ironic mimicry of projects' premises and presumptions became a forceful mode of social criticism in the 1700s precisely because it harnessed the grippingly confident language of the proposals it sought to ridicule. It was the potency of project writing, in other words, that made its travesty so incisive and entertaining. In highlighting the rhetorical similarities between projection and its parody, this chapter shows how antiprojectors established an air of disinterested authority by willing so-ciety's improvement through their performances in the satirical mode, what J. M. Treadwell calls satire's "own scheme to reform the world."[7] At stake in delineating project satire from satire's project is a clearer idea of how authors resist persuasive argumentation by inhabiting its language, and how a tradition of British writing solidified around the goal of refuting scheme-mongering futurists.

Eighteenth-century project culture found a prolific satirist (and occasional sponsor) in Jonathan Swift, the Anglo-Irish author who devised, endorsed, impugned, and laughed off efforts to better Britain and Ireland through proj-ects. Throughout his career, Swift pivoted between proposing improvement and attacking improvers. In *A Tale of a Tub* (1704), Swift mocks the vainglori-ous Peter for projecting outlandish schemes, styling himself "*Monarch of the Universe*," and possessing a brain that "*shook* it self, and begun to *turn round*."[8]

Only five years later, Swift published the straightforwardly didactic *Project for the Advancement of Religion and the Reformation of Manners* (1709), which self-identifies as a project within its title. "Among all the Schemes offered to the Publick in this projecting Age," the tract laments, none addresses "the Improvement of Religion and Morals."[9] This statement appears to validate the project as a worthwhile vehicle for reform by regretting (and then purporting to remedy) its lack.

Three years later, Swift would adapt a more dismissive attitude toward projects. He addressed his 1712 proposal to establish an English language academy to Robert Harley, Lord High Treasurer, whom he credits with carrying out reforms faster "than the most visionary Projector can adjust his Schemes."[10] This dedicatory praise faults the vigorous but ineffectual projector who cannot convert high-minded ideals into tangible public benefits. Given the pamphlet's own grand ambition to standardize language, it is likely that Swift is making fun of his own petitioning. He raises this possibility in the final lines, wherein he fears "my self turning Projector," before excusing his untoward ambition by submitting it to the discretion of "*Your* Lordship's."[11] Swift evokes and then refuses the terminology of projects (and the identity of projector) in order to preempt critics who would use those same categories to attack his linguistic enterprise.

By the 1720s, projection had become such a widespread mode for imagining change that when Swift protested English schemes for Irish improvement, he inscribed his resistance through literary ventures that took the form of project proposals. Most famously, his pseudonymous creation, M. B. Drapier, presages the "projet contre projet" of Georges Bataille when he characterizes the monetization of Wood's copper pence as a "Destructive Project," and then proposes his own scheme to disrupt their circulation.[12] "Project" encompasses both a corruption of royal favor through the despised institution of monopoly and a worthwhile countermeasure against fiscal oppression.[13] This piling up of projects for dominance and dissent complicates Swift's prose, which reveals the self-serving empiricism of Ireland's colonizers by speaking through their signature instrument.

No work more comprehensively demonstrates Swift's belief in society's capacity to make and unmake itself through discrete enterprise than *Travels into Several Remote Nations of the World* (1726), more commonly known as *Gulliver's Travels*. Swift's protagonist, the Nottinghamshire-born surgeon and sailor Lemuel Gulliver, works through and against projects within all four of his voyages. However, it is in the journey to Laputa and Balnibarbi that

projection receives its most sustained critique. The third book's survey of Balnibarbi's desolate landscape and tour through the Academy of Projectors jux-
tapose scenes of intellectual self-flattery alongside displays of failed statecraft,
crumbling infrastructure, and unhinged citizens. It is this sojourn that has
made the *Travels* come to seem like the last word on eighteenth-century projecting, a resounding rejection of experimental enterprise, and therefore an
ideal site for assessing the role of satire in the service of antiproject thought.

It is also the book that readers tend to enjoy least. We know that Swift
composed this narrative last, set it aside to take up the role of Drapier, and later
inserted it into his *Travels* as the penultimate voyage.[14] The fragmentary plot
meanders between five islands and lacks the escalating action of the Lilliput
and Brobdingnag episodes. John Arbuthnot told Swift that "the part of the
projectors is the least Brilliant."[15] The twentieth-century critic J. M. Treadwell
echoes this opinion, claiming, "it would be perverse not to admit that at best
the third voyage will always remain the least satisfactory of the four."[16] Readerly disappointment with what Ronald Paulson calls the "traditional satiric
anatomy" of book 3 accompanies widespread disagreement as to whom or
what exactly the story is meant to attack.[17] Critics have traditionally read the
academy's scenes of botched knowledge production as a satire on the Royal
Society and the scientific claims (and claims to scientificity) issued in its journal, the *Philosophical Transactions*.[18] Other proposed satirical targets include
the South Sea Company, the University of Leiden, Irish colonization, the epistemological quarrels between Ancients and Moderns, and Swift himself, who
we know drafted proposals on a variety of topics.[19]

This abundance of interpretive frames testifies to both the rigorous historicism of Swift scholarship and the intricacy of *Gulliver's Travels*, which indeed
appears to comment on the blunders of the Royal Society, the speculative
frenzies of the Georgian era, and the subjugation of Ireland. That said, these
topic-bound hunts for singular referents have yielded "no equivalent gains in
the wider interpretation of the third book," according to Treadwell, who argues
that what the academy passages ultimately question is the "notion of the projector" and Swift's occupation of this role as reform-minded satirist.[20] McKeon
likewise claims that the purpose of the third voyage is to reveal the capacity of
the "solid character of the materialistic projector" to conceal the "subjective
heresy of psychological projection."[21] Swift's satire, he claims, shatters the ve-
neer of a seemingly "progressive protagonist" to reveal the "ugly core of hypo-
critical opportunism."[22] The satirical object according to McKeon and

Treadwell is the projector's dissembling brain. What Swift makes risible are the concealed motives driving projection, whether cunning or naive, benevolent or self-serving.

Such a portrayal fixes the projector as a static character, a phantom of self-reproach or straw man for parodic dismemberment. Given what we now know about the practices of scheming and dreaming in eighteenth-century Britain, this chapter proposes a new explanation of the voyage to Balnibarbi. I argue that book 3 does not merely psychologize the projector by auditing his motives and sources of institutional support, but more fundamentally confronts the logic of projects themselves by addressing the individual stages through which enterprise moved from mind to world: language, publication, and undertaking. Having mapped these procedures in Chapters 1–3 and investigated their interface with self-consciously literary writing in Chapter 4, we can see that Swift does not just ironically refute enterprise (or a given instance of it), but rather uncovers the reconciliations of language and action that propelled endeavor toward reality.

Or failed to do so. Where Defoe imagined better futures through the completion of plans, Swift treasured the meantime bought from the breakdown of projects. Based in Dublin, Swift saw firsthand how forestalled schemes occasioned cooperative resistance, even opened space for Irish self-determination. The revocation of Wood's patent revealed how the distance between design and action could provide vulnerable societies with temporary refuge from their self-appointed improvers. Book 3 documents the social debris left by the execution of bad plans while exploring the open temporality of projects that never conclude. Gulliver observes enterprises in medias res, absorbs their promises, but never sticks around to see how experiments turn out. That Lagado's experiments remain incomplete reflects Swift's personal experience of projection not only as an untrustworthy medium, but as an ongoing condition of eighteenth-century life.

By transposing visionary schemes into plot action, *Gulliver's Travels* illustrates enterprise once it has left the page but before its results are known. Swift's fiction restores for us the ongoingness of old projects. It also provides an ample view of the projector, not merely as a disembodied voice that solicits us from the grave, but as an attired character who inhabits the present tense and grammatical third person. The academy's inmates, I will show, are the misbegotten offspring of projection's search for language that can explain action gone awry. Where Treadwell and McKeon argue that Swift builds his

satire around the reviled projector, I will show that in Lagado it is the trial of
projecting—the perpetual challenge of adjusting schemes to reality—that
forms (and deforms) its authors.

My argument begins by chronicling the development of antiproject satire
in early modern British literary history, a tradition that Swift knowingly inherited and modified. I contrast this tradition's figurations of projectors in plays
and pamphlets with Gulliver's own encounters with projects in the first two
books of the *Travels*. I argue that these episodes presage Balnibarbi, where Swift
voices and eviscerates the fact-making fictions of projection, giving particular
emphasis to the words and actions of one benighted academy member toiling
to extract sunlight from cucumbers. The chapter concludes by placing the
voyage to Balnibarbi in the context of Swift's later career, as he continued
partaking in projects against projects, though with decreasing faith in their
efficacy.

The Antiproject Tradition

Incensed by patent monopolists and a king who indulged them, Caroline
satirists blamed projectors for all that seemed wrong about the spread of new
enterprise during the years of Charles I's Personal Rule. Early modern plays
and pamphlets depict the projector not as a fleshed-out, multidimensional
character, but rather as a conniving perpetrator or dimwitted victim. Richard
Brome's comedy *The Court Beggar*, first performed between 1640 and 1641,
features a triad of projectors known simply by number (Projector 1, Projector
2, and Projector 3), who approach Andrew Mendicant with schemes for gaining wealth and filling "Coffers Royall."[23] Mendicant, himself "an old Knight
turned projector," appears in the final scene "attir'd all in Patents, a Windmill
on his Head."[24] Festooned with monopolistic documents while donning a
replica windmill, symbolic of fen drainage schemes and perhaps also the knight
errantry of Don Quixote, Mendicant appears to be made of projects. The
name Mendicant, synonymous with begging, connotes material privation and
a poverty of ideas. He is the dupe of projectors and a projecting lunatic who
embodies Caroline England's frenzied culture of privilege seeking.

Three years later, the opening procession of William Shirley's 1634 masque
The Triumph of Peace featured "six Proiectors" whose apparel evoked the content of its wearer's scheming. A doctor who wants to turn carrots into poultry
fodder wears "a Hat with a bunch of Carrots, a Capon perched upon his fist."[25]

A seaman who has contrived a vessel to "sail against the winds" is fittingly nautical in his array, "a Shippe upon his head and holding a Line and Plummet in his hand." These projectors are chased from the stage by "many Beggars," legions of mendicants who personify the ruinous aftermath of scheming.[26] The beggars, with their "timerous lookes and gestures," embody the human cost of crown-licensed projection in a brazen performance "before the King's and Queen's majesties" at the Inns of Court.[27]

Dramatists and masque scriptors made projecting farcical onstage at the same time pamphleteers mocked new enterprise in print. Several tracts from the early 1640s blamed the English craze for projecting on Charles I, who sold patent monopolies to raise revenue.[28] John Taylor's broadside ballad *The Complaint of M. Tenter-Hooke* (1641) links patent awards to court corruption through a woodcut that depicts the projector as a grotesque monster patched together from soap, starch, tobacco, pipes, butter, cards, and dice—goods he sought to monopolize. Addressing "Sir Thomas Dodger, the patentee," Tenter-Hooke recalls that he once possessed "the Art to Cheat the Common-weal" but laments that "time" had since "pluck'd the *Vizard* from my face."[29] Exposé was the explicit aim of another pamphlet, the anonymous *Projectors Downfall; or, Times Changeling* (1642), which proclaimed it would render projectors "unmasked to the View of the World."[30] The implication is that the projector's roguish nature becomes visible only by peeling away his verbal artifice.

Thomas Brugis attempts a similar act of unveiling in his *Discovery of a Proiector* (1641), which unveils the projector as a "pretended reformer of the old" and the reckless "Corne-cutter of the age," referring to unscrupulous surgeons who jeopardized the health of their patients to treat minor ailments.[31] Brugis accuses projectors of seeking only the "faire outside of a reformation."[32] The playwright and pamphleteer Thomas Heywood invoked the same figure to attack those who pursued the semblance of improvement at the cost of its actual implementation.[33] His *Hogs Character of a Projector* (1642) describes the projector as "a Mongrill by birth, his father was an *Hittite*, his mother was an *Amorite*; his education in his youth was with a Peer, and by him infected with strange raptures and whimsees, which he strives to put in practise, and calls them Projectors. His riper years were corrupted with abominable termes of Lawyers latine, and Pedlers French."[34] Heywood's bastard projector embodies the flightiness of the aristocrat, the fastidiousness of the lawyers, and the blood of the Hittites and Amorites, enemies of ancient Israel. He dabbles in many fields but masters none. Like Brugis's projector, who "vowes to forsake the plaine pathway of all Trades, Professions, and Mysteries whatsoever" in the hopes of raising "fortunes on a sodaine," Heywood's projector combines a lack of discipline with baseless self-faith.[35] His heterogeneous birth and miscellaneous education cast him as the modern Proteus, a shape-shifter who becomes society's "Canker."[36] Heywood's projector abandons legitimate trade to promote undertakings he knows nothing about.[37] One example is his scheme for rebuilding central London, a half-baked plan that would leave the metropolis in chaos: "He is an excellent Architector, he will pull down *Whitehall*, and build the King a new Pallace, to which the *Banqetting-house* shall be but half the Porters Lodge, and all at his own cost and charges; if the King will but give him leave. He will turn an Hospitall into a Court, and next the *Savoy* to *Somerset-house* if the *Dutchy* were not between."[38] This vision of urban renewal, which seems to anticipate Balnibarbi's infrastructural confusion, privileges reform for its own sake without accounting for the actual needs of Londoners. Heywood's projector so fetishizes redevelopment that he razes Inigo Jones's iconic Whitehall Palace—and the central government it metonymizes—simply to create space for future building. An unchecked desire for originality also guides the projector's scheme to modernize urban transportation: "He will turn all Wagons, Carts, and Coaches, into the nature of Wind-mills, to saile to their stages for the benefit of the Kingdom, in sparing Horse-flesh for the Warres, and to that intent hath got a Patent to make wooden horses fit for Brewers, Butchers, Maulsters, and Carriers, that shall do as good service as if they were alive, carry greater burthens, and fast much longer."[39] Armed with a patent, the projector plans to convert all horse-drawn carts to "wooden ones" powered by wind. This invention, again tellingly synechdochized by the quixotic windmills of Cervantes, would reserve a store of horse flesh to feed soldiers and a more durable fleet of vehicles. Heywood's projector, like Brugis's, fails to consider the already-functional aspects of horse-powered transportation, such as the fact that it can move people and goods on calm days. Nor does he acknowledge the danger that his single-minded pursuit of marginal benefits could render all Londoners immobile. *Hogs Character* places the projector at the center of a society that will paralyze itself for the sake of novelty.

In the 1660s and 1670s, the Royal Society provoked a new generation of antiprojectors. We have seen how Henry Stubbe urged his readers to oppose "these projectors," claiming that even a peasant would dismiss the Royal Society's "*superlatively* ridiculous" ventures as "but projecting."[40] John Wilson took this same line of attack in *The Projectors* (1665), a theatrical comedy that accuses the Royal Society of pursuing far-fetched inventions and exploiting investors. Wilson's play features an aspirant virtuoso and "Projecting Knight," Sir

Gudgeon Credulous, and a diabolical schemer, Jocose, who seduces him with the promise of fictitious whirligigs to drain the sea, devices to "stop up Rivers, a "plegnicke screw," and a "*Horse-Wind-Water-Mill*."[41] Jocose preys also on the miser, Suckdry, who invests in a project to build a mechanical horse, and the merchant, Gottam, who abandons his shop to chase fantastical inventions and subsequently embezzles from the parish stock to gratify his projecting habit.[42]

This tradition of Menippean caricature extended after the Glorious Revolution in pamphlets like *Angliae Tutamen* (1695), which laments how "Knots of Projectors" have drawn the nation into "pernicious Projects," and *Exchange-Alley; or, The Stock-Jobber Turn'd a Gentleman* (1720), a "Tragi-Comical Farce" that laments how "numerous Inhabitants of this great Metropolis . . . deserted their Stations, Businesses, and Occupations; and given up all pretensions to Industry, in pursuit of an imaginary Profit."[43] In 1722, a satirical pamphlet by A.M., entitled *Thoughts of a Project for Draining the Irish Channel*, promised nothing less than to turn the sea dry, and thereafter to replace packet boats with "Post-Horses and Post-Boys, not only from *Dublin*, to the *Head*, but also from opposite Port to Port, on each side the Channel, which (I also presume) will very much encrease his Majesty's Revenue."[44] Drainage promised to make Ireland more accessible to British traders and governable by Britain's Parliament. The author, one "A.M. in Hydrostatistics," planned to finance this fantasy of imperial control through its exposure of sunken treasure, lucre that could "retrieve the Reputation of our Affairs" following the South Sea fiasco.[45] A.M. fails to address what would seem to be the most obvious obstacle facing his enterprise: how to pump forty-thousand square miles of salt water elsewhere. He simply assumes that the endeavor would succeed "if some of the ablest Projectors of our Kingdom, and those adjoining, would but incorporate (by Charter or otherwise) and lay in heartily and willingly but One Hundred Thousand Pounds."[46]

Like the monopoly-seeking bandits who staggered through early Stuart print culture, the bumbling scientists who paraded across Wilson and Shadwell's stages, and the devious stockjobbers who infiltrated Exchange Alley, the single-minded public works engineer illuminates the specious logic by which enterprise became believable. By adapting strategies of characterization from these earlier works, *Gulliver's Travels* exposes the derivative behavior of projectors within a richly precedented satire. However, Swift alters the course of this tradition by reversing its causal logic. Where early modern pamphleteers and dramatists treat schemes as the product of an already-deranged or feckless individual, Swift shows how projects can make anyone dangerous to themselves and society. This includes his hero, Gulliver, whose darkening worldview throughout the *Travels* reflects the fallout of projects gone bad.

Approaching the Academy

Before entering the Academy of Projectors, Gulliver divulges that "I had my self been a sort of a Projector in my Younger Days."[47] Critics have understood this line to refer to the author of *Travels*: claims Treadwell, there is "nothing in the career of Lemuel Gulliver to support such a confession, but there is a good deal in the career of Jonathan Swift."[48] This conclusion ignores several details from Gulliver's biography as well as his activities in the first two books. The third son to a "small Estate," Gulliver raises his station in the world through a peripatetic education at Cambridge and Leyden and apprenticeship to a surgeon, one Master Bates.[49] He applies a modest allowance to study "Navigation, and other Parts of the Mathematicks," essential knowledge for an aspirant mariner.[50] Gulliver eventually sails to the Levant, the Caribbean, and East Indies as a ship's surgeon, resolving at the end of each voyage to settle permanently in England. He marries "to alter my Condition," establishes a practice in London, and later tries to drum up "Business among the Sailors" at Wapping.[51] When these ventures fail to support his family, Gulliver resolves to sail for the South Sea on May 4, 1699.

Swift's protagonist hazards life and limb to make money, though he does so judiciously. Gulliver adapts to but is not determined by his conditions. He is a third son but bears no ill-starred genealogy. He is profit seeking and restless, but not pathologically so. Gulliver projects out of the necessity of circumstances, but unlike Andrew Mendicant and Gudgeon Credulous, he is not a projector a priori. It is after shipwreck maroons Gulliver on Lilliput that he schemes in the service of its government. Most famously, Gulliver communicates "to his Majesty a Project" for seizing the enemy fleets of Blefuscu, which he accomplishes by knotting together the warships' anchor lines and towing them back to Lilliput.[52] Gulliver receives popular praise and the high title of Nardac for this heroic deed. But the maneuver also enflames the Lilliputian monarch with dreams of conquering Blefuscu and enslaving its subjects. Gulliver counsels against these imperial "schemes and politics," which his ruse made possible, and loses royal favor as a result. Gulliver's enemies subsequently contrive a "Project of starving" him. Upon discovering this treachery, the English surgeon contemplates his own vengeful "Project" of pummeling

Mildendo with rocks until the metropolis lies in ruins.[53] Gulliver rejects this violent fantasy and departs Blefuscu, his misadventures in court politics having given him the sobering realization that even well-executed enterprise can breed discord and danger.

In Lilliput, Gulliver leverages his immense size to execute certain projects, like stealing ships and extinguishing a palace fire by urination, while blocking others, such as the colonization of Blefuscu. In Brobdingnag, the now-diminutive Gulliver finds himself an object of condescension. Here the queen "contrived [a] Project" to construct a floodable trough that gave Gulliver an opportunity to practice his seamanship.[54] This basin degrades Gulliver's marine craft into a spectacle of courtly diversion at a time when he had no access to the coast, and thereby could not "form any Project" to escape by sea.[55] "Project," in this context, emphasizes the hopelessness of Gulliver's captivity by contrasting the work of regaining civilization with the performance of human behavior for the entertainment of others. When Gulliver solicits Brobdingnag's king with a "Proposal for much Advantage" to manufacture gunpowder, the monarch recoils, astonished that his guest would recommend such vicious machinery while remaining "wholly unmoved."[56] Though the king otherwise delights in "new Discoveries in Art or in Nature," he orders Gulliver to suppress this secret at penalty of death.[57] The gunpowder project, he fears, would empower even the "impotent and groveling" Gulliver to reduce society to "Blood and Desolation."

"Blood and Desolation" are apt themes for Gulliver's third journey, which explores the kind of suicidal society that haunted Brobdingnag's king. When Gulliver descends from the floating court of Laputa to the "firm Ground" of Balnibarbi, he finds a landscape of dilapidated buildings, wasted tillage, and weary inhabitants who "walked fast, looked wild, their Eyes fixed, and were generally in Rags."[58] The continent is full of activity, Gulliver observes, yet this grim bustle of "busy Heads, Hands, and Faces" yields only "Misery and Want."[59] Gulliver's host, the former governor Lord Munodi, explains Balnibarbi's distress by way of story. Forty years earlier, some local inhabitants visited Laputa, the ponderous society that hovered and ruled over Balnibarbi. These travelers were exposed to the levitating island's famous geometric discourses, musical recitals, and fatalistic astronomy. They met brooding Laputians "so wrapped up in Cogitation" that they routinely drifted off from conversation (and sometimes into ditches).[60] The visitors eventually returned to Balnibarbi "with a very little smattering in Mathematicks, but full of Volatile Spirits acquired in that Airy Region."[61] Eager to institutionalize their newfound expertise, the improvers petitioned to put "all Arts, Sciences, Languages, and Mechanicks upon a new Foot," forcing Balnibarbi to live by Laputian knowledge.[62]

The first act of these high-minded reformers was to obtain a royal patent "for erecting an Academy of PROJECTORS" in the capital city of Lagado.[63] The conspicuously capitalized term "PROJECTORS" refers to a variety of Balnibarbian adventurers, including engineers, chemists, linguists, physicians, and politicians.[64] The academy housed many of these schemers, each striving to establish "new Rules and Methods of Agriculture and Building" and aspiring to invent "new Instruments and Tools for all Trades and Manufactures."[65] Such innovation, they promised, would permit one man to do the work of ten. A palace could be built in a week "of Materials so durable as to last for ever without repairing."[66] Fruit would ripen in the dead of winter.

The only problem with all this ingenious novelty is that "none of these Projects are yet brought to Perfection, and in the mean time the whole Country lies miserably waste, the Houses in Ruins, and the People without Food or Cloths."[67] Projects, it turns out, mortgage the society they pledge to better. So-called improvement programs waste labor and materials that would have better served conventional industry, while disrupting the lives of citizens, who suffer perpetual inconvenience as a result of official projection. *Gulliver's Travels* presents Balnibarbi as a cautionary case study in licensing freelance visionaries to operate under the aegis of state power. Swift draws attention both to the absence of sound solutions and to the imposition of faulty ones by a self-appointed technological vanguard. Borrowing the subtitle of James Scott's critique of twentieth-century planning regimes like Soviet collectivization and China's Great Leap Forward, we could say that Swift's endeavor was to show how "certain schemes to improve the human condition have failed."[68]

This failure becomes most palpable when Gulliver tours the academy for himself. Here he finds projectors engaged in a panoply of ridiculous experiments: reconstituting food from human excrement, roasting ice into gunpowder, spinning textiles from spider webs, breeding woolless sheep, abolishing spoken language, and sundry other schemes. The academy's inmates apply conceptual knowledge haphazardly acquired in Laputa to endeavors reflecting a misguided belief that "the Regulation and Management of the World require no more abilities than the handling and turning of a Globe."[69] Swift's projectors mistake theoretical suppositions for the realities they would model. Their experiments founder on unforeseen difficulties while society disintegrates around them.

What these schemes share is their incomplete yet ongoing status. Shifting focus from the much-scrutinized contents of particular experiments to their orchestrations of language and action can resituate *Gulliver's Travels* from eighteenth-century discourses of natural science and partisan politics to broader traditions of proposal making that advanced and unsettled early modern society. Both Gulliver's own endeavors and the experiments he witnesses at the academy confirm Swift's view that visionary scheming is not itself evidence of an addled brain, inauspicious blood, or unseemly motives. Rather, it is the hardship of launching and finishing schemes that reduces their authors to madness. Books 1 and 2 show how under the right circumstances anyone can become the author or object of projects. Book 3 shows how the effects of such transformation touch every aspect of society.

Promise Versus Performance

In Lilliput and Brobdingnag, projects circulate orally and then are immediately executed or rejected out of hand. By contrast, the experiments of book 3 are always stuck partway between conception and completion (or abandonment). Swift implies that these schemes are hopeless, but we never see an experiment conclusively fail, a projector evicted from his laboratory, or a school of inquiry shut down. Dogged patience guides the academy's activities, along with a willingness to persevere in the face of dispiriting evidence. Gulliver is himself reluctant to write off any endeavor. He finds one project "at that time not very perfect" and reflects that the success of another "hath not hitherto been answerable."[70] All endeavors seem to him "capable of improvement"—able to mature themselves and the society they act on—even if they have not yet achieved concrete gains.

Gulliver reaches these nonconclusions by speaking with the projectors, who eagerly promote their labors. Like Andrew Yarranton, the academy's inmates formulate persuasive justifications for their schemes. Like Aaron Hill, they obsess over the media that would transmit those words to an audience. This combination of rhetorical sensitivity and "bibliographic self-consciousness" manifests in the boasts of several academy projectors who pledge to disseminate their findings in "treatises."[71] Another composes a "large Paper of Instructions for discovering Plots and Conspiracies against the Government" within a discourse "written with great Acuteness."[72]

Despite this desire to exploit technologies of communication, intelligible exchange proves rare in the third voyage, which casts writing as a fool's errand. In this sense, Lagado's fellows take after their Laputian forbearers, who, while dexterous "upon a Piece of Paper in the management of the Rule, the Pencil, and the Divider," show no inclination to "attend to the Discourses of others." The academy's levitating progenitors reel up petitions from their Balnibarbian subjects, though it seems unlikely that these intercessions are ever seriously considered. In response to language's perceived unreliability, the academy dedicates an entire family of projects to enhancing or eliminating discursive transmission. One projector schemes to make language more concise by removing all "Verbs and Participles" under the assumption that "in reality all things imaginable are but Nouns."[73] Another projector proposes to abolish "all Words whatsoever" and replace them with the physical objects they signify as "every Word we speak is in some Degree a Diminution of our Lungs by Corrosion."[74]

Converting words into things is the goal of another projector, whose contraption enables "the most ignorant Person at a reasonable Charge, and with a little bodily Labour, [to] write Books in Philosophy, Poetry, Politicks, Law, Mathematicks, and Theology, without the least Assistance from Genius or Study."[75] The inventor exhibits the machine's output to date, including "several Volumes in large Folio already collected, of broken Sentences, which he intended to piece together, and out of those rich Materials to give the World a compleat Body of all Arts and Sciences."[76] The achievement of mechanized language finds proof in the prestigious folio format, which implies an elite readership and predicts the eventual procurement of comprehensive scholastic knowledge. Meanwhile, a scheme from the academy's Mathematical School aims to circumvent the labors of reading by transcribing theorems onto edible wafers that would convey knowledge to the brain by digestion.[77] Like the rhetorical machinist, this inventor turns expression into matter to guarantee its absorption. His dream of eating ideas betrays a lack of faith in the written word, whose simultaneous overproduction and supersession was making Balnibarbian society unintelligible to itself.

Where Yarranton and Hill circulated proposals to guide enterprise into existence, Lagado's projectors report on their undertakings to rebut evidence of their futility. Their words do not expedite undertaking but instead deny the material reality that was frustrating those efforts. This rhetoric of denial shines through the speech of one projector who schemes to capture and retail the sunlight absorbed by cucumbers:

The first Man I saw was of a meager Aspect, with sooty Hands and Face, his Hair and Beard long, ragged and singed in several places. His Cloths, Shirt, and Skin were all of the same Colour. He had been eight Years upon a Project for extracting Sun-Beams out of Cucumbers, which were to be put into Vials hermetically Sealed, and let out to warm the Air in raw inclement Summers. He told me, he did not doubt in eight Years more, he should be able to supply the Governors Gardens with Sun-shine at a reasonable Rate; but he complained that his Stock was low, and entreated me to give him something as an Encouragement to Ingenuity, especially since this had been a very dear Season for Cucumbers.[78]

The cucumber man is a sooty, monochromatic burn victim whose long beard confirms his protracted labors. Another academy projector, who is trying to turn human waste back into food, sports a "pale yellow" beard and "Clothes dawbed over with Filth."[79] In both cases, the projector becomes a synecdoche for his projects and is disfigured by its residue. Neither man bears a name nor any biographical detail beyond the amount of time he has been at work. Both forge their limited identities from the materials they experiment on— vegetables and excrement. And these projectors, the first that Gulliver encounters on his tour, are the most elaborately detailed of any in the academy. Most residents receive not even this degree of individuating description and are instead referred to collectively as projectors, professors, physicians, artists, students, apprentices, or simply as "a Man" or "another."[80]

In Lagado, projectors exist to explain their projects. They are anonymous placeholders who put into words what their experiments cannot make evident. The disparity between this speech and the undertakings it purports to explain forms the core of Swift's antiproject satire. The academy scenes pit proposal rhetoric against physical implementation, sabotaging enterprise from within by misdeploying its argumentative conventions. In tracing the divergence of language from the action it would spur, my reading of the cucumber man's speech does not identify real world antecedents for his experiment.[81] Nor do I simply confirm Swift's appropriation of project language the way others have sourced Gulliver's use of jargon from discourses of seamanship, political economy, and empiricism.[82] Rather, I am showing how Swift contorts the cucumber projector's language to rationalize its botched performance.[83] By sounding proposal language beside its execution, *Gulliver's Travels* accentuates the deadening perpetuity of unfinished enterprise, while laying bare the projector's habit of adjusting his forecasts, timelines, and definitions of progress.

The cucumber projector struggles to reconcile his current state, where eight years of toil have yielded only soot and burns, with a fantasized future in which he has triumphantly commodified sunlight for purchase by a grateful public. He attempts this temporal and modal leap by professing that he "did not doubt" his future success.[84] In another chamber, Gulliver observes, "it is not doubted" that a project to use hogs to furrow through fields in place of plows will succeed.[85] One of the academy's political projectors contends that his proposal to make legislators vote against bills they sponsor, and thereby remedy partisan bickering, would "infallibly terminate in the Good of the Publick."[86] As academy experiments grind on hopelessly, their authors attempt to negate doubt through perforce denial. To "not doubt" is to shift a discourse's modal grounding from an account of how things are to an understanding of what they might be. But this projector is not content to articulate the future through mere probabilistic claims. For him, cucumber solar power achieves the status of fact, an epistemological entity comprising what Mary Poovey calls "noninterpretive (numerical) descriptions of particulars *and* systematic claims that were somehow derived from those particularized descriptions."[87] The topos of doubtlessness permits a subjunctive proposition ("he should be able to supply the Governors Gardens with Sun-shine") to masquerade as "incontrovertible data."[88] Swift shows how project language can place a risky venture beyond the realm of argument by making argumentative claims for its causal determinacy.[89]

Oral promises alone could not will projects into being. Balnibarbi's ruinous state gives the lie to the academy's boasts of enhancing society. The projector's certitude only reminds readers (and the listener Gulliver) of the contingency built into any proposed endeavor—in this case a vegetable power project entering its eighth year. Swift learned how excessive guarantee could subvert itself from his own attempts at proposal writing. His *Project for the Advancement of Religion and the Reformation of Manners* claims that even though "Faith and Morality are declined among us, I am altogether confident, they might in a short time, and with no very great Trouble be raised as high a Perfection as Numbers are capable of receiving."[90] Swift links an absolutist assertion ("I am altogether confident") to the modal verb ("might") to the superlative clause ("as high a Perfection . . . capable"), issuing an extravagant promise, backing away from its certitude, and then attesting its singularity. It was precisely this kind of fluctuating syntax that Swift would scrutinize seventeen years later in his treatment in *Gulliver's Travels* of projectors driven on by "Hope and Despair."[91]

Gulliver's Travels pokes fun at Swift's juvenile reform efforts—efforts that might already have been self-satirizing according to Leo Damrosch—but the academy passage performs more than self-deprecation.[92] Swift ridicules the very forms of language he used to convey certitude. Other projects employed the same rhetoric. Samuel Fortrey alleged, "it cannot be doubted . . . but we might be sufficiently stored with wealthy and industrious people" in his 1663 commercial treatise *England's Interest and Improvement*. He later asserts that if his plans are followed, "there is no doubt but the people, and riches of the kingdom might be greatly increased and multiplied."[93] John Smith, the author of *England's Improvement Reviv'd*, promises "if any Person of Honour should so imploy me . . . I doubt not that I should answer his utmost Expectation."[94] John Houghton claims that his *Proposal for Improvement of Husbandry and Trade* will be of "undoubted Utility and publick Advantage."[95] Nothing suggests that Swift had these specific improvers in mind when he wrote *Gulliver's Travels*. His goal, rather, was to teach readers to recognize how the rhetorical construction of doubtlessness facilitates projection.

Brimming with assurance, the cucumber projector sharpens his pitch by declaring that the whole enterprise will culminate in a timely manner. Having labored for eight years, he needs but "eight Years more" to complete the scheme.[96] This phrase implies that the undertaking has reached its exact midpoint. The numerical specificity assures Gulliver that what might seem like haphazard experimentation actually adheres to a master timetable and progressive teleology. With less precision but equal certitude, the academy's "universal artist," who had been "thirty Years employing his Thoughts for the Improvement of human Life" promises to propagate a new breed of woolless sheep "in a reasonable time."[97] Likewise, Swift's *Project for the Advancement of Religion* promises that its patronage scheme would yield pedagogical benefits in a "short time," placing a finite but unspecified duration between the implementation of reforms and discernible moral progress.[98] In this vein, the cucumber projector makes an innovated future more tangible by scheduling it. He contrives quantitative benchmarks that recast idle bumbling as progressive labor toward a fixed goal.

The cucumber project will end when its author can supply sunlight to the public. Projectors, we have seen, were virtually unanimous in pledging that their enterprises would further the common good by strengthening commerce, employing the poor, and improving the collective quality of life for citizens.

The cucumber experimenter aspires to heat the Governor's Gardens in inclement weather, making Balnibarbi's ornamental state grounds more hospitable. He appears to balance entrepreneurial self-interest with patriotic munificence by pledging to sell bottled sunshine at a "reasonable Rate." The word "rate" implies both that the projector will supply a regular amount of power over time and that he will charge a fair price for the service. The inventor of the word machine similarly proposes a "reasonable Charge" for anyone wanting to try his engine.[99] How such costs could ever be reckoned is, of course, beside the point: by assigning future exchange value to enterprise stuck in an interminable present, Swift shows how projects presume the world it is their business to bring about.

The projector's preposterous benevolence often harbored what Samantha Heller calls "contorted articulations of self-interest and semi-disguised hopes for profit possibilities."[100] Take, for example, Carew Reynell's 1674 treatise *The True English Interest*, which delivers an inventory of essential national improvements that would give the kingdom "some advance, by our own Art and Industry."[101] Reynell proposes "publick actions," in the form of stricter laws against vice, the tripling of duties on imports, and the erection of a North Sea Fishery, that could serve the "general good."[102] The national interest dictates that England's wealthy subjects commit their land and money to "publick actions" that could "employ the poor people in general works, as building of Houses, Colleges, Bridges, or the like, Improving of Grounds, cutting of Rivers, discovering of Mines, and digging of Quarries, planting of wood, and many other things might be Invented also."[103] Reynell's championing of public works appears as pure civic devotion until we account for his professional ambitions, argues V. E. Chancellor, who notes that the publication of *The True English Interest* coincided with the author's campaign to secure a seat on England's Board of Trade.[104] Reynell used his pamphlet's exhibition of commercial knowledge to audition for the budgetary authority necessary to realize its plans.

It is unclear whether Reynell drafted *True English Interest* to earn a sinecure or sought office to implement his vision—or whether both desires played a part in his projecting. Swift understood that many schemes were reducible to neither motivation—that the majority of projectors sought fame and fortune, but also sincerely endeavored to raise the state of their countrymen. While he had no reservations savaging someone like William Wood as a villainous profiteer, Swift simultaneously appreciated that British society presented relatively few real-life Tenter-Hookes and projecting knights. This critical but open-minded attitude toward projects is evident in Gulliver, who refrains from judging anyone's character or motives in the academy and, with only a few exceptions, keeps open the possibility that their demonstrations could one day positively shape the world.

Public-minded projectors characterized their plans as feasible interventions that would, in Defoe's words, "tend to the Improvement of Trade, and Employment of the Poor, and Circulation and Increase of the publick Stock of the Kingdom."[105] Those proposals that fashioned themselves as operable and advantageous faced the further obstacles of having to distinguish their solutions from earlier attempts to remedy those same problems. The welfare projector needed to account for the continued existence of poor Londoners despite a history of relief efforts, and then explain how a new proposal would succeed where earlier efforts failed. Drainage projectors perhaps most acutely felt the burden of having to show how their designs would surmount obstacles that had sunk preceding ventures. Convincing enterprise needed at once to feel familiar and yet appear groundbreaking.

Lagado's projectors skirt this justificatory work by fretting over false obstructions. Swift's cucumber experimenter complains that "his Stock was low," meaning that he is out of cucumbers, with a pun on "stock" suggesting that he lacks investment, a noteworthy hardship given that "this had been a very dear Season for Cucumbers."[106] The projector frames a difficult, perhaps intractable problem of bio-thermal engineering as a monetary deficit. The project will doubtlessly benefit the public if only its author is allocated "eight Years more" and sufficient subsidy to replenish his gourd supply. Likewise, the engineer of the academy's word loom promises to manufacture "a compleat Body of all Arts and Sciences" if only the "Publick would raise a Fund for making and employing five hundred such Frames."[107] The inscription of infinite knowledge depends on the construction of an arbitrary number of machines. The projector who wanted to abolish signification by substituting things for the words complains, "this Invention would certainly have taken Place . . . if the Women in conjunction with the Vulgar and Illiterate had not threatened to raise a Rebellion, unless they might be allowed the Liberty to speak with their Tongues, after the manner of their Ancestors."[108] The goal of eliminating talk is farcically obstructed by chatty women leagued with the lower classes. Meanwhile, the obvious problem with this project, that one cannot carry around all speech referents, is passed off as a mere "inconvenience." Still another academy projector believed he could ameliorate political conflicts by pairing off each member of the legislature with his factional opponent. An "operator" would then lop off the back half of each politician's brain and transplant it to the other's skull. Of this surgery, the projector commented, "it seems indeed to be a Work that requireth some exactness," but "if it were dexterously performed, the Cure would be infallible."[109]

The cucumber projector wants cucumbers. The language reformer wants masculine consensus. The political surgeon wants dexterity. Swift mocks projectors who complain about a lack of money, will, or skill in order to avoid addressing the more recondite difficulties that plagued such endeavor (the complexities of botanical respiration, the materiality of speech objects, the delicacy of neural anatomy). Reasoning almost as specious organized proposals from the same period. One probable source of an academy scheme claimed that England could manufacture silk domestically, because silk worms require "nothing but the want of its Food." Its author, John Apletre, reduces all project costs to "raising the Tree, and managing the Silk, and nothing else."[110] One contributing correspondent to the *Philosophical Transactions* understood that England's slow-growing mulberry trees could not support silk worms and proposed as an alternative the cultivation of cobwebs, a forbearer to the academy's own spider project. This author laments that the only problem with his scheme was the "prejudice that is entertained against so common and dispicable an Insect" and not, of course, anything to do with the durability or comfort of woven webs.[111] Further afield, Walter Blith argued that river improvements would offer great advantage to the English Commonwealth, "it costing nothing but labour."[112] Yarranton argued that his plan to establish a registry of lands was blocked by lawyers who feared that the rationalization of English property law would deny them lucrative casework.[113] Aaron Hill blamed the failure of his beech oil factory on "the *Envious*, and the *Ignorant*" rather than the absence of consumer demand.[114]

The cucumber experimenter boasts that he will reverse photosynthesis if given enough time and money. In so doing, he imitates British projectors who collapsed theoretical challenges into finite needs. Swift reveals how the "nothing-but" rhetorical construction brings false clarity to a project proposing the violation of natural law. The academy's projectors test the capacity of language to resolve dilemma by turning misunderstanding into a kind of rhetorical strategy. By deliberately fixating on the wrong issues, the experimenters defend their efforts but do nothing to overcome that which inhibits them. Their words merely apologize for unmet expectations. Where Swift's satire opens straightforwardly on a projector singed by his own machinations, it quickly sets aside the low-hanging fruit of "simple parody" to infiltrate projection's shaping of word to action. It is this reconciliation that *Travels* exposes in order to mount its resistance to badly planned futures.

Quitting Projects

Gulliver makes a small donation to the cucumber projector before proceeding with his tour of the academy. On this count, the experimenter's plea succeeds. His self-faith, claims of public benefit, and papering over of conceptual predicaments yields a subsidy. But Gulliver remains suspicious of the venture's merits, explaining that Lord Munodi "furnished me with Money on purpose, because he knew [the projector's] Practice of begging from all who go to see them."[115] The projector, we learn, is a tourist attraction, an earnest but ridiculous clown. He resembles a Bedlamite, suggests *Gulliver's Travels* editor Albert Rivero, in a time when Londoners paid admission to watch inmates at the Hospital of Saint Mary, an institution Swift had been appointed governor of in 1714.[116] Gulliver's perfunctory charity turns the cucumber experimenter into an object of entertainment and pity. He is humorous and humored. Projection's compulsive uprooting of tradition has become such a routine aspect of Balnibarbian life as to render alms obligatory. Gulliver abides by local custom in a decorous gesture that hastens that place's destruction.

The habit of scheming is strangely irrepressible, even when Gulliver stands in the shadow of so much ingenious failure. Despite the cautionary experience of Balnibarbi, Gulliver later returns to projecting, after his deportation from Houyhnhnmland—where Yahoos hatch "projects" to ambush one another—and forced return to human society.[117] Specifically, Gulliver endeavors to raise his family from their own "yahoo" vulgarity by inculcating the virtue of the Houyhnhnms. This reform program motivates the composition of *Travels*, of which "my sole Intention was the 'PUBLICK GOOD.' "[118] Gulliver renounces this undertaking in a letter to his Cousin Sympson, asking why he ever "attempted so absurd a Project as that of reforming the *Yahoo* Race."[119] Unable to refine his uncouth family, Gulliver retreats to his Redriff stables and forswears "visionary Schemes for ever."[120] Where Swift's protagonist began his travels as a sympathetic, sharp-minded, and conversant Englishman, he now resembles the caricatured projector of seventeenth-century pamphlets and plays: a beleaguered misanthrope and convener of equine counterpublics.

Gulliver renounces projecting. The same could not be said of Swift, whose next major publication mounted a bracing attack against English colonial policy and social engineering that, like *Gulliver's Travels*, caustically reveled in the forms of rhetoric and habits of thought that made possible these forms of control. "A Modest Proposal for Preventing the Children of Poor People from Being a Burthen to Their Parents or Country, AND for Making Them Beneficial to the Publick" (1734) assaults Ireland's administrators for their unfeeling application of political arithmetic to human misery by making infanticide and cannibalism the final imperative of progressive mercantilism. The searing burlesque of "Proposal" assigns the ruins, famine, and weary faces of Balnibarbi to nonfictional geographical coordinates and locates in the offices of Irish government and the bookstalls of London the same compulsive search for improvement that ran rampant in Lagado's academy.[121]

Gulliver's Travels renders absurd the assumptions of projects by voicing them inopportunely. "A Modest Proposal" inhabits and bristles against the cold logic of the project itself. Its author professes "no doubt" that his scheme will feed Ireland's poor and that a newborn's flesh "will equally serve in a Fricasie, or a Ragoust."[122] Like the cucumber projector, the author promises that his scheme will make a natural resource—children—"Beneficial to the Publick."[123] Having "maturely weighed the several *Schemes of other projectors*," the modest proposer elevates his solution over other schemes for taxing absentee landholders, incentivizing the consumption of domestic products, and encouraging landholders to treat their tenants mercifully.[124] The projector can imagine only one potential obstacle: "that some scrupulous people might be apt to censure such a Practice (although indeed very unjustly) as a little bordering upon Cruelty."[125] The end of famine requires only that the Irish overcome their squeamishness.

It is not cannibalism, however, that the author fears his readers will find objectionable. Rather, it is his dissemination of policy recommendations through the degraded project mode. The proposer confesses that charges of inhumanity "hath always been with me the strongest Objection against any Project, how well soever intended."[126] Swift shows how the cruelty of Ireland's colonizers articulates through "any Project" aspiring to demolish existing economic and cultural orders to clear the way for new programs, epistemologies, and idealized patterns of life. It is the instrumentation of this power, perilously bestowed on England's burgeoning corps of unaffiliated adventurers, that also forms the wordy substance of *Gulliver*'s anxious comedy.

Three years later, Swift would return to projecting in his *Proposal for Giving Badges to the Beggars* (1737), a seemingly earnest scheme to police Irish vagrants by affixing the resident poor of each parish with shoulder badges. He proclaims that if his program were implemented, "we should in a few Weeks clear the Town of all Mendicants, except those who have a proper Title to our Charity."[127] Despite this confident proposition, Swift fears that no one would go to the trouble of implementing the scheme, having "well discovered the Disposition of our People, who never will move a Step towards easing themselves from any one single Grievance."[128] Likewise, Swift advances, then undercuts, a program for remedying Irish poverty in his *Proposal That All the Ladies and Women in Ireland Should Appear Constantly in Irish Manufactures* (1729, published 1765).[129] Concluding that no "reformation can be brought about by law," he settles for the idea that "every senator, noble or plebeian" could pledge to wear home manufactures and "prevail on their tenants, dependants, and friends, to follow their example."[130] Swift tempers his goals, settling for symbolic affirmation rather than concrete legal change.[131]

Swift's illustration of misused knowledge makes a decisive contribution to Britain's antiproject tradition, even if it was neither the first nor last of its kind.[132] The perennially popular *Travels* continues to mediate our understanding of eighteenth-century enterprise through its satiric filter, warning modern readers to scrutinize novelty and its presumptions. Antiproject sentiment continues to manifest itself in the stock caricatures of crackpot visionaries, mad scientists, unscrupulous capitalists, and delusional planners, figures guilty of professing ambitions beyond their moral ambit and material means. The academy of Lagado remains a popular site for readerly tourism today, while its figural cousin, the ivory tower, is regularly leveraged against the institutional denizens of colleges and universities. The enduring handiness of these archetypes attests to Swift's success in hollowing out the rhetorics of innovation—one project of Balnibarbian insight that seems to have worked.

Coda

Imaginary Debris in Defoe's New Forest

"I cannot omit to mention here a Proposal made a few years ago," proclaims the speaker of Daniel Defoe's *A Tour thro' the Whole Island of Great Britain* (1724) upon entering the New Forest of Hampshire.[1] The infinitive verb "mention" momentarily pauses the *Tour*'s rambling circuit through southern England. "Here" opens a parenthesis off the road and outside the present tense of the travelogue that surrounds it. The speaker "cannot omit" this foray. The "proposal made a few years ago" needs mentioning in order for *Tour* to deliver a complete report of the New Forest. It does not matter that the proposal in question remained only a proposal, a gathering of unrealized volition, a passively voiced object of the past. Defoe is emphatic that the "here" of *Tour*'s New Forest encompass both the woodlands the speaker traverses, and an imagination of what they could have become were this plan fulfilled. The past's former future returns as an obligation to account for the intersection of reality and unreality that marks this "very Spot."[2]

Seventeenth- and eighteenth-century ideas for endeavor formed in minds and strived to matter—be of consequence and substance—in the world. More often than not something went awry, reducing old proposals to records of visionary obsolescence. When left unenacted, the sweeping plan to reform society faces what E. P. Thompson calls "the enormous condescension of posterity."[3] A more sympathetic reader might detect in defunct projects "the single voice, the isolated scandal, the idiosyncratic vision, the transient sketch," the telltale traces of fragmentary life whose salvage New Historicism compels.[4] But in his tour of the New Forest, Defoe forges a relationship to past potential more radical than reverential, and with aims more ambitious than simply retrieval. *Tour*'s text superimposes an old project on British land, conducting readers over actual ground while immersing them within the details of an enterprise that never spurred action. Reading this proposal from the perspective of its afterlife reveals how questions into projection's unconsummated futures can be as old as endeavor itself. To understand what Defoe meant by "here," we need to ask what an old project does when it appears to do nothing, and how the recollection of nonaction compromises our ability to talk about the past.

This story begins "a few years" before Defoe's *Tour*, fifteen to be precise. In July 1709, Queen Anne's Board of Trade announced that it would hear proposals to solve an emerging crisis of human suffering and budgetary drain: the arrival of the Palatines. "Palatine" was the name, often erroneous, that English writers assigned to the approximately fifteen thousand immigrants who flooded into London that spring and summer.[5] The "Palatine refugees" or "poor Palatines," as they were often dubbed, hailed from villages in and around the Holy Roman Empire's Rhenish Palatinate, on the border with France. Famine, plague, and a trail of destruction left by the French army during the War of the Palatine Succession (1688–97) and the War of the Spanish Succession (1701–14) devastated the region's farms and vineyards, compelling many residents to seek new lives elsewhere. In 1709, they sailed by droves down the Rhine for Rotterdam in hopes of crossing to London.[6]

England became a popular Palatine destination following the Foreign Protestants Naturalization Act of 1708, which "deemed natural-born subjects" all Protestant immigrants who pledged loyalty to the crown.[7] News of this legislation spread throughout the Continent, leading many Palatines to expect a warm greeting in London, kinder than Walloons and Huguenots had received in earlier years.[8] The Whig Party, whose members drafted the law and whose 1708 rise to power secured its passage, lobbied for Palatine settlement by equating the country's "Greatness, Wealth, and Strength" with its quantity of residents.[9] Meanwhile, rumors held that the proprietors of Pennsylvania and Carolina would grant the Palatines free passage from England to North America, and either free tillage or "peppercorn rents" in those colonies. Perceived as a religious shelter and gateway to the New World, Britain seemed to promise a standard of living and opportunity for wealth unobtainable in the Holy Roman Empire.

But when thousands of Palatines actually arrived in London in the summer of 1709, they found themselves at first crammed into Deptford warehouses and Walworth barn lofts, and later, confined to ramshackle camps on the city's eastern edge. Wage-earning opportunities were few. Plans for American settlement did not immediately materialize. Queen Anne helped the Palatines survive for a time by distributing relief funds from her personal coffers, but this

charity rankled those subjects who resented the royal subsidization of strangers. "I think our Charity ought to begin, at Home, both in Peace and War,
before we extend it to our Neighbours," huffed one "English Merchant" in a
1709 dialogue.[10]

Faced with this grim and divisive spectacle, Anne appointed a new body,
the Commissioners for the Relief and Settlement of the Poor Palatines, to work
with the Board of Trade to identify and implement permanent solutions. The
board went to work placing advertisements in the *London Gazette* notifying
shipmasters of the city's fresh supply of German tradesmen. The commission,
meanwhile, solicited proposals from anyone with bright ideas for employing
Palatines. They convened six days a week at the Chapter House of St. Paul's to
hear project proposals. The Palatines could mine for silver and copper in Wales,
proposed one organization, or tin in Cornwall, suggested another. They could
establish a colony in South America called Rya de la Plata, force Spaniards out
of the Canary Islands, or toil alongside slaves in Jamaica. They could man
fisheries in Newfoundland or enlist in the navy. The Lord Lieutenant of Ireland
transported five hundred Palatine families to British plantations outside Dublin.[11] The Marquis of Kent offered to house Palatines in Herefordshire and
Gloucestershire, but the commissioners found the cost of this scheme prohib-
itive. What these haphazard proposals shared was a commitment to recasting
downtrodden refugees into the portable muscle that would cultivate Britain's
countryside and populate its imperial periphery.

One proposal asserted that the Palatines would best serve Britain at home
by converting the realm's royal forests and wastes into agricultural colonies. Its
author was the pamphleteer, projector, and Whig intelligencer Daniel Defoe,
who dedicated several issues of his periodical the *Review* to explaining and
promoting the scheme: "My Proposal is in short thus—That the *Palatine
Strangers* may be planted in small Townships, like little Colonies, in the several
Forrests and Wastes of *England*, where the Lands being rich and good, . . .
upon their Application to Husbandry, and Cultivation of the Ground, so not
only subsist them, but encourage them."[12] Domestic settlement, claimed Defoe, would be most "satisfactory to the People, honourable to the Queen,
beneficial to the Nation, least expensive."[13] Conceiving of labor as the "Wealth
and Strength of a Nation," he urges readers to see this influx of foreigners as
an opportunity for human ingenuity to supply the "Essentials of Commerce."[14]
At a time when some feared that the Palatines would devour Britain's food
supply, Defoe reasoned that immigrants, when put to work, would enrich the
nation by planting new farms, increasing crop yields, and consuming

surpluses. His proposal would settle England's most underexploited terrains, identifying "Forrests and Wastes" as desolate grounds in want of improvement. The German immigrants he characterizes as human blank slates, an anonymous labor force that would toil at the state's pleasure.

Defoe also appealed to the charity of English protestants who had themselves arrived as "*Refugees* and *Shelterers* in the Shadow of *Britain*'s Wealth and Fertility," or descended from such people.[15] He reminds readers how England once suffered under Catholic monarchs, like Mary Tudor, who drove some eight hundred Protestants to live as "Marian Exiles" in the United Provinces, France, Switzerland, and Scandinavia. Defoe proposes Palatine settlement as a means of returning the favor, "for the kind Entertainment they gave many of our learned Divines and others, who were forc'd to take Shelter beyond Seas in the Time of Queen *Mary*'s Persecution."[16] To expedite the integration of Palatines into British society, Defoe advises capping settlements at one hundred families each, encouraging their "mingling themselves with us, [to] become the same People with our selves."[17] His proposal assimilates a German "themselves" to a British "our selves" by ensuring readers that a shared Protestant heritage and indubitable work ethic would bridge cultural and linguistic difference.

The July 9 issue of Defoe's *Review* names several particular "Forrests and Wastes" where Palatine colonies could take root. The first site chosen was the New Forest, along the southern coast of Hampshire. The "new" forest was actually over six centuries old by the early 1700s. The name derived from a 1079 decree by William of Normandy, who designated the area a royal game preserve, "Nova Foresta," in the Domesday Book. Defoe describes the creation of this forest as the cruel handiwork of a marauding despot: "All our Histories mention *William* the Conqueror, as committing a horrid Waste in depopulating the Country, destroying 30 Churches, and a great many Villages, driving the Inhabitants from their Houses, to lay this Tract of Land open into a Forrest, a Habitation for wild Beasts, and restoring primitive Desolation; and without doubt it was a most barbarous Usage of them."[18] According to Defoe's gloss of "all our histories," William's forestation entailed the seizure of land and displacement of people. Saxon civil society reverts to the "primitive Desolation" of wilderness to field the blood sport of kings.[19] The Norman conqueror would pay for his crime, suggests Defoe, through the death of his heir, William Rufus, who was impaled by an arrow while hunting in the woods his father enclosed. But the forest itself endured as sparse crownland to the reign of Queen Anne.

Defoe proposed to unmake forest in order to give Palatines a place to live, and England an opportunity to shake off a lingering vestige of Norman tyranny. His project of patriation sought to liberate England from William I's legacy by making subjects of the Holy Roman Empire "True-Borne-Englishmen," the same epithet Defoe conferred eight years earlier on his Dutch-born hero William III.[20] But, as we know from the case of Alexander Pope's Windsor Forest, deforestation entailed more than felling trees. In 1709, the word "forest" did not necessarily mean a sylvan landscape but rather signified a legally proscribed domain that could contain "both woody ground and open pasture . . . heaths and bogs, villages and parish churches, roads and dwellings."[21] Forest was a place where "the law of the land at once ceased to run, and the rights of property only existed under conditions which were *mainly*, but not entirely, directed to the preservation of game."[22] While Defoe intended to scrap the odious legacy of William the Conqueror, his plan also called for dismantling an intricate jurisdiction of Swainmote, Woodmote, and Eyre courts, and a time-honored source of patronage for the verderers, regarders, agisters, and wardens who administered the enclosure. A Norman tyrant may have established the New Forest, but subsequent sovereigns chose to leave it intact. Defoe's scheme asked Queen Anne not only to surrender 150 square miles of land, but also to break seven hundred years of executive tradition.

The commissioners were unsure this could be done. Upon receiving Defoe's proposal on May 30, 1708, they wrote to the attorney and solicitor general to inquire "whether her Majesty has a right and power by law to grant parcels of lands in her forests, chaces and wasts to any of her subjects with license to build cottages and inclose the said lands, in order to convert the same to tillage and husbandry."[23] That the New Forest had, over its long history, incorporated acres of commons and populations of commoners presented further obstacles and opponents. Defoe himself acknowledged that his project might violate law and affront royal prerogative. He concedes in the *Review* that "the Forrest Laws and the Right of the Common being annex'd to the several mannors and Lands adjoining to the said Forrests, with the Privilege of Town-Poor, &c. will be objected in this case."[24] Nonetheless, Defoe believed that Anne's concern for the welfare of Continental protestants and the growth of Britain's economy would move her to cede an ancient holding in return for a more populous and prosperous realm. The livelihoods of commoners and integrity of crownland, he argued, were small costs for the benefit of reclaiming the New Forest from its artificial desolation. Defoe dedicated several issues of the *Review* to the cause and used his friendship with Sidney Godolphin, Lord of the Treasury, to advance the plan before Anne's commissioners.

And then nothing happened. No evidence suggests that the commissioners or the Board of Trade ever signed off on the plan. The *Review* mentions the scheme less and less frequently toward the end of 1709. The project's failure we can infer both from Defoe's silence and a straightforward examination of land: the New Forest remained a forest throughout the eighteenth century, and in 2005 it became England and Wales's twelfth national park. There are many potential reasons why the Palatine project never got off the ground. New Forest soil was never as arable as Defoe assumed, and it is likely that readers would have suspected this based on the pastoral practices of its commoners.[25] Opponents questioned Anne's authority to alienate her own forests, a point that was never decisively settled.[26] Many continued to want the Palatines out of England, especially when several thousand of them turned out to be Roman Catholic.[27] Historians have shown that Defoe sensationalized his account of bloody William the Conqueror, and notwithstanding accuracy, his invocation of the "Norman yolk" was unlikely to persuade commissioners desperate for practical solutions.[28]

Several competing proposals did manage to secure treasury funding. A report from the Board of Trade to Queen Anne outlines one such victorious scheme, which sent two thousand Palatines to the Hudson Valley to make pitch and rosin from pine tar.[29] This industrial project aimed to liberate England from its dependence on Scandinavian naval staples but ultimately failed owing to the region's harsh winter weather and the disobedience of German migrants who opted to start their own farms rather than make pitch.[30] Other Palatines eventually did make it to Pennsylvania and Carolina. Others, tired of waiting and unable to withstand confinement and poverty in London, returned to their native Rhineland villages. The singularly dauntless Defoe moved on to other undertakings, like ingratiating himself to the new Tory ministry of Robert Harley and managing the *Review*.

It had been almost two decades since the summer of 1709 when the Palatine project returned to life in an unlikely place: *A Tour thro' the Whole Island of Great Britain*, Defoe's panoramic exploration of Anglo-Scotch society. The first volume of this massive travelogue tracks Defoe's speaker through Hampshire, where he enters the New Forest and locates the very ground that his author petitioned to populate. "I cannot omit to mention here a Proposal made a few years ago," announces the speaker, before enumerating the 1709 scheme's most attractive features. But these twelve pages do more than "mention" the fact that Defoe once petitioned the Commission for the Relief and Settlement of the Poor Palatines. They adapt the original proposal's persuasive language, inviting readers to imagine a future world through its expired scheme. The speaker recites, rather than reports on, an unrealized vision in a passage whose anachronistic explorations stand out in a work otherwise dedicated to describing the present state of British land.

The New Forest passage signals a digression from *Tour*'s factual and timely account of Britain, its comprehensive effort to illuminate the "now" of the mid-1720s. Writing topography to the moment was no easy task for Defoe, whose preface expounds on the frustrated art of capturing the "present state of the country" in fixed prose:[31] "The Fate of Things gives a new Face to Things, produces Changes in low Life and innumerable Incidents; plants and supplants Families, raises and sinks Towns, removes manufactures, and Trade; Great Towns decay, and small Towns rise; new Towns, new Palaces, new Seats are Built every Day; great Rivers and good Harbours dry up, and grow useless; again, new Ports are open'd, Brooks are made Rivers, small Rivers; navigable Ports and Harbours are made where none were before, and the like."[32] This sentence pairs paradigmatic images of development and dissolution. Pat Rogers observes that Defoe "set[s] off an idiom of growth . . . against counter-images of exhaustion."[33] Families obtain place and are displaced. Towns flourish and rot. Navigational arteries dilate and shut. Britain changes literally "every day." The nation's daily ongoingness vexed and invigorated Defoe no less in his second volume, where he reflects: "New Foundations are always laying, new Buildings always raising, Highways repairing, Churches and public Buildings erecting, Fires and other Calamities happening, Fortunes of Families taking different Turns, new Trades are every Day erected, new Projects enterpriz'd, new Designs laid; so that as long as *England* is a trading, improving Nation, no perfect Description either of the Place, the People, or the Conditions and State of Things can be given."[34] The gerunds "laying," "raising," "repairing," "erecting," and "happening" give readers the exciting impression of a nation in process with each new "project enterprised" and "design laid," a sense of immediacy reinforced by the present-tense copulatives "are" and "is." Given the rapid pace of social and topographical change, Defoe reflects that no sooner could a "finished account" of Britain be composed than "cloaths be made to fit a growing Child."[35]

When Defoe occasionally delves into past events ranging from civil war battles to the demise of the Cinque Ports, his purpose is almost always to explain some aspect of the landscape before him. *Tour* invokes history only to thicken description of things "as they are."[36] The New Forest detour therefore appears anomalous, an anecdotal eruption in a text that aspires to factual solidity. Nothing in these woods presages a changeful present. The soil instead inspires Defoe to tell a story that is neither fiction nor fact: "I had the Honour to Draw up the Scheme, and argue it before the Noble Lord, and some others who were principally concern'd at that time in bringing Over, *or rather providing for when they were come Over* the poor Inhabitants of the Palatinate; a Thing it self Commendable, but as it was manag'd, made Scandalous to *England*, and Miserable to those Poor People."[37] The tortuous shifts in tense reflect the project's undefined status. The speaker *had* the honor to pitch his scheme, a plan that *is* "commendable" except it *was* botched. Defoe introduces another temporal layer by adapting the continuous past tense: "the Proposal was as follows." When exactly "was" was is unclear. The speaker suggests that while the plan belongs to some duration of the past its motivating principles remain valid. *Tour*'s readers must distinguish between the failure of a particular plan to make hardy German émigrés atone for Norman tyranny while appreciating the enduring truth of the maxim that "every laboring Man is an Eucrease to the publick Wealth, by how much, what he gains by his Labour."[38] Readers know that the Palatine project "was," in contrast to the New Forest, which is a "waste and wilde part of the country," at the same time they can perceive how wasted woodlands still called for improvement.

The *Review* asked readers to ponder a live proposal. *Tour* imposes the Palatine project's lapsed possibility on top of fact. To make this imposition convincing, Defoe alternates between the past, present, and future conditional tenses. The speaker recalls that "it was propos'd" to single out twenty Palatines to settle farms, men who "should be recommended as honest industrious Men."[39] This statement places the project's proposal in the past while hitching its advice to "should," a verb that gestures from the present—either 1709 or 1724—toward a future, idealized state of affairs. The Palatines "should have no Rent to pay," "should have Occasion" to build houses, and "should be oblig'd to go to Work," insists the speaker, whose ambiguous diction grants old ideas renewed urgency.[40] Defoe visualizes these timeless desires in a diagram of the New Forest agricultural colony, an image that appeared neither in the pages of the *Review* nor in his *Brief History of the Palatines* (1709) (Figure 3). A rectangle encloses four thousand acres of forest. Two highways intersect to form 4 one-thousand-acre plots, leaving land at the crossroads for a church, market, shambles, town hall, wells, and houses. A caption states that the "Form of the several Farms would be laid out thus," lending assurance to a scheme of land

*The Form of the several Farms would be laid
out thus.*

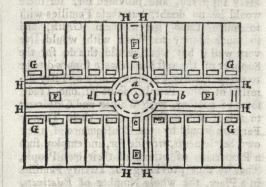

a the Church, *b* the Shambles, *c* the Mar-
ket House, *d* a Town Hall, *e* a Conduit with
Stocks, *&c. F* the Conduits, or Wells, *G* Houses,
H the Lands enclosed behind, *I* Streets of
Houses for Tradsemen.

To each of these Families, who I wou'd now
call Farmers, it was propos'd to Advance 200 *l.*
in ready Money, as a Stock to Set them to Work,
to furnish them with Cattle, Horses, Cows,
Hogs, *&c.* and to Hire and pay Labourers, to
Enclose, Clear, and Cure the Land; which
it would be suppos'd the first Year would not
be so much to their Advantage as afterwards;
allowing them Timber out of the Forest to
Build themselves Houses, and Barns, Sheds,
and Offices, as they should have Occasion;
also for Carts, Waggons, Ploughs, Harrows,
and the like necessary Things, Care to be
E   taken

Figure 3. Map of proposed Palatine settlement from Daniel Defoe's *A Tour thro' the Whole
Island of Great Britain.* RB 121829, Huntington Library, San Marino, California.

distribution that was never actually tested. The twenty "honest industrious Men" selected by the project undertakers would each cultivate a two-hundred-acre strip (marked by the letter G). *Tour* explains how these pioneers, "who I wou'd now call Farmers," would work these plots rent-free for twenty years and receive advances of £200 to purchase cattle and tools, and pay laborers to clear woods and build fences.[41]

This drawing encompasses both the design and culmination of the New Forest project—the map can be interpreted either as an aspirational schema or a bird's eye view of a community already built, or in the process of being built. It sketches in shapes the attempted construction of a new society. *Tour* explains that each of the twenty homesteads would employ more Palatines because "Twenty Farmers would be the Consequence of their own Settlements, provide for, and employ such a Proportion of others of their own People."[42] Defoe connects this first "Consequence" to others: new material desires and commercial obligations arise at every stage in the colonization of the New Forest. As farmers find themselves in need of barrels, carts, and other implements, so would wheelwrights, cartwrights, and various other Palatine tradesmen gravitate from London to meet this need. Population growth spurs new divisions of labor, including the specialized trades of butchers, shoemakers, glovers, and shopkeepers, a class in charge of distributing goods made by others. A full-fledged market town develops within the bounds of the rectangle as Teutonic industry transforms a lonely deer park into a bustling township.

Though thrilled by his rediscovery of old ideas, Defoe ultimately consigns his project to a doomed subjunctive clause: "twenty such Villages might have been erected, the poor Strangers maintain'd, and the Nation evidently better'd by it."[43] These three parallel clauses deny the benefits they enunciate by locking momentarily reanimated possibility in the past. Defoe then delivers final punctuation: "I reserv'd this Account to this Place, because I pass'd in this Journey over the very Spot where the Design was laid out; namely near *Lindhurst*, in the Road from *Rumsey* to *Limington*, whether I now directed my course."[44] An "account" belongs to ground that is conspicuous because nothing happened there. The "very Spot"—an intensification of the textual and spatial "here" that opens the New Forest passage—remembers past ambition through its enduring emptiness, its silent but steadfast refusal of old projects. The passive syntax ("was laid out") even makes the author vanish. What Defoe's tourist confronts here is not destruction or decay, the diminution of things that are or were, but the felt effacement of something that failed to be—not a declining port or ruined town, but the wreckage of intention itself.

Why does Defoe choose to relive his failure? One might argue that he uses the *Tour* to vindicate himself from the disgrace of a miscarried project by carrying its text back to the land that refused it. This seems plausible given Defoe's habit of recounting his disastrous investments in diving engines and civet cats in bitter, self-exculpating diatribes.[45] More optimistically, Defoe may have seen the *Tour* as a vehicle for refloating old ideas in the hopes that someone might undertake them in the age of George I.[46] Both of these explanations posit the New Forest excursion as the retrial of old ideas, if only in the court of readerly opinion. Why Defoe would undertake this work in the midst of a travelogue, and at such length and detail, is unclear. Given its miscellaneous itinerary and great length, *Tour* hardly seems like an auspicious place to resuscitate an old project (or rehabilitate an old projector), especially for an ambidextrous writer like Defoe, who had nimbler vehicles at his disposal.

Rather, the point of the New Forest detour is to press failed plans in the service of narrative. The Palatine project may not have moved people or land, but Defoe is able to convert its imaginary debris into a resource of literary invention, the grist of a more dramatic and personal story. When Defoe embeds an old proposal within travel writing, he draws attention to the residue of failed plans in an experience of space, an experience shaped as much by the invisible traces of his personal ambition—the "should" of 1709 and 1724—as by the actual groves before him. The speaker's sylvan apostrophe invokes a virtual New Forest to convey a richer sense of the real one in terms of what Gallagher and Greenblatt call "lived life, at once raw and subtle, coarse and complex."[47] *Tour* invites readers to consume its record of "lived life" not, as the preface suggests, through exacting chorography, but precisely the opposite: land's archive of imaginary interventions restored to life through Defoe's heavy-handed touch of the unreal.

All projects contain an aspect of the unreal to the extent that they try to bring nonexistent things—places, practices, identities—into being. Defoe knew this as early as his first publication, *An Essay upon Projects*, which gripes that the 1690s "swarmed" with projectors who issue "Innumerable Conceptions which dye in the bringing forth, and (like Abortions of the Brain) only come into the Air, and dissolve."[48] The insect metaphor emphasizes the weightlessness of cancelled ideas: a phenomenon so ephemeral as to barely exist. Later in the *Essay*, Defoe identifies the Tower of Babel as the quintessential project, "too big to be manag'd, and therefore likely enough to come to nothing."[49] But even though Babel's edifice came to a ruinous "nothing," its narrative, Genesis 11:4–9, transforms the failed tower into an etiology of polylingualism and

cautionary tale of hubris that retains explanatory power within multiple religious and folk traditions today. This unfinished project enjoys immortality in
the matter of myth.

Likewise, the empty New Forest sponsors its own literature in the form of
the "account" Defoe reserved "to this Place." The unrealized action that attends
"here" spurs an imaginative story that thematizes its own incompletion.[50] But
Defoe's New Forest passage does more than aestheticize its source plans and
setting. This passage draws and denies a clear division between historical fact
and counterfactual fiction. Defoe's entanglement of temporality and mood—
his warp and weave of "was," "would," and "should"—compels the *Tour*'s
speaker to long for an imaginary landscape as he treads across the real one.
Palatines haunt grounds they never got to inhabit. A rehearsed plan abolishes
but does not disturb a Norman retreat. In Defoe's exhibition of alternative
history we see how cultural interest in the stakes of unrealized enterprise is not
simply the imposition of modern scholars, but a possibility of salvage encoded
in history's former blueprints. Even this book's attempt to trace old schemes
and reventilate their expired worlds finds precedent in the narrative art of a
projector who battles against the inevitability of his failure and inevitability
itself.

Defoe's project sunders time, unzipping a split plot between realist travelogue and imaginary forecast. His Palatine scheme took on speculative life in
the language of the *Review* and an afterlife, or more accurately, an after-unlife,
in *Tour*. Projects, he demonstrates, cannot fit within a single temporal point:
either a validating green check or annulling red "X," on a constant timeline of
human innovation. This is because as long as a proposal remains legible, as
long as its language conveys to readers what a future can be—or what it should
have been—its anticipation of action endures through the act of reading. The
Palatine scheme resurfaced fifteen years after its apparent death, daring readers
to weigh the sanctity of forests against the utility of habitation. In a certain
sense, the text reconstitutes itself as a project each time it is rewritten and re-
read under the sign of action's possibility. "Such a project it is,"[51] claimed the
anonymous author of *Designe for Plentie* in reference to his 1652 call for universal fruit plantation, a statement as true in Commonwealth England as it is
today. Even the most timeworn scheme can persist past wreckage, its counsel
defunct, recuperable, waiting.

Notes

INTRODUCTION

1. *A Designe for Plentie, by an Universall Planting of Fruit-Trees* (London: Richard Wodeno-the, 1652), 7, 4. An editorial preface by the renowned husbandry reformer and scientific intelli-gencer Samuel Hartlib attributes the tract to a nameless "Minister of the Gospel" (A2v). That Hartlib signed this preface has led some critics to credit him with writing the entire work.

2. *Designe for Plentie*, A2r.

3. Ibid., 5.

4. Ibid., 15.

5. Ibid., 10.

6. Ibid., 3.

7. Ibid., 11.

8. Ibid., 3.

9. Ibid.

10. "Project, n." *OED Online*. June 2015. Oxford University Press. http://www.oed.com (accessed July 13, 2015). Vera Keller, *Knowledge and the Public Interest, 1575–1725* (Cambridge: Cambridge University Press, 2015), 132.

11. On foreign affairs, see Edward Little's *A Project of a Descent upon France* (London: Rich-ard Baldwin, 1691) and the anonymous *A Project for Establishing the General Peace of Europe* (London: [s.n.], 1712). On resolving domestic disputes, see Francis Nethersole's *A Project for an Equitable and Lasting Peace* (London: [s.n.], 1648).

12. See respectively Henry Maurice's *Project for Repealing the Penal Laws and Tests* (London: [s.n.], 1688); Jonathan Swift's *A Project for the Advancement of Religion and the Reformation of Manners* (London: Benjamin Tooke, 1709); and James Kirkwood's *A Copy of a Letter Anent a Project, for Erecting a Library, in Every Presbytery, or at Least Every County in the Highlands* (Edin-burgh: [s.n.], 1702).

13. On crown fundraising, see L.G.'s *A Project, Humbly Offered to Both Houses of Parliament, for the Ready Raising of a Million* (London: L.G., 1693); the anonymous *A New Project Humbly Offer'd to the Consideration to the Honourable House of Commons for the More Effectual Encourage-ment of a General Trade* (London: [s.n.], 1695); F.S.'s *The Anatomy of a Project for Raising Two Millions* (London: [s.n.], 1698); and *The Eyes of Ireland Open: Being, a Short View of the Project for Establishing That Intended Bank of Ireland* (London: J. Roberts, 1722). On land improvement, see *An Essay on the New Project for a Land-Mint* (London: [s.n.], 1705). On urban development, see *The Case of the New Project for Bringing Water to London and Westminster, Considered* (London: [s.n.], 1725). Attempts to colonize foreign land were often labeled projects. See, for instance,

Walter Harries's *An Enquiry into the Caledonian Project*, which examines the failure of Scotland's Darien Scheme (London: John Nutt, 1701).

14. See Joan Thirsk's *Economic Policy and Projects: The Development of a Consumer Society in Early Modern England* (Oxford: Clarendon, 1978) for a comprehensive list of early modern industrial projects (including the manufacture of stockings, buttons, pins, nails, linens, soap, and lace) and projects of agriculture (including the cultivation of oil-bearing plants like rape; the dye crops woad and madder; and mulberry groves to feed silk worms) (6).

15. On the use of patent monopolies "to wring a profit solely from the control . . . over some quite traditional economic activity," see J. M. Treadwell, "Jonathan Swift: The Satirist as Projector," *Texas Studies in Literature and Language* 17.2 (Summer 1975), 441.

16. On "unwanted and unnecessary" drainage projects, see Julie Bowring, "Between the Corporation and Captain Flood: The Fens and Drainage after 1663," in *Custom, Improvement and the Landscape in Early Modern Britain*, ed. Richard Hoyle (Burlington, Vt.: Ashgate, 2011), 237.

17. The later coinages "projectress" (1631) and "projectrix" (1709) referred to women who projected, such as Lady Tailbush in Jonson's *Devil Is an Ass* (London: [s.n.], 1641). Neither of these terms became more popular than the phrase "female projector."

18. Christopher Hill, *The Century of Revolution: 1603–1714* (London: Routledge, 2002), 152.

19. (London: John Wright, 1652), e2v.

20. Ibid., 3. "Project" would retain its negative connotations throughout the Interregnum. When veterans of the New Model Army criticized Oliver Cromwell and Henry Ireton for negotiating with Charles I to restore the toppled monarchy, they regarded this perceived treachery as projection. Several Leveler tracts used the word to express their fear of an untoward design meant to return England to tyranny. See John Wildman, *Putney Proiects; or, The Old Serpent in a New Forme* (London: [s.n.], 1647); and Victor Verity, *The Royal Project; or, A Clear Discovery of His Majesties Design in the Present Treaty* (London: [s.n.], 1648). The title page of one news pamphlet, *Tricks of State; or, More Westminster Projects* (London: [s.n.], 1648), accuses Cromwell's commanding elite of selling out their supporters: "They juggle still on all hands, and like knaves / Project all wayes to make the *People* slaves" (A1r).

21. *Legends, No Histories: A Specimen of Some Animadversions upon the History of the Royal Society* (London: [s.n.], 1670), 42.

22. *The History of the Royal Society* (London: J. Martyn and J. Allestry, 1667), 77.

23. Defoe categorizes Noah's Ark and the Tower of Babble as projects but places the beginning of the "Projecting Age" in 1680. *An Essay upon Projects*, ed. Joyce Kennedy, Michael Seidel, and Maximillian Novak (New York: AMS, 1999), 14. Tracing Defoe's periodization, Novak calls projecting "the mode of the age, even if a great many of the schemes were unrealizable." Introduction to *The Age of Projects* (Toronto: University of Toronto Press, 2008), 7.

24. *Essay*, 9, 11. Defoe similarly distinguished between useful "Improvements and Discoveries" and "dangerous and impracticable Projects, such as mad Men cannot, and wise Men will not meddle with" three decades later in *A General History of Discoveries and Improvements in Useful Arts* (London: J. Roberts, 1725–26), vi.

25. *Actions and Objects from Hobbes to Richardson* (Stanford, Calif.: Stanford University Press, 2010), 3.

26. *The Idler and the Adventurer*, ed. W. J. Bate, John Bullitt, and L. F. Powell, *The Yale Edition of the Works of Samuel Johnson* (New Haven: Yale University Press, 1958–2005), 2:435.

27. *Theology and the Scientific Imagination from the Middle Ages to the Seventeenth Century* (Princeton, N.J.: Princeton University Press, 1986), 156.

28. Ibid., 153.

29. *Science, Reading, and Renaissance Literature: The Art of Making Knowledge, 1580–1670* (New York: Cambridge University Press, 2004), 27.

30. Lubomir Doležel, *Heterocosmica: Fiction and Possible Worlds* (Baltimore: Johns Hopkins University Press, 2000), x.

31. Christine Rees, *Utopian Imagination and Eighteenth-Century Fiction* (New York: Longman, 1996), 3, 74.

32. "The Rise of Fictionality," in *The Novel*, vol. 1, *History, Geography, and Culture*, ed. Franco Moretti (Princeton, N.J.: Princeton University Press, 2006), 340.

33. Ibid., 36, 346.

34. Ibid., 346.

35. *The Origins of the English Novel, 1600–1740* (Baltimore: Johns Hopkins University Press, 1987), 419.

36. *Utopian Geographies and the Early English Novel* (Charlottesville: University of Virginia Press, 2014), 5.

37. Simon Schaffer and Steven Shapin, *The Leviathan and the Air-Pump: Hobbes, Boyle, and the Experimental Life* (Princeton, N.J.: Princeton University Press, 2011), 6.

38. One late eighteenth-century author still riled by the idea of projects was Adam Smith, who condemned projectors as fickle arbitrageurs, "a corn merchant this year, and a wine merchant the next, and a sugar, tobacco, or tea merchant the year after." *The Wealth of Nations*, ed. Edwin Cannan (New York: Modern Library, 2000), 131. Smith's friend Jeremy Bentham would refute this characterization by praising projectors as "a most meritorious race of men, who are so unfortunate as to have fallen under the rod of your displeasure." *Defence of Usury* (London: T. Payne, and Son, 1787), 132.

39. *Aramis; or, The Love of Technology*, trans. Catherine Porter (Cambridge, Mass.: Harvard University Press, 1996), 23.

40. *Economic Policy and Projects*, 26.

41. *Economics and the Fiction of Daniel Defoe* (Berkeley: University of California Press, 1963), 31.

42. *The Rise of the Novel: Studies in Defoe, Richardson, and Fielding* (Berkeley: University of California Press, 1962), 12.

43. Ibid., 13, 12.

44. Lennard Davis, *Factual Fictions: The Origins of the English Novel* (New York: Columbia University Press, 1983), 221.

45. *The Galesia Trilogy and Selected Manuscript Poems of Jane Barker*, ed. Carol Shiner Wilson (New York: Oxford University Press, 1997), 12.

46. John Milton, *John Milton: The Complete Poems*, ed. John Leonard (London: Penguin Books, 1998), 151.

47. *A Tale of a Tub: Written for the Universal Improvement of Mankind* (London: John Nutt, 1704), 95.

48. See *Gulliver's Travels*, ed. Albert J. Rivero (New York: W. W. Norton, 2002), 147–60.

49. *The Dunciad, in Four Books* (London: M. Cooper, 1743), 120.

50. (London: Richard Marriot and Thomas Dring, 1653), O1v.

51. *The Projectors* (London: John Playfere, 1665), A1r, 38, 21. References to projects and projectors abound in Restoration comedies. In William Wycherley's *The Country Wife* (1675), Horner's impotence trick inducts him into a brotherhood of "projectors," according to the physician Quack (*The Broadview Anthology of Restoration and Early-Eighteenth Century Drama*, ed.

Douglas Canfield [Toronto: Broadview, 2001], 1078). When another sexual schemer, the courtesan Angellica Bianca, is seduced into gratis intercourse by the dashing but penniless Willmore in Aphra Behn's *The Rover* (1677), her exasperated business partner, Moretta, bemoans, "Is all our project fallen to this? to love the only enemy of our trade?" (in *Broadview Anthology*, ed. Canfield, 609).

52. *Robinson Crusoe*, ed. Evan R. Davis (Toronto: Broadview, 2010), 77.

53. Ibid., 210, 213.

54. *Essay*, 9, 11. In this vein, Moll Flanders rejects "two or three unlucky projects" of high-risk theft, and at that same time she refers to her subsequent transportation and salvation as "my project for Virginia." *Moll Flanders*, ed. G. A. Starr (Oxford: Oxford University Press, 1971), 209, 159.

55. Samuel Richardson, *Pamela; or, Virtue Rewarded*, ed. Thomas Keymer and Alice Wakely (Oxford: Oxford University Press, 2001), 99.

56. Ibid., 227.

57. Samuel Richardson, *Clarissa; or, The History of a Young Lady*, ed. Angus Ross (London: Penguin Books, 1985), 125, 952. Other projectors of eighteenth-century fiction include Tobias Smollett's Peregrine Pickle, who "projected a thousand salutary schemes" (*The Adventures of Peregrine Pickle*, ed. James L. Clifford [London: Oxford University Press, 1964], 217); Jonathan Cleland's Fanny Hill, who likens sodomy to a "project of preposterous pleasure" (*Fanny Hill; or, Memoirs of a Woman of Pleasure*, ed. Peter Wagner [New York: Penguin Books, 1985], 194); Jane Austen's Henry Crawford, who was "full of ideas and projects" (*Mansfield Park*, ed. Kathryn Sunderland [New York: Penguin Books, 2003], 91); and Henry Fielding's Mr. Allworthy, who occupied himself "with intended alterations in the house and gardens, and in projecting many other schemes" (*The History of Tom Jones a Foundling*, ed. Fredson Bowers (Middletown, Conn.: Wesleyan University Press, 1975), 108).

58. In this vein, Sandra Macpherson has shown how a "logic of strict liability" can restrict the autonomy and personhood of characters in eighteenth-century novels by treating them as the agents and victims of "accident and injury." *Harm's Way: Tragic Responsibility and the Novel Form* (Baltimore: Johns Hopkins University Press, 2010), 16.

59. Jonson, *Devil Is an Ass*, 66.

60. *The Complete Poems* (London: Penguin Books, 2005), 192.

61. *A Treatise of Human Nature*, ed. David Fate Norton and Mary J. Norton (Oxford: Oxford University Press, 2000), 82, 381.

62. Ibid., 1.

63. "Introduction," 3.

64. "Montaigne's Forays into the Undiscovered Country," in *The Uses of the Future in Early Modern Europe*, ed. Andrea Brady and Emily Butterworth (New York: Routledge, 2010), 42.

65. *Foregone Conclusions: Against Apocalyptic History* (Berkeley: University of California Press, 1994), 3.

66. *Futures Past: On the Semantics of Historical Time*, trans. Keith Tribe (New York: Columbia University Press, 2004), xxiv.

67. *Foregone*, 70.

68. Morson, *Narrative and Freedom: The Shadows of Time* (New Haven, Conn.: Yale University Press, 1994), 6.

69. *The Whig Interpretation of History* (New York: W. W. Norton, 1965), 23. Walter Benjamin offers a similarly useful metaphor when he rejects the singular thread of universal histories "bound up with the notion of progress," in favor of a "frayed bundle unraveling into a thousand

strands that hang down like unplaited hair," until gathered up by the historian. "Paralipomena to 'On the Concept of History,'" in *Selected Works*, vol. 4 (Cambridge, Mass.: Harvard University Press, 2003), 403.

70. *Narrative*, 6.

71. For instance, "project" is not one of Raymond Williams's famous keywords, though related terms like "industry," "improve," "reform," and "science" are. See *Keywords: A Vocabulary of Culture and Society* (New York: Routledge, 2011). To take another example, "project" does not possess a stand-alone entry in the *Stanford Encyclopedia of Philosophy*, though some form of the word appears in over a thousand of its articles.

72. Adam Smith called John Law's Mississippi Company "the most extravagant project . . . the world ever saw" in *Wealth of Nations*, 346. Thomas Macaulay, meanwhile, characterized Scotland's efforts to establish a colony on the isthmus of Panama as William Patterson's "esoteric project" in *The History of England*, ed. Hugh Trevor-Roper (New York: Penguin Books, 1986), 515.

73. For example, Andrew Yarranton's 1663 clover plantation treatise *The Improvement Improved by a Second Edition of the Great Improvement of Lands by Clover* refers to an earlier edition of the work, but according to Ernest Clarke, "no copy of the first is known." See "Yarranton, Andrew (1619–1684)," rev. P. W. King, in *Oxford Dictionary of National Biography*, ed. Lawrence Goldman (Oxford: Oxford University Press, 2008).

74. On possibility's incorporation of nonpossibility, see Giorgio Agamben's assertion that "to be potential means: to be one's own lack, *to be in relation to one's own incapacity.*" "On Potentiality," in *Potentialities: Collected Essays in Philosophy*, ed. Daniel Heller-Roazen (Stanford, Calif.: Stanford University Press, 1999), 182.

75. Thomas Brugis, *The Discovery of a Projector: Showing the Beginning, Progresse, and End of the Projector and His Projects* (London: [s.n.], 1641), 2. See Koji Yamamoto's related claim that "reformers shared what those following Erving Goffman would call 'stigma consciousness'— awareness that their attempts at promoting useful knowledge could be discredited as unreliable, even nefarious, 'projects.'" "Reformation and the Distrust of the Projector in the Hartlib Circle," *Historical Journal* 55.2 (June 2012), 379.

76. Thomas Brugis anticipated Bentham's argument a century earlier, when he observed how projectors took credit for various products and conveniences, "to affirme that all Arts, Trades, Crafts, Sciences, Mysteries, Occupations, Professions, Devises, and flights whatsoever, were meerely *Projects.*" See *Discovery*, 3.

77. The major exceptions are *The Age of Projects* (2008), a multiauthor collection of essays edited by Novak that identifies projection as a pervasive spirit of the age in eighteenth-century Britain, and Joan Thirsk's *Economic Policy and Projects* (1978), a history of profit-minded schemers and their impact on agriculture and industry during the late sixteenth and early seventeenth centuries. However, neither Thirsk's monograph nor any of the essays in Novak's collection tries to define projection outside its particular manifestations. "Project," in these works, is a means to exploring different fields of early modern activity, rather than the end goal of historical investigation.

78. *Rise of the Novel*, 11.

79. See *Economic Policy*, 51–78.

80. *Age of Projects*, ix.

81. *Aaron Hill: The Muses' Projector, 1685–1750* (Oxford: Oxford University Press, 2003), 4.

82. *The Sinews of Power: War, Money, and the English State, 1688–1783* (Cambridge, Mass.: Harvard University Press, 1990), 68.

83. Thomas Heywood, *Hogs Character of a Projector, Being a Relation of His Life and Death, with His Funerall* (London: [s.n.], 1642), 2. Dwight Codr aptly defines the projector not as a professional type, but as a "form of subjectivity" that expressed itself within many fields of early modern activity. *Raving at Usurers* (Charlottesville: University of Virginia Press, 2016), 109.

84. *Metaphors of the Mind* (Baltimore: Johns Hopkins University Press, 2016), 1.

85. Projection for Martin Heidegger entails overcoming or "throwing off" conventions and limitations thrust on humans by virtue of their accidental position in the world. *Being and Time*, trans. John Macquarrie and Edward Robinson (New York: Harper and Row, 1962). Freud outlined his theory of "projektion," the attribution of one's own negative characteristics to another, within *A Project for a Scientific Psychology. The Origins of Psycho-Analysis: Letters to Wilhelm Fliess, Drafts and Notes, 1887–1902*, trans. James Strachey (London: Imago, 1954): 347–445. Sartre defines man as a "project," an entity that "propels itself toward a future," and attains existence only "when he is what he purposes to be." "Existentialism Is a Humanism," in *Existentialism from Dostoevsky to Sartre*, ed. Walter Kaufmann (New York: Meridian Books, 1966), 291. Marx critiqued Ludwig Feuerbach for describing God as a projection (*vergegenstandlicht*) of man's inner nature in his *Essence of Christianity*, trans. Marian Evans (London: John Chapman, 1854), and then used this idea to formulate his theory of religion as a manifestation of man's alienated consciousness.

86. *The Arcades Project*, trans. Howard Eiland and Kevin McLaughlin (Cambridge, Mass.: Belknap Press of Harvard University, 2002), xi.

87. Ibid., 410.

88. Ibid., 460. *Arcades Project* manifests Benjamin's career-long interest in the reciprocity between past and future. He defines politics in "World and Time" as "the fulfillment of an unimproved humanity," and happiness in "On the Concept of History" as the redemption of past conditionals: "air we could have breathed, among people we could have talked to, women who could have given themselves to us." *Selected Works*, trans. Michael W. Eiland. (Cambridge, Mass.: Harvard University Press, 2006): 1: 226; 4: 389. In this counterfactual spirit, a recent work of experimental scholarship by David Kishik asks what would have happened if Benjamin had escaped the Gestapo, settled in New York, and composed a sequel to the *Arcades Project*. For this "study of a manuscript that was never written," see *The Manhattan Project* (Stanford, Calif.: Stanford University Press, 2015).

89. The ubiquity of the word "system" poses a similar challenge to Clifford Siskin, who claims that "we have forgotten that system, like the novel, *is* a genre and not just an idea—it's a form of writing that was crucially important to the eighteenth and early nineteenth centuries." See "Novels and Systems," *NOVEL: A Forum on Fiction* 34.2 (Spring 2001), 202.

90. *Inner Experience*, trans. Leslie Ann Boldt (Albany: State University of New York Press, 1988), xiii.

CHAPTER I

1. Samuel Pepys, *The Concise Pepys*, ed. Tom Griffith (Ware, Herts.: Wordsworth Editions, 1997), 44.

2. *Astraea Redux: A Poem on the Happy Restoration & Return of His Sacred Majesty Charles the Second* (London: Henry Herringman, 1660), 5, 14.

3. (London: Henry Herringman, 1667), 5. Dryden modeled *Annus Mirabilis* on two prognosticatory tracts, which, by contrast, proclaimed that England would suffer divine retribution

for its dissolution of the Puritan Republic. See *Eniaytos Terastios Mirabilis Annus* (1661) and *Mirabilis Annus Secundus; or, The Second Part of the Second Years Prodigies* (1662).

4. *The History of the Royal Society of London for the Improving of Natural Knowledge* (London: J. Martyn and J. Allestry, 1667), 78.

5. Ibid.

6. Annabel Patterson, "Dryden and Political Allegiance," in *The Cambridge Companion to John Dryden*, ed. Steven N. Zwicker (Cambridge: Cambridge University Press, 2004), 222.

7. Charles Webster, *Samuel Hartlib and the Advancement of Learning* (Cambridge: Cambridge University Press, 1970), 70.

8. Paul Slack, *From Reformation to Improvement: Public Welfare in Early Modern England* (Oxford: Clarendon, 1999), 2.

9. The late seventeenth century saw scores of proposals promising to enhance society bit by bit, such as Samuel Fortrey's *England's Interest and Improvement* (Cambridge: John Field, 1663); John Smith's *England's Improvement Revived* (London: Thomas Newcomb, 1670). (Roger Coke's *England's Improvements in Two Parts* (London: Henry Brome, 1675); and Andrew Yarranton's *England's Improvement by Sea and Land* (London: R. Everingham, 1677). These tracts often drew on earlier works from the Commonwealth era like Walter Blith's influential husbandry manual *The English Improver Improved; or, The Survey of Husbandry Surveyed* (London: John Wright, 1652). That Blith proclaimed "VIVE LA REPUBLICK" on the title page did not prevent royalist pamphleteers from praising its wisdom and citing its precepts.

10. Paul Slack, *The Invention of Improvement: Information and Material Progress in Seventeenth-Century England* (Oxford: Oxford University Press, 2014), vii.

11. See Patrick Edward Dove's *Account of Andrew Yarranton: The Founder of English Political Economy* (Edinburgh: Johnston and Hunter, 1854). Philip William Flower also refers to Yarranton as the "Founder of English Political Economy" in his *History of the Trade in Tin* (London: G. Bell and Sons, 1880), 101. Chris Upton observes that Yarranton "has been called England's first canal engineer." "Andrew Yarranton the Forgotten Visionary," *Birmingham Post* (UK) August 17, 2011, http://www.birminghampost.co.uk/lifestyle/andrew-yarranton-the-forgotten-visionary-3918876. A. W. Skempton praises Yarranton as the "first to appreciate the value of *clover*" in *A Biographical Dictionary of Civil Engineers in Great Britain and Ireland: 1500–1830* (London: Thomas Telford, 2002), vol. 1, 809. On Yarranton's involvement with wagon rail construction, see M. J. T. Lewis, *Early Wooden Railways* (London: Routledge and Kegan Paul, 1970), 244–46.

12. *England's Improvement by Sea and Land*, a4r, a3v.

13. The tract's full title reflects its breadth of contents: *England's Improvement by Sea and Land: To Out-do the Dutch without Fighting, To Pay Debts without Moneys, To set at Work all the Poor of England with the Growth of our own Lands. To prevent unnecessary SUITS in Law; With the Benefit of a Voluntary REGISTER. Directions where vast quantities of Timber are to be had for the Building of SHIPS; With the Advantage of making the Great Rivers of England Navigable. RULES to prevent FIRES in London, and the Great CITIES; With Directions how the several Companies of Handicraftsmen in London may always have cheap Bread and Drink.*

14. An example of a more straightforwardly organized project proposal is Carew Reynell's *The True English Interest; or, An Account of the Chief National Improvements* (London: Giles Widdowes, 1674), which distributes its contents under chapter headings like "money," "husbandry," and "manufacture." Verging on pedantic is Roger Coke's *England's Improvements in Two Parts* (1675), which arranges its material by "propositions," "theorems," "corollaries," and "annotations."

15. *The Industrial Revolution in the Eighteenth Century: An Outline of the Beginnings of the Modern Factory System in England* (Abingdon Oxfordshire: Routledge, 2006), 121.

16. *Economic Policy and Projects: The Development of a Consumer Society in Early Modern England* (Oxford: Clarendon, 1978), 1. Various books borrow Thirsk's definition, including Elizabeth Rivlin's *The Aesthetics of Service in Early Modern England* (Evanston, Ill.: Northwestern University Press, 2012); Malcom Thick's *Sir Hugh Plat: The Search for Useful Knowledge in Early Modern London* (Totnes, Devon: Prospect Books, 2010); Phyllis Whitman Hunter's *Purchasing Identity in the Atlantic World: Massachusetts Merchants, 1670–1780* (Ithaca, N.Y.: Cornell University Press, 2001), and Christopher Breward's *The Culture of Fashion: A New History of Fashionable Dress* (Manchester: Manchester University Press, 1995).

17. *Essay upon Projects*, ed. Joyce Kennedy, Michael Seidel, and Maximillian Novak (New York: AMS, 1999), 13.

18. *The True English Interest*, A6v.

19. *Angliae Tutamen; or, The Safety of England* (London: [s.n.], 1695), 34. See also Richard Brome's stage comedy *The Court Beggar*, which names its protagonist projector "Sir Andrew Mendicant" (London: Richard Marriot and Thomas Dring, 1653), N4r.

20. (London: William Gilbertson, 1662), 1.

21. *The Discovery of a Proiector: Showing the Beginning, Progresse, and End of the Projector and His Projects* (London: [s.n.], 1641), 2.

22. *The History of England*, ed. Hugh Trevor-Roper (New York: Penguin Books, 1986), 489.

23. *The Wealth of Nations*, ed. Edwin Cannan (New York: Modern Library, 2000), 388.

24. Ibid., 196.

25. *Essay upon Projects*, 8.

26. It is possible that poorer projectors left behind less biographical evidence than their middle- and upper-class counterparts. Still little is known about most projectors beyond what they wrote. As of 2016, the *Oxford Dictionary of National Biography* lacks entries for the improvement projectors John Blanch, William Carter, Gabriel Reeve, William Woodford, and George Carew, among others.

27. Defoe derided Phips's attempt to salvage sunken treasure as "a mere Project, a Lottery of a Hundred thousand to One odds; a hazard, which if it had fail'd, every body wou'd have been asham'd to have own'd themselves concern'd in." *Essay upon Projects*, 11.

28. Paul Warde, "The Idea of Improvement, c. 1520–1700," in *Custom, Improvement and the Landscape in Early Modern Britain*, ed. Richard W. Hoyle (Burlington, Vt.: Ashgate, 2011), 144.

29. *England's Improvement*, b3v.

30. Ibid., a3r.

31. "The Idea of Improvement," 139.

32. *England's Interest and Improvement* (Cambridge: John Field, 1673), 2.

33. *England's Improvements*, 112.

34. *True English Interest*, A3r.

35. Ibid., A4r.

36. *England's Improvement*, a3r.

37. *England's Interest and Improvement*, 3.

38. *A Discourse of Trade* (London: Nicholas Barbon, 1690), A2r.

39. Joyce Appleby, *Economic Thought and Ideology in Seventeenth-Century England* (Princeton, N.J.: Princeton University Press, 1978), 97. Appleby notes that "the Dutch displayed unheroic qualities; they popularized the value of commercial virtues. Searching for the origins of

Dutch wealth, English writers found it in the mundane world of herring, efficient labor, low interest rates, and land registers" (97).

40. *England's Improvement*, c1r, c1v.

41. Ibid., c1v.

42. Ibid., 1.

43. Ibid., 7.

44. Yarranton was not the only projector to suggest that England do "as the Hollanders do at Amsterdam," but his tract was the first to offer explicit directions for actually implementing Dutch institutions and practices. See Reynell's *True English Interest*, 45–46, 60.

45. *England's Improvement*, a3r.

46. Ibid., b3v. On the role sixteenth-century Dutch immigrants played in the development of English ethnicity, see Marjorie Rubright, *Doppelgänger Dilemmas: Anglo-Dutch Relations in Early Modern English Literature and Culture* (Philadelphia: University of Pennsylvania Press, 2014).

47. *English Improver* (London: John Wright, 1653), C2r. On the unnerving character of projectors, see Joanne Myers's observation that "while most critics have been content to attribute contemporary disdain for projecting to its ties to financial speculation, projecting's perceived enthusiastic potential helps to explain the depth of negative feeling the practice evokes," in "Defoe and the Project of 'Neighbours Fare,'" *Restoration: Studies in English Literary Culture, 1660–1700* 35.2 (Fall 2011), 4.

48. *England's Improvement*, a4r.

49. Ibid., a3v.

50. On the politically fraught but mutually dependent relationship between court and port in the late seventeenth century, see Gary S. De Krey, *Restoration and Revolution in Britain: A Political History of the Era of Charles II and the Glorious Revolution* (New York: Palgrave Macmillan, 2007), 205–6.

51. *England's Interest and Improvement*, title page.

52. Smith, *England's Improvement Reviv'd*, A2r.

53. Coke, *England's Improvements*, A2r.

54. Yarranton, *England's Improvement*, b1r.

55. Ibid.

56. Ibid., b3r.

57. Ibid., b3v.

58. Ibid., b3r.

59. Ibid.

60. Ibid., c2v.

61. Ibid., 193.

62. Ibid.

63. Ibid.

64. Yarranton remarks cryptically that he "sometimes had the Honour and Misfortune to lodg and dislodg an Army," which seemingly could refer either to his task of encamping parliamentary troops, or to his role in displacing Charles I's forces through battle (*England's Improvement*, 193).

65. See *A Coffee-House Dialogue; or, A Discourse Between Captain Y—— and a Young Barrester of the Middle Temple* ([s.l.]: [s.n.], 1679), discussed in the final section of this chapter.

66. *England's Improvement*, 194.

67. National Archives, Kew, State Papers Domestic 46/104/fo103.

68. Ian Gentles, "The Management of the Crown Lands, 1649–60," *Agricultural History Review* 19.1 (1971), 40.

69. Christopher Hill, *The Century of Revolution, 1603–1714* (New York: Routledge, 2002), 120.

70. *England's Improvement*, 194. Joan Thirsk, "Agricultural Policy: Public Debate and Legislation, 1640–1750," in *Agricultural Change: Policy and Practice, 1500–1750*, ed. Joan Thirsk (Cambridge: Cambridge University Press, 1990), 298.

71. *England's Improvement*, 194.

72. *Calendar of State Papers: Domestic Series, 1660–61* (London: H. M. Stationery Office, 1860–1949), 356–57.

73. *England's Improvement*, a3v.

74. Ibid., 6.

75. Ibid.

76. Ibid., 37, 7.

77. Ibid., 38. For an explanation of how British writers came to distinguish between rape and seduction on the basis of female agency, see Toni Bowers, *Force or Fraud: British Seduction Stories and the Problem of Resistance 1660–1760* (Oxford: Oxford University Press, 2011).

78. On the history of Dutch land registration, see Jaap Zevenbergen, *Systems of Land Registration: Aspects and Effects* (Delft: Nederlandse Commissie voor Geodesie, 2002).

79. *England's Improvement*, 13.

80. Ibid., 8.

81. Ibid.

82. Ibid.

83. Ibid., 9.

84. Ibid.

85. Ibid.

86. Ibid.

87. Ibid., 11.

88. *English Improver*, 169.

89. Ibid.

90. *England's Improvement*, a3r.

91. Ibid., a4r.

92. Ibid., c2v. Folded into a quarto, *England's Improvement* contained twenty-seven sheets.

93. *England's Interest and Improvement*, a3r, a4r.

94. (London: Walter Kettilby, 1694), 2.

95. (London: R. Wilkin, 1694), 6.

96. (London: Thomas Bever, 1694), A3v.

97. Projectors long sought to legitimate their proposals by selling short their persuasive skills. Hugh Plat's *A Discouerie of Certaine English Wants* (London: William Ponsonby, 1595) refers to its author as the "boldest, though the meanest of many thousands to take so waighty a task in hand" (A2v). Plat prides himself on artless prose, presenting "meaness" as evidence of his sincerity. Blith aspired to "deliver my self in our naturall Country Language, and in our ordinary & usuall home-spun tearmes," hoping that his unstylized proposal text would vanish behind its prescriptive contents (*English Improver*, 2). The possessive "our" inducts Blith into the fellowship of (literate) farmers. He professes a linguistic deficit ("I can speak no other") to portray himself as a plain-speaking promoter of artisanship rather than a slick artificer.

98. *Economic Policy and Projects*, 1.

99. *England's Improvement*, a4r.

100. Ibid., a3v.

101. Ibid., 170.

102. Ibid., 66.

103. *English Improver*, 173.

104. *Account of the Rise and Progress of the Beech-Oil Invention* (London: [s.n.], 1715), 8.

105. *England's Improvement*, 39.

106. Ibid., 40.

107. Ibid., 179.

108. Ibid., 40.

109. Ibid., 43.

110. Ibid., 50.

111. Ibid., 47.

112. *England's Interest and Improvement*, 12.

113. *England's Interest Asserted* (London: Francis Smith, 1669), 23.

114. Ibid., 30.

115. *True English Interest*, 42.

116. *England's Improvement*, c2v.

117. *England's Interest and Improvement*, 4.

118. *England's Interest Asserted*, 14, 8.

119. *An Essay to the Restoring of Our Decayed Trade* (London: Giles Widdowes, 1675), 7.

120. *Economic Policy and Projects*, 70.

121. (London: H. Gosson, 1620), A2v.

122. (London: [s.n.], 1650), 2.

123. Ibid., 24.

124. *England's Improvement*, 38.

125. *Windsor-Forest* (London: Bernard Lintott, 1713), 16.

126. *England's Improvement*, 39.

127. Ibid., 195.

128. Ibid.

129. "Poets and Projectors: Profit, Production, and Economic Paradigms in Early Modern England," PhD diss., Columbia University, 1999, 16.

130. *Discouerie of Certaine English Wants*, A2r. Plat's contemporary Rowland Vaughan (1559–1629) likewise touts his design of an irrigation system for supposedly giving two thousand Herefordshire residents "meanes to worke, and so to lieu." See *Most Approved, and Long Experienced Water-Workes* (London: [s.n.], 1610), E2v.

131. *True English Interest*, 27.

132. Ibid., 51.

133. *Remarks on the Founding and Carrying on the Buildings of the Royal Hospital at Greenwich* (London: [s.n.], 1728), 7.

134. *England's Improvement*, 135.

135. Ibid., 113.

136. Ibid., 138.

137. *True English Interest*, 56.

138. *England's Improvement*, 67–71.

139. Ibid., 97.

140. Ibid., 99.

141. *Apology for the Builder* (London: Cave Pullen, 1685), 23.

142. Ibid.

143. Ibid., 26.

144. Ibid., 3. The grotesque figuration of London as an oversized skull affixed to a feeble body dates at least to the work of John Graunt, who prefaced his mortality study by observing that London is "perhaps a Head too big for the Body, and possibly too strong." See *Natural and Political Observations Mentioned in a Following Index, and Made Upon the Bills of Mortality* (London: John Martin, James Allestry, and Thomas Dicas, 1665), A5r.

145. *Apology*, 30. Likewise, Yarranton observed, "London is as the Heart is in the Body, and the great Rivers are as its Veins; let them be stopt, there will then be great danger either of death or else such Veins will apply themselves to feed some other part of the Body, which it was not properly intended for." *England's Improvement*, 179.

146. *Apology*, 31.

147. *England's Improvement*, 193.

148. *Coffee-House Dialogue*, A1r.

149. Ibid.

150. Ibid.

151. Ibid.

152. Ibid.

153. Ibid., 2.

154. Ibid., A1v.

155. *England's Improvements Justified* (London: [s.n.], 1680), 1.

156. *The Coffee-House Dialogue Examined and Refuted* (London: [s.n.], 1680), 1.

157. "An Account of Three Books," *Philosophical Transactions of the Royal Society* 11 (1676), 798.

158. *Aubrey's Brief Lives*, vol. 2, ed. Andrew Clark (London: Henry Frowde, 1898), 316.

159. *England's Improvement*, a4r.

CHAPTER 2

1. Ed. Joyce Kennedy, Michael Seidel, and Maximillian Novak (New York: AMS, 1999), 7.

2. Ibid.

3. "Foreword," in *Essay Upon Projects*, xv.

4. "Projecting Fictions: *Gulliver's Travels*, *Jack Connor*, and *John Buncle*," *Modern Philology* 100.3 (2003), 331.

5. Carole Fabricant, "Geographical Projects in the Later Eighteenth Century: Imperial Myths and Realities," in *The Age of Projects*, ed. Max Novak (Toronto: University of Toronto Press, 2008), 318.

6. *Marxism and Literature* (Oxford: Oxford University Press, 1977), 128.

7. Philip Gaskell, *A New Introduction to Bibliography* (New Castle: Oak Knoll, 1995), 47.

8. "'What's Past Is Prologue': The Bibliographical Society and History of the Book," in *Making Meaning: "Printers of the Mind" and Other Essays*, ed. Peter D. McDonald and Michael F. Suarez (Amherst: University of Massachusetts Press, 2002), 262.

9. Introduction to *The Cambridge History of the Book in Britain*, vol. 5, ed. Michael F. Suarez and Michael L. Turner (Cambridge: Cambridge University Press, 2009), 1.

10. *Knowing Books: The Consciousness of Mediation in Eighteenth-Century Britain* (Philadelphia: University of Pennsylvania Press, 2011), 4.

11. Ibid., 6.

12. "Introduction: Knowledge and Its Making in Early Modern Europe," in *Making Knowledge in Early Modern Europe: Practices, Objects, and Texts, 1400–1800*, ed. Pamela Smith and Benjamin Schmidt (Chicago: University of Chicago Press, 2008), 4.

13. See Brewster, *Aaron Hill: Poet, Dramatist, Projector* (New York: AMS, 1913), and Gerrard, *Aaron Hill: The Muses' Projector, 1685–1750* (Oxford: Oxford University Press, 2003).

14. *An Impartial Account of the Nature, Benefit, and Design, of a New Discovery* (London: [s.n.], 1714), 4.

15. Christine MacLeod describes patent review as an "unnecessarily lengthy and tortuous procedure" costing "between £70 and £100 in money and from two weeks to six months in time." "The 1690s Patents Boom: Invention or Stock-Jobbing?" *Economic History Review* 39.4 (1986), 551. Maxine Berg observes that the eventual rewards of patenting were "sometimes questionable." See "From Imitation to Invention: Creating Commodities in Eighteenth-Century Britain," *Economic History Review* 55.1 (2002), 21. The rolls reveal some projector patentees, including Thomas Hale, author of *An Account of Several New Inventions and Improvements Now Necessary for England* (1691), who received a patent for milling lead to fortify ship hulls. John Apletre refers to his patent for silk cultivation in the pamphlet *Proposals for an Undertaking to Manage and Produce Raw-Silk . . . Pursuant to a Patent Granted to John Apletre, Esq: Under the Great Seal of England* (London: [s.n.], 1718).

16. Bennet Woodcroft, *Subject-Matter Index of Patents of Invention from March 2, 1617 (14 James I.) to October 1, 1852 (16 Victoriae) Part II* (London: George Edward Eyre and William Spottiswoode, 1854), 89.

17. 21 Ja. 1. Cap. 3.

18. Christopher Hill, *The Century of Revolution, 1603–1714* (New York: Routledge, 2002), 31.

19. Aaron Hill, *Impartial Account*, 13. See Berg, "In Pursuit of Luxury: Global History and British Consumer Goods in the Eighteenth Century," *Past and Present* 182.1 (2004), 85–142. Domestic oil production had been the elusive goal of seventeenth-century projects to grow hemp and coleseed on reclaimed marsh. See Joan Thirsk, *Economic Policy and Projects: The Development of a Consumer Society in Early Modern England* (Oxford: Clarendon, 1978), 69. Despite heavy agricultural experimentation and widespread mercantilist desire to curb imports and employ the king's subjects in improvement projects, eighteenth-century Britain continued to import foreign oil.

20. National Archives, Kew, C 66/3494/6/185.

21. Technical specification arose from the 1778 case of *Liardet v. Johnson*. See John Adams and Gwen Averley, "The Patent Specification: The Role of Liardet v. Johnson," *Journal of Legal History* 7.2 (1986), 156–77.

22. "1690s Patents Boom," 552.

23. Ibid., 550. Hill made his patent sound more impressive by implying that Queen Anne had personally signed off on the award. In his second pamphlet, *Proposals for Raising a Stock*, Hill makes the monarch the grammatical subject of the patenting process: "Her Majesty by *Letters Patents*, under the Great Seal of *Great Britain*, bearing Date the 23d Day of *October* last, was graciously pleas'd to Grant to *Aaron Hill*, Esq; and his Assigns, the *Sole* Priviledge and Exercise,

for 14 Years, of a *New Invention*, to make *Oil* from the *Fruit* of the *Beech-Tree*, commonly call'd *Beech-Mast*" (London: [s.n.], 1714), 3. This claim is technically true to the extent that all patents bore the royal insignia, but it misleads readers by suggesting that Hill's invention had garnered exclusive royal favor.

24. *Impartial Account*, 4.

25. Ibid.

26. Ibid., 5.

27. *Post-Boy*, October 27–29, 1713.

28. Ibid.

29. *Post-Boy*, December 31, 1713–January 2, 1714.

30. Hill informs readers in a postscript to *An Impartial Account* that "Till Places proper for the Business can be prepar'd and fitted in the Heart of the Town, The Oil Annuity-Office will be kept at the Patentee's-House, against the Upper-End of the Duke of Mountague's, in Great Russel-street, *in* Bloomsbury: Where the Books are now open'd, in Order to receive Subscriptions" (30).

31. "Projecting Fictions," 336.

32. "Swift's Modest Proposal: The Biography of an Early Georgian Pamphlet," *Journal of the History of Ideas* 4.1 (1943), 89.

33. Samantha Heller, "Poets and Projectors: Profit, Production, and Economic Paradigms in Early Modern England," PhD diss., Columbia University, 1999, 52.

34. Joad Raymond, *Pamphlets and Pamphleteering in Early Modern Britain* (Cambridge: Cambridge University Press, 2006), 72.

35. For a more detailed explanation of this kind of imposition, see Gaskell, *New Introduction to Bibliography*, 83.

36. Nutt published and sold the Gardyner-printed *Funeral Poems* in 1700. Nutt was succeeded at his Royal Exchange print shop by John Morphew, who would publish Hill's *The Dedication of the Beech-Tree* (London: John Morphew, 1714).

37. John Feather, "The Commerce of Letters: The Study of the Eighteenth-Century Book Trade," *Eighteenth-Century Studies* 17.4 (1984), 409.

38. John Smith self-published the first edition of *England's Improvement Reviv'd* (1670). Moses Pitt self-published his prison reform treatise *The Cry of the Oppressed* (1691) and arranged for its sale by the unspecified "Booksellers of London and Westminster." Charles Povey did the same with his commercial treatise *The Unhappiness of England* (1701).

39. *Impartial Account*, 7.

40. Ibid., 6.

41. Ibid.

42. *Pamphlets*, 54.

43. *Knowing Books*, 4.

44. *Proposals*, 9.

45. Michael Harris notes that in eighteenth-century London, coffeehouses not only "became a crucial centre for access to printed newspapers" but also were "crucial to the development of the newspaper as a form." "London Newspapers," in *The Cambridge History of the Book in Britain*, vol. 5, ed. Michael Suarez and Michael L. Turner (Cambridge: Cambridge University Press, 2009), 414.

46. *Account of the Rise*, 6.

47. *Impartial Account*, 6.

48. *Account of the Rise*, 8.

49. Ibid., 4.

50. Ibid., 8.

51. Ibid., 7.

52. *Impartial Account*, 31.

53. Ibid.

54. Hill also enclosed a "sample of a product new to Britain" in a letter to Lord Oxford on April 12, 1714, and requested that the peer "Present her Majesty a Specimen of this Oil" because it would "greatly Influence to my advantages." British Library Stowe MS 143 f.128.

55. *Impartial Account*, 21.

56. See John McCusker, *Essays in the Economic History of the Atlantic World* (London: Routledge, 1997), 101–105.

57. Ibid., 102. Economic historians have shed little light on eighteenth-century British oil consumption. B. R. Mitchell's *Abstract of British Historical Statistics*, for instance, tabulates the importation of "Oils, Seeds and Nuts for Expressing Oil, Gums and Tallow" beginning only in 1805. (Cambridge: Cambridge University Press, 1962), 287.

58. (London: A. Bell, W. Taylor, and J. Baker, 1715), 15. Likewise, in her compilation of trade statistics, Elizabeth Boody Schumpeter makes no mention of olive oil, though she does record that Britain imported over £45,173 of train oil derived from whale blubber, which could have been used as an illuminant or ingredient for making soap. *English Overseas Trade Statistics 1697–1808* (Oxford: Clarendon, 1960), 48.

59. Schumpeter, *English Overseas Trade Statistics*, 12.

60. Another analysis of commerce, William Edgar's *Vectigalium systema; or, A Complete View of That Part of the Revenue of Great Britain* (1714) mentions that olive oil was one of twenty-five commodities subject to an "aliens duty," imposed on British sailors who imported goods on foreign ships (8). This tax, along with Hill's patent, suggests that oil importation was significant enough to shape the formulation of state policy.

61. *Impartial Account*, 21.

62. Ibid., 17–19.

63. *Account of the Rise*, 22.

64. Evelyn's *Sylva* qtd. in Hill, *Proposals*, 23.

65. *Proposals*, 23.

66. Ibid.

67. Ibid., 23-24.

68. *Post-Boy*, January 12–14, 1714.

69. *Proposals*, 3.

70. (London: [s.n.], 1695), 19.

71. *Proposals*, 5.

72. Ibid.

73. *London Gazette*, June 19-22, 1714.

74. *Dedication*, 5.

75. Hill refers to the poem in a letter to Harley dated April 12. In it he claims that *Dedication* constitutes "an honest Man's Poor acknowledgement of Duty," an expression of praise that "stoops not to the modern mercenary motives of Poetic Application," namely, patronage seeking. British Library Stowe MS 143 f.128.

76. *Aaron Hill*, 43.

77. *Dedication*, 5.

78. Ibid., 6.

79. *Post Man and Historical Account,* June 25–28, 1714.

80. *Post-Boy,* February 26–March 1, 1715.

81. Ibid.

82. Ibid.

83. Aaron Hill, *An Impartial State of the Case Between the Patentee, Annuitants, and Sharers, in the Beech-Oil Company* (London: Aaron Hill, 1716), 6.

84. *Aaron Hill,* 44.

85. *Post-Boy,* May 24–26, 1715.

86. Benedict Webb received a patent for "Making oil from rapeseed and other like seeds sown in England and Wales" in 1624. Lewis Bailey patented a press for making rapeseed and linseed oil in 1647. See Woodcroft, *Subject-Matter Index of Patents of Invention.*

87. *Daily Courant,* September 30, 1715.

88. The notations can be found in *Account of the Rise,* 77–79.

89. Ibid., 3.

90. Ibid., A2r.

91. Ibid., 8.

92. Ibid., 33–39.

93. *Impartial Account,* 7.

94. Ibid., 26.

95. *Account of the Rise,* 50.

96. Ibid., 66.

97. Ibid., 67–70.

98. Ibid., 67.

99. Ibid., 103–4.

100. *Post-Boy,* February 26–March 1, 1715.

101. *Account of the Rise,* 96.

102. *Post-Man and Historical Account,* April 19–21, 1716.

103. Similar invitations to purchase stock at the Essex Street office appeared in the *Daily Courant* on June 7, 8, 12, 1715.

104. *Daily Courant,* May 12, 15, 23, 24, 25, and 28, 1716.

105. *Daily Courant,* July 7, 1716.

106. *Impartial State,* title page.

107. Ibid., 1.

108. Ibid., 15.

109. (London: Thomas Baston, 1716), 11.

110. Ibid., 4.

111. Ibid., 11.

112. Ibid.

113. Ibid., 4.

114. *Historical and Chronological Deduction of the Origin of Commerce,* vol. 3 (London: J. Robson and W. Clarke, 1787), 103. Building off Anderson's work, an anonymous 1825 volume titled *South Sea Bubble* listed Hill's beech oil scheme as one of the "numerous fraudulent projects" that led to the 1720 crash. (London: Thomas Boys, 1825), 79.

115. *Historical and Chronological Deduction,* 103.

116. See William Robert Scott, *The Constitution and Finance of English, Scottish and Irish Joint-Stock Companies to 1720,* vol. 3 (Cambridge: Cambridge University Press, 1910), 127–30.

117. (London: T. Jauncy, 1721), 2.

118. Ibid., 13.

119. Ibid., 34.

CHAPTER 3

1. Della Pollock, *Exceptional Spaces: Essays in Performance and History* (Chapel Hill: University of North Carolina Press, 1998), 20. Bruno Latour, *Aramis; or, The Love of Technology*, trans. Catherine Porter (Cambridge, Mass.: Harvard University Press, 1996), 24.

2. Daniel Defoe, *Robinson Crusoe*, ed. Evan R. Davis (Toronto: Broadview, 2010), 77. Italics mine.

3. *An Essay upon Projects*, ed. Joyce Kennedy, Michael Seidel, and Maximillian Novak (New York: AMS, 1999), 32.

4. Ibid.

5. While Defoe disowns "undertaking" here, he boasts elsewhere in *Essay* of the practical experience he gained executing projects, like his brick and pantile factory in Tilbury.

6. (London: R. Wilkin, 1694), 172.

7. "Writing the Unwritten: Morris Dance and Theatre History" in *Representing the Past: Essays in Performance Historiography*, ed. Charlotte M. Canning and Thomas Postlewait (Iowa City: University of Iowa Press, 2010), 86.

8. Ibid.

9. *The Archive and the Repertoire: Performing Cultural Memory in the Americas* (Durham, N.C.: Duke University Press, 2003), xvii.

10. *Performance Studies: An Introduction* (New York: Routledge, 2002), 22.

11. In the eighteenth century, Samuel Johnson defined "performance" as the "completion of something designed; execution of something promised," "composition; work," and "action; something done." *Dictionary of the English Language*, vol. 2 (London: J. and P. Knapton, T. and T. Longman, C. Hitch and L. Hawes, A. Millar, and R. and J. Dodsley, 1755), 19Mr.

12. *The Draining of the Fens* (Cambridge: Cambridge University Press, 1940), 28.

13. Anne Reeves and Tom Williamson, "Marshes," in *The English Rural Landscape*, ed. Joan Thirsk (Oxford: Oxford University Press, 2000), 150.

14. Ian Rotherham, *The Lost Fens: England's Greatest Ecological Disaster* (Stroud: History Press, 2013), 201.

15. Christopher Taylor, "Fenlands," in *The English Rural Landscape*, ed. Thirsk, 167.

16. 43 Eliz. Cap. 11.

17. H. C. Darby, *The Changing Fenland* (Cambridge: Cambridge University Press, 1983), 56.

18. H. C. Darby records that "the lords of manors and the majority of the commoners in any common fen, together with the owners of any flooded land lying near, might deliver up a portion of their fens to any person or persons who would undertake their 'draining and keeping dry perpetually.'" Ibid. For an attempt at tabulating the total acreage claimed by seventeenth-century drainage projectors, see N.N., *A Narrative of All the Proceedings in the Drayning of the Great Level of the Fenns, Extending into the Counties of North'ton: Lincoln, Norffolk, Suffolk, Cambridge, and Huntington, and the Isle of Ely; From the Time of Queen Elizabeth Untill This Present May, 1661* (London: N.N., 1661).

19. Thomas Badeslade, *The History of the Ancient and Present State of the Navigation of the Port of King's-Lyn, and of Cambridge* (London: Thomas Badeslade, 1725), 24.

20. William Dugdale claims that Hatfield commoners sabotaged Vermuyden's drainage by "pull[ing] up the Floudgates of *Snow* Sewer, which by letting in the tides from the River of *Trent*, soon drowned a great part of *Hatfield* Chase." *The History of Imbanking and Draining of Divers Fens and Marshes, Both in Foreign Parts and in This Kingdom, and of the Improvements Thereby* (London: [s.n.], 1662), 146.

21. *The Anti-Projector* (London: [s.n.], 1646), 8.

22. Joan Thirsk, "Vermuyden, Sir Cornelius (1590–1677)," in *Oxford Dictionary of National Biography*, ed. Lawrence Goldman (Oxford: Oxford University Press, 2006).

23. Dugdale, *History of Imbanking*, 82.

24. Vermuyden, *A Discourse Touching the Drayning of the Great Fennes* (London: [s.n.], 1642), 1.

25. Ibid., 1–2.

26. Ibid., 2.

27. *History or Narrative of the Great Level of the Fenns* (London: Moses Pitt, 1685), A1v.

28. *History of the Ancient and Present State of the Navigation*, 14.

29. H.C., *A Discourse Concerning the Drayning of Fennes and Surrounded Grounds in the Six Counteys of Norfolke, Suffolke, Cambridge with the Isle of Ely, Huntington, Northampton, and Lincolne* (London: [s.n.], 1629), A3v.

30. Ibid.

31. H.C., *Discourse*, A3v. H.C. popularized ways of seeing fen that would be adapted by William Dugdale, Samuel Fortrey, and Thomas Badeslade, whose histories also conceive of drainage as pastoral care, commercial stimulus, and salvage expedition. Dugdale lifted numerous passages directly from H.C. For treatments of these metaphors and the epistemologies of fenland they reveal, see Eric Ash's essay "Amending Nature; Draining the English Fens," in *The Mindful Hand: Inquiry and Invention from the Late Renaissance to Early Industrialisation*, ed. Lissa Roberts, Simon Schaffer, and Peter Dear (Amsterdam: Edita, 2007), 117–43. See also Vittoria Di Palma's chapter on swamps in *Wasteland: A History* (New Haven, Conn.: Yale University Press, 2014), 84–127.

32. H.C., *Discourse*, A3r, C1r.

33. *A Scheme for Draining the Great Level of the Fens* (London: J. Roberts, 1729), 3.

34. Vermuyden, *Discourse*, 3.

35. Ash, "Amending Nature," 129, 132.

36. Vermuyden, *Discourse*, 7.

37. Vermuyden was not the first drainer to propose rebedding fenland rivers, though prior to his *Discourse*, no one had imagined the creation of artificial rivers on such a comprehensive scale.

38. Vermuyden, *Discourse*, 12.

39. Ibid., 13.

40. *A Desperate and Dangerovs Designe Discovered Concerning the Fen-Countries* (London: Robert Constable, 1642), 1.

41. Ibid., 17.

42. *Brief Relation Discovering Plainely the True Causes Why the Great Levell of Fenns . . . Have Been Drowned and Made Unfruitfull for Many Yeares Past* (London: Francis Constable 1642), A2v. *Exceptions Against Sir Cornelius Virmudens Discourse* (London: Robert Constable, 1642), 3.

43. *Exceptions*, 3, 9.

44. Burrell, *Brief Relation*, 8.

45. Ibid., 20.

46. *The Designe for the Perfect Draining of the Great Level of the Fens* (London: [s.n.], 1665), A4v.

47. Ibid.

48. H.C. Darby, *The Draining of the Fens* (Cambridge: Cambridge University Press, 1940), 70.

49. "Pretended Act for Draining the Great Level (1649)," in Samuel Wells, *The History of the Drainage of the Great Level of the Fens*, vol. 2 (London: Samuel Wells, 1830), 370.

50. Margaret Albright Knittl, "The Design for the Initial Drainage of the Great Level of the Fens: An Historical Whodunit in Three Parts," *Agricultural History Review* 55.1 (2007), 39.

51. BL Lansdowne MS 722/4. Frances Willmoth argues that this figure is likely exaggerated. *Sir Jonas Moore: Practical Mathematics and Restoration Science* (Rochester: Boydell, 1993), 91.

52. *Draining of the Fens*, 42.

53. Samuel Wells, *The History of the Drainage*, 372.

54. J. Korthals-Altes, *Sir Cornelius Vermuyden* (New York: Arno, 1977), 29.

55. Nottingham University, Stovin, HCC 9111/1.

56. Dugdale, *History of Imbanking*, 145.

57. This sartorial coding apparently did not discourage some Scottish workers from deserting, often with the "open encouragement of surrounding commoners." *Fenland Riots and the English Revolution* (London: Heinemann Educational Books, 1982), 175.

58. Describing the windmill-driven reclamation of Haddenham Level in Cambridgeshire in the 1740s, Nicholas James breaks drainage down into five basic tasks: "clearing drains; banking; building bridges and other features; millwrights' work; and milling." These activities demanded of workers "skills of observation and of walking, hauling, grappling, digging and lifting." "The 'Age of the Windmill' in the Haddenham Level," *Proceedings of the Cambridge Antiquarian Society* 98 (2009): 118–19.

59. Charles Labelye, *The Result of a View of the Great Level of the Fens* (London: [s.n.], 1745), vol. 1, 12.

60. Dodson, *Designe for the Perfect Draining*, 2.

61. *Desperate and Dangerous Design*, 20.

62. "The Making of the Bedford Level: Archives and Archaeology," in *Drowned and Drained: Exploring Fenland Records and Landscape*, ed. Susan Oosthuizen and Frances Willmoth (Cambridge: University of Cambridge Institute of Continuing Education, 2009), 8.

63. Ibid., 8.

64. *English Improver Improved* (London: John Wright, 1652), 45.

65. Ibid.

66. Ibid.

67. *Result of a View*, 2.

68. *English Improver Improved*, recto to 68.

69. *Designe for the Perfect Draining*, 10. Andrews Burrell accused Vermuyden of using cheap inch-thick deal boards to make sluice doors instead of quality oaken planks in conjunction with an earlier drainage venture. *An Explanation of the Drayning Workes vvhich have beene Lately Made for the Kings Maiestie* (London: [s.n.], 1641), 9.

70. *Pretended Act*, 370.

71. *England's Improver*, 51.

72. Ibid.

73. Ibid., 64.

74. Ibid.

75. Wells, *History of the Drainage of the Great Level of the Fens*, vol. 1, 228.

76. *Explanation of the Drayning Workes*, 10.

77. Nottingham University, Stovin, HCC 9111/1.

78. (London: Richard Baddeley, 1653), 2.

79. *The History or Narrative of the Great Level of the Fenns, Called Bedford Level* (London: Moses Pitt, 1685), 72.

80. Vermuyden, *Discourse*, 23.

81. Fortrey, *The History or Narrative*, 74.

82. Ibid., 75.

83. "Lynn Law (1630)," in Wells, *History of Drainage*, vol. 2, 103.

84. "An Act for Settling the Draining of the Great Level of 1663," in Wells, *History of Drainage*, vol. 2, 386.

85. *Result of a View*, 55.

86. The Bedford Level Corporation's manuscript records, held in the Cambridgeshire Archives, provide a day-to-day glimpse into this struggle from the perspective of drainers. For a history of drainage derived from scrupulous examination of these documents, see Eric Ash's *The Draining of the Fens: Projectors, Popular Politics, and State Building in Early Modern England* (Baltimore: Johns Hopkins University Press, 2017).

87. H.C., *Discourse*, C11.

88. Furrowing pigs posed another problem. The bylaws of the Bedford Level Corporation, the successor to the Adventurers, stipulated that "no Person or Persons whatsoever, shall at any time hereafter put, or cause any *Swine* to be put or kept, into or upon any of the *Banks* or *Forelands* of any of the *Rivers* or *Sewers* within or without the said *Great Level*. Fortrey, *History or Narrative*, 58.

89. *Designe for the Perfect Draining*, 14.

90. In this spirit of self-sabotaging work, Keith Lindley mentions a 1630 account of some drainage workers in Chippenham who dug a drain during the day, and returned at night to "fill up the said River again by flinging in the earth which they were paid for flinging out." *Fenland Riots*, 40.

91. Badeslade, *History*, 11.

92. Vermuyden, *Discourse*, 5, 12. Dodson shared the belief that weeds were "of very dangerous consequence." *Designe for the Perfect Draining*, 27.

93. *Changing Fenland*, 107.

94. *Draining*, 114.

95. Qtd. in Knittl, "The Design for the Initial Drainage," 42.

96. For example, John Leaford surveyed the "remaining two Arches, part of the old Sluice at *Denver*, call'd *Colonel Russel's two Eyes*," and surmised that these ruins were "strong and fit to support Slice-Doors to shut upon the Flux of the Tides." *Some Observations Made of the Frequent Drowned Condition of the South Level of the Fenns* (London: [s.n.], 1740), 17.

97. Nottingham University, Stovin, HCC 9111/1, 168.

98. "Act for the Settling of the Draining" in Wells, *History of Drainage*, vol. 2, 396.

99. "Enquiries Concerning Agriculture," *Philosophical Transactions of the Royal Society* 5. (1665), 94.

100. C. Taylor, "Fenlands," 187. The tenuousness of drainage has shown itself in modern times. On January 31, 1953, a North Sea storm surge overwhelmed East England's seawalls, resulting in floods that killed 307 people in what Peter Baxter calls "the worst natural disaster to befall Britain during the twentieth century." See "The East Coast Big Flood, 31 January–1 February 1953:

A Summary of the Human Disaster," *Philosophical Transactions of the Royal Society* 363 (June 2005), 1293.

    101. *England's Improver*, 58.

    102. *History of Imbanking*, 145.

    103. Lindley, *Fenland Riots*, 6.

    104. *The Fleece: A Poem. In Four Books* (London: J. Dodsley, 1757), 53.

    105. Ibid., 54.

CHAPTER 4

    1. Rachel Crawford, "English Georgic and British Nationhood," *ELH* 65.1 (1998), 124.

    2. *The Georgic Revolution* (Princeton, N.J.: Princeton University Press, 1985), 119.

    3. Courtney Weiss Smith, *Empiricist Devotions: Science, Religion, and Poetry in Early Eighteenth-Century England* (Charlottesville: University of Virginia Press, 2016), 174.

    4. "The Maritime Georgic and the Lake Poet Empire of Georgic," *ELH* 75.3 (Fall 2008), 532.

    5. "An Essay on the Georgics," printed on unnumbered, unsignatured leaves between pages 48 and 49 in Dryden's *The Works of Virgil: Containing His Pastorals, Georgics, and Aeneid: Adorn'd with a Hundred Sculptures* (London: Jacob Tonson, 1697).

    6. Pat Rogers observes that *Cyder* and *Windsor-Forest* processed agricultural writing "in the light of topical concerns, party loyalties, and competing versions of English history" in "John Philips, Pope, and Political Georgic," *Modern Language Quarterly* 66.4 (2005), 414. Chris Mounsey reads Christopher Smart's *Hop-Garden* (1752) as a "digest" of Richard Bradley's pamphlet *The Riches of a Hop-Garden Explain'd* in *Christopher Smart: Clown of God* (Lewisburg, Pa.: Bucknell University Press, 2001), 75.

    7. "Roman Georgic in the Georgian Age: A Theory of Romantic Genre," *Texas Studies in Literature and Language* 33.2 (1991), 184.

    8. *Georgic Modernity and British Romanticism: Poetry and the Mediation of History* (Cambridge: Cambridge University Press, 2004), 21, 3.

    9. "Essay on the Georgics," fourth un-numbered verso page after 48.

    10. "Husbandry Manuals and the Language of Agrarian Improvement," in *Culture and Cultivation in Early Modern England*, ed. Michael Leslie and Timothy Raylor (Leicester: Leicester University Press, 1992), 52.

    11. *The Seasons*, ed. James Sambrook (Oxford: Clarendon, 1981), 95.

    12. *Georgic Revolution*, 123.

    13. *The Agrarian History of England and Wales*, vol. 5.2 (Cambridge: Cambridge University Press, 1985), 553.

    14. *A Treatise of Fruit-Trees Shewing the Manner of Grafting, Setting, Pruning, and Ordering of Them in All Respects* (Oxford: William Hall, 1665), 10. In this vein, Clare Bucknell observes that "predominantly, the changing topography of eighteenth-century Britain was the result of the localised ventures of tenants, agents and smallholders." "The Mid-Eighteenth-Century Georgic and Agricultural Improvement," *Journal for Eighteenth-Century Studies* 36.3 (2013): 335.

    15. *Samuel Hartlib: His Legacy* (London: Richard Wodenothe, 1655), 174.

    16. *The English Improver Improved; or, The Survey of Husbandry Surveyed* (London: John Wright, 1652), 173.

17. *Husbandry and Trade Improv'd: Being a Collection of Many Valuable Materials Relating to Corn, Cattle, Coals, Hops, Wool, &c.*, vol. 4 (London: Woodman and Lyon, 1727), 80. Several other authors describe the hostile reception of their works in terms that evoke antiprojection without using the term: John Evelyn despaired that horticultural improvers of the Restoration era suffered "the ugly affronts of *Clowns . . .* who laugh and scorn at every thing which is above their understanding." *Pomona; or, An Appendix Concerning Fruit-Trees in Relation to Cider* (London: [s.n.], 1670), 13.

18. *Sylva; or, A Discourse on Forest-Trees and the Propagation of Timber in His Majesty's Dominions* (London: Royal Society, 1670), 2.

19. Ibid., 1670., a1v.

20. *Some Considerations Touching the Vsefulnesse of Experimental Naturall Philosophy Propos'd in Familiar Discourses to a Friend, by Way of Invitation to the Study of It* (Oxford: Richard Davis, 1663), 4.

21. *Legends, No Histories: A Specimen of Some Animadversions upon the History of the Royal Society* (London: [s.n.], 1670), 42.

22. Ibid., 51, 44. Stubbe would use the same line verbatim in *A Specimen of Some Animadversions upon a Book Entituled, Plus Ultra; or, Modern Improvements of Useful Knowledge Written by Mr. Joseph Glanvill, a Member of the Royal Society* (London: [s.n.], 1670), 44.

23. *Plus Ultra; or, The Progress and Advancement Knowledge Since the days of Aristotle* (London: Iames Collins, 1668), 5.

24. "Reformation and the Distrust of the Projector in the Hartlib Circle," *Historical Journal* 55.2 (2012), 378.

25. Vol. 3 (London: J. Robson and W. Clarke, 1787), 108.

26. *Cyder: A Poem. In Two Books* (London: H. Hills, 1708), 1.

27. Juan Christian Pellicer, "John Philips (1676–1709), Life, Works, and Reception," PhD diss., University of Oslo, 2002, i.

28. *Agrarian History*, vol. 5.1, 160.

29. *Cyder*, 31.

30. Ibid., 89.

31. Thirsk, *Agrarian History*, vol. 5.1, 160.

32. Patrick Woodland, "Beale, John (*bap.* 1608, *d.* 1683)," in *Oxford Dictionary of National Biography*, ed. David Cannadine (Oxford: Oxford University Press, 2004).

33. Mayling Stubbs, "John Beale, Philosophical Gardener of Herefordshire: Part I. Prelude to the Royal Society (1608–1663)," *Annals of Science* 39 (1982): 466.

34. Michael Leslie, "The Spiritual Husbandry of John Beale," in *Culture and Cultivation*, ed. Leslie and Raylor, 152.

35. *Herefordshire Orchards, a Pattern for All England: Written in an Epistolary Address to Samuel Hartlib, Esq.* (London: [s.n.], 1657), 2. This tract originated as letters that Beale sent to Hartlib in 1656. When Hartlib asked Beale to translate some of his Latin quotations of Horace and Columella into "plain and common *English*, that all the vulgar capacities may understand them," Beale replied that the work "must fly abroad . . . in the free garb of a natural simplicity; written with speed, and with more care of truth, than of fit words." *Herefordshire Orchards*, 60.

36. In an ironic twist, Beale's suspected royalist allegiances led the government to sequester his estate at Sock Dennis. For a review of the "various readings of Beale's ideological and political allegiance," see Leslie, "Spiritual Husbandry," 153.

37. Besides Crawford, Mary Gwyneth Lloyd Thomas identifies Beale's tract as a topical sourcebook for Philips, along with Evelyn's *Pomona* and *Sylva* and Worlidge's *Vinetum*

Britannicum (1678). See *The Poems of John Philips*, ed. Mary Gwyneth Lloyd Thomas (Oxford: Blackwell, 1927).

38. *Herefordshire*, 37.

39. Ibid., 39.

40. Ibid., 6.

41. Ibid., 37.

42. *Most Approved, and Long Experienced Water-Workes* (London: [s.n.], 1610), B1r.

43. *Herefordshire*, 32.

44. Mark Overton, *Agricultural Revolution in England: The Transformation of the Agrarian Economy 1500–1850* (Cambridge: Cambridge University Press, 1996), 141, 142.

45. *Herefordshire*, 7.

46. Ibid., 7, 33.

47. Ibid., 39.

48. Ibid., 40.

49. Ibid., 8.

50. *Cyder*, 2.

51. Ibid., 1.

52. Ibid., 23.

53. Ibid., 21.

54. *Herefordshire*, 1.

55. *Cyder*, 7, 35, 8.

56. Ibid., 34.

57. Ralph Austen's *Treatise on Fruit-Trees* refers to the possibilities and problems in his recommendation that fruit trees be planted twenty yards apart in "Corne, Pasture, & hay grounds," and that planters permit "no branches to spread, within two yards from the ground, that so they may be out of the reach of Cattle & may not be troublesome to workmen in *plowing, sowing, reaping*, and other works" (4).

58. *A Designe for Plentie, by an Universall Planting of Fruit-Trees* (London: Richard Wodenothe, 1652), 7.

59. *Cyder*, 52.

60. Ibid., 59.

61. Ibid., 12, 14, 15.

62. Ibid., 12.

63. Ibid., 14.

64. *Empiricist Devotions*, 202.

65. *Cyder*, 88. 89.

66. "Shall, v." *OED Online*. September 2012. Oxford: Oxford University Press.

67. Karen O'Brien, "Imperial Georgic: 1660–1789," in *The Country and City Revisited: England the Politics of Culture, 1550–1850*, ed. Gerald MacLean, Donna Landry, and Joseph P. Ward (Cambridge: Cambridge University Press, 1999), 161.

68. Goodman, *Georgic Modernity*, 8.

69. *The Dunciad, in Four Books* (London: M. Cooper, 1743), 120.

70. *The Temple of Fame: A Vision* (London: Bernard Lintott, 1715), 19.

71. *Windsor-Forest* (London: Bernard Lintott, 1713), 10, 18.

72. Joseph Roach, *Cities of the Dead: Circum-Atlantic Performance* (New York: Columbia University Press, 1996), 139, 141.

73. Pat Rogers offers the most exhaustive study of *Windsor-Forest*'s "inherited systems of

202   Notes to Pages 132–135

signification" and their relation to historical local customs, forestry law, and regional history. *The Symbolic Design of* Windsor-Forest: *Iconography, Pageant, and Prophecy in Pope's Early Work* (Newark: University of Delaware Press, 2004), 223. By establishing the poem's context within histories of projection, I am challenging Rogers's claim that Pope "largely accepts the royalist vision of the greenwood, as a place untainted by commerce and a site of harmonious social relations" (147).

74. *England's Improvement by Sea and Land* (London: R. Everingham, 1677), 189.

75. *An Impartial Account of the Nature, Benefit, and Design, of a New Discovery* (London: [s.n.], 1714), 10.

76. R. R. Tighe and J. E. Davis, *Annals of Windsor Forest*, vol. 2 (London: Longman, Brown, Green, Longmans, and Roberts, 1858), 87.

77. *Windsor-Forest*, 24.

78. Rogers, *Symbolic Design*, 143.

79. But then in a later comment, Defoe reflects that if one sets aside considerations of "Trade, River, Navigation, Meal, and Malt," Windsor affords "the most beautiful, and most pleasantly situated Castle, and Royal Palace, in the whole Isle of Britain." *A Tour thro' the Whole Island of Great Britain, Divided into Circuits or Journies*, vol. 1 (London: G. Strahan, 1724), 84 of letter 2, 73 of letter 1.

80. *Windsor-Forest*, 2.

81. Ibid., 3.

82. "Ephemerides 1650 Part 3, Hartlib," *The Hartlib Papers*, 2013, https://www.hrionline .ac.uk/hartlib/view?docset=main&docname=28_01_60.

83. Adam Zucker, *The Places of Wit in Early Modern English Comedy* (Cambridge: Cambridge University Press, 2011), 31.

84. Tighe and Davis, *Annals*, 240.

85. *England's Improver Improved* (London: John Wright, 1653), 183.

86. *A Discours of Husbandrie Used in Brabant and Flanders* (London: [s.n.], 1650), 14.

87. Ibid. Peter Heylyn also compared Westphalia's Bishoprick of Bremen to Windsor Forest, claiming that it was "full of dry sands, heaths, and unfruitfull thickets, like the wilde parts of *Windsor Forrest* betwixt *Stanes* and *Fernham*" (*Cosmographie in Four Books* (London: Henry Seile, 1652), 113).

88. "Ephemerides 1649 Part 3, Hartlib," *The Hartlib Papers*, 2013, https://www.hrionline .ac.uk/hartlib/view?docset=main&docname=28_01_26&termo=transtext_vpon&term1=transtext _experimented#highlight.

89. *Windsor-Forest*, 4.

90. Ibid., 3, 4.

91. Ibid., 7, 4.

92. Robert P. Irvine, "Labor and Commerce in Locke and Early Eighteenth-Century English Georgic," *ELH* 76.4 (Spring 2009), 980.

93. Pope, *Windsor-Forest*, 11, 14.

94. Ibid., 14.

95. Thirsk, *Agrarian History*, vol. 5.1, 314.

96. *An Olde Thrift Nevvly Reuiued VVherein Is Declared the Manner of Planting, Preserving, and Husbanding Yong Trees of Diuers Kindes* (London: Richard Moore, 1612), 8.

97. Tighe and Davis, *Annals*, 242.

98. G.S., *Anglorum Speculum; or, The Worthies of England, in Church and State* (London: Thomas Passinger, 1684), 31.

99. O'Brien, "Imperial Georgic: 1660–1789," 200.

100. *Windsor-Forest*, 34.

101. *Cyder*, 35.

102. *Rural Sports* (London: Jacob Tonson, 1713), 1.

103. *The Seasons*, 95.

104. Ibid., 60.

105. Ibid., 95. Patricia Meyer Spacks, *The Varied God: A Critical Study of Thomson's The Seasons* (Berkeley: University of California Press, 1959), 14.

106. *Seasons*, 206.

107. Ibid., 252.

108. Ibid., 146–47.

109. Ibid., 149.

110. Ibid., 247, 248.

111. Ibid., 232.

112. *English Literature in History 1730–80: An Equal, Wide Survey* (New York: St. Martin's, 1983), 54.

113. *Varied God*, 177.

114. "'The Year Runs Round': The Poetry of Work in Eighteenth-Century England," in *Ritual, Routine, and Regime: Repetition in Early Modern British and European Cultures*, ed. Lorna Clymer (Toronto: University of Toronto Press, 2006), 163–64.

115. "Mid-Eighteenth-Century Georgic," 339.

116. "Hard Pastoral: Frost, Wordsworth, and Modernist Poetics," *Criticism* 29.1 (1987), 74.

117. *Seasons*, 204.

118. John Hervey, *Some Materials Towards Memoirs of the Reign of King George II*, ed. R. Sedgwick, vol. 1 (London: Eyre and Spottiswoode, 1931), 24.

119. Thomas Brugis, *The Discovery of a Projector: Showing the Beginning, Progresse, and End of the Projector and His Projects* (London: [s.n.], 1641), 2.

120. *An Account of the Life of Mr. Richard Savage, Son of the Earl Rivers* (London: J. Roberts, 1744), 120.

121. Ibid., 121.

122. *Georgic Modernity*, 8–9.

CHAPTER 5

1. *The Origins of the English Novel, 1600–1740* (Baltimore: Johns Hopkins University Press, 1987), 20.

2. Daniel Defoe, *Moll Flanders*, ed. G. A. Starr (Oxford: Oxford University Press, 1971), 159.

3. (London: Charles Rivington, 1728), 321–23.

4. Ed. Louis Landa (Oxford: Oxford University Press, 2010), 170.

5. Defoe, *Roxana*, ed. John Mullan (Oxford: Oxford University Press, 1996), 144. *Robinson Crusoe*, ed. Evan R. Davis (Toronto: Broadview, 2010), 77.

6. I take the word "antiprojection" from the 1646 pamphlet *The Anti-Projector* (London: [s.n.], 1646), which accuses wetlands reclamation schemes of overstating their talents, bilking investors, and coercing the poor. Other tracts in this mode include the anonymous *Angliae Tutamen; or, The Safety of England* (London: [s.n.], 1695) and Thomas Baston's *Thoughts on Trade, and Public Spirit* (London: Thomas Baston, 1716), esp. 9–17. These pamphlets adapted content from Caroline-era works, including Thomas Brugis's *The Discovery of a Projector: Showing the*

Beginning, Progresse, and End of the Projector and His Projects (London: [s.n.], 1641), Thomas Heywood's *Hogs Character of a Projector, Being a Relation of His Life and Death, with His Funerall.* (London: [s.n.], 1642), and the anonymous *Projectors Downfall; or, Times Changeling* (London: Thomas Paine, 1642).

7. J. M. Treadwell, "Jonathan Swift: The Satirist as Projector," *Texas Studies in Literature and Language* 17.2 (1975), 460.

8. *A Tale of a Tub: Written for the Universal Improvement of Mankind* (London: John Nutt, 1704), 103.

9. Swift, *A Project for the Advancement of Religion and the Reformation of Manners* (London: Benjamin Tooke, 1709), 7.

10. *A Proposal for Correcting, Improving, and Ascertaining the English Tongue* (London: Benjamin Tooke, 1712), 7.

11. Ibid., 48.

12. *The Drapier's Letters to the People of Ireland,* ed. Herbert Davis (Oxford: Clarendon Press, 1965), 30. Catherine Skeen calls the drapier's letters an "antiproject project." "Projecting Fictions: *Gulliver's Travels, Jack Connor,* and *John Buncle,*" *Modern Philology* 100.3 (2003), 338.

13. Swift similarly resents a "Project *on Foot*" that would force Irish subjects to buy "yearly so many *Tun of Straw-Hats* for the use of our Women" in the context of his own piece of industrial projection *A Proposal for the Universal Use of Irish Manufacture* (Dublin: E. Waters, 1720), 10–11.

14. Skeen, "Projecting Fictions," 341.

15. Letter: John Arbuthnot to Swift, November 5, 1726. *Correspondence of Jonathan Swift,* vol. 3, *1724–1731,* ed. Harold Williams (Oxford: Clarendon, 1963), 179.

16. "Jonathan Swift," 439.

17. *The Fictions of Satire* (Baltimore: Johns Hopkins University Press, 1967), 172.

18. Marjorie Nicolson and Nora M. Mohler, "The Scientific Background of Swift's 'Voyage to Laputa,'" *Annals of Science* 2.3 (1937), 299–334.

19. See Pat Rogers, "Gulliver and the Engineers," *Modern Language Review* 70.2 (1975), 260–70; Dolores Palomo, "The Dutch Connection: The University of Leiden and Swift's Academy of Lagado," *Huntington Library Quarterly* 41.1 (1977), 27–35; Douglas Lane Patey, "Swift's Satire on 'Science' and the Structure of *Gulliver's Travels,*" *ELH* 58.4 (1991), 809–39. There is considerable debate over the purpose and sincerity of Swift's *A Project for the Advancement of Religion and the Reformation of Manners* (1709), *A Proposal for Correcting, Improving, and Ascertaining the English Tongue* (1712), and *A Proposal for the Universal Use of Irish Manufacture* (1720). Leo Damrosch, for instance, characterizes *Project for the Advancement of Religion* as a "booby trap" and example of "Swiftian impersonation" in *Jonathan Swift: His Life and His World* (New Haven, Conn.: Yale University Press, 2013), 213. Treadwell, by contrast, argues that the pamphlet's "specific proposals are so close to Swift's known preferences as to be above suspicion" in "Jonathan Swift," 448.

20. Ibid., 439.

21. *Origins,* 337.

22. Ibid., 418. *Theory of the Novel: A Historical Approach,* ed. Michael McKeon (Baltimore: Johns Hopkins University Press, 2000), 395.

23. *The Court Beggar* (London: Richard Marriot and Thomas Dring, 1653), N8r.

24. Ibid., S6r.

25. William Shirley, *The Triumph of Peace* (London: Iohn Norton, 1634), 2.

26. Ibid., 3.

27. Ibid., 3. Of *Triumph*'s depiction of projectors, Bulstrode Whitelock remarked that the antimasque "pleased the spectators [all the] more, because by it an *information was covertly given to the King* of the unfitness and ridiculousness of these Projectors against the law." Qtd. in Annabel Patterson, *Censorship and Interpretation: The Conditions of Writing and Reading in Early Modern England* (Madison: University of Wisconsin Press, 1984), 116. Other dramatic depictions of projecting from this period can be found in Philip Massinger's *The Emperour of the East* (London: Iohn Waterson, 1632), when the protectress, Pulcheria, summons a projector to court and then rails against him for proposing divisive tax schemes. See also William Cavendish's *The Country Captaine* (London: Humphrey Robinson, 1649), in which Sir Francis refers to the projector, Engine, as "one that liues like a moth upon the comon wealth" (32).

28. On Charles I's scandalous associations with project culture, see the anonymous *Stage-Players Complaint*, in which one player proclaims, "For Monopolers are down, Projectors are down, the High Commission Court is down, the Star-chamber is down, and (some think) Bishops will down; and why should we then that are far inferior to any of those not justly fear least we should be down too?" (London: Thomas Bates, 1641), 4. Projects, along with monopolies, the Star Chamber, and William Laud synechdochize Charles I's abuse of royal prerogative and embattled authority.

29. John Taylor, *The Complaint of M. Tenter-Hooke the Projector* (London: Francis Coles, 1641).

30. *Projectors Downfall*, A1r.

31. Brugis, *Discovery of a Proiector*, B2r.

32. Ibid.

33. Heywood, *Hogs Character*, 2.

34. Ibid., 2.

35. *Discovery of a Proiector*, 12.

36. Ibid., 3.

37. Brugis also describes the projector as pathologically restless, likening projects to contractions of the human colon: "Feeling a consumptive weaknesse in his Shop and Warehouse, and continuall most terrible Convulsions in his Counterbox, he began most grievously to complaine, and cry out of the Collick, suddenly expecting an Eruption" (*Discovery of a Proiector*, 7). By contrast, Thomas Herbert's *Newes Out of Islington* (London: [s.n.], 1641), features one "honest clod the plough-man" who resists a "navish projector," attempts to lure him from the fields: "no indeed Mr. Projector, I had rather work with my plow at home then to play at hazard abroad" (7).

38. *Hogs Character*, 3.

39. Ibid.

40. Henry Stubbe, *Legends, No Histories: A Specimen of Some Animadversions upon the History of the Royal Society* (London: [s.n.], 1670), 36, 42.

41. John Wilson, *The Projectors* (London: John Playfere, 1665), 38, 21. On satirical responses to the *Transactions* by William King, Charles Hanbury Williams, and others, see Barbara Benedict, "Collecting Trouble: Sir Hans Sloane's Literary Reputation in Eighteenth-Century Britain," *Eighteenth-Century Life* 36.2 (2012), 111–42, and T. Christopher Bond, "Keeping Up with the Latest Transactions," *Eighteenth-Century Life* 22.2 (1998), 1–17.

42. So regularly was the Royal Society accused of projection that Thomas Sprat answered the charge directly in his *History of the Royal Society of London* (London: J. Martyn and J. Allestry, 1667). Sprat specifically repudiates his institution's detractors for failing to recognize how their respective trades rely on scientific innovation: "The little *Tradesmen*, conspire against [inventors],

and indeavor to stop the Springs whence they themselves receive nourishment: The common titles with which they are wont to be defam'd are those of *Cheats* and *Projectors*" (402).

43. *Angliae Tutamen*, 19, 4. *Exchange-Alley; or, The Stock-Jobber Turn'd a Gentleman* (London: T. Bickerton, 1720), 5. Dedicated to the "Gentlemen daily attending at Jonathan's *Coffee-House*," *Exchange* depicts the adventures of a projector named Bubble, whose many schemes include the construction of flying ships, insurance against cuckoldry, and a patent "to shew Bears, Monkies, and Monsters" (14–15). On the abandonment of steady jobs to pursue projects, see also *A Letter to a Livery-Man, Occasion'd by His Commencing Projector* (London: Author, 1737), in which the author chastises a member of his company who "left the City behind you and run headlong into Measures you had no Business with" (4). For the rare example of a work in which a tradesman's transformation into projector yields positive consequences, see Barnaby Slush, *The Navy Royal; or, A Sea-Cook Turn'd Projector* (London: B. Bragge, 1709). Slush describes himself as "quitting his Nets, and the catching of Souls, and fell strait upon Angling for Projects" and then uses his experience as a low-ranking seaman to propose sensible reforms from below (A2v).

44. (Dublin: [s.n.], 1722), 12.

45. Ibid., 5.

46. Ibid., 11.

47. Jonathan Swift, *Gulliver's Travels*, ed. Albert J. Rivero (New York: W. W. Norton, 2000), 151.

48. "Jonathan Swift," 456.

49. *Gulliver's Travels*, 15.

50. Ibid.

51. Ibid., 16.

52. Ibid., 42.

53. Ibid., 60.

54. Ibid., 100.

55. Ibid., 116.

56. Ibid., 111, 112.

57. Ibid., 113.

58. Ibid., 147, 148.

59. Ibid.

60. Ibid., 134.

61. Ibid., 149.

62. Ibid.

63. Ibid.

64. On Swift's orthographic rendering of this term, see Martin Gierl, "Science, Projects, Computers, and the State: Swift's Lagadian and Leibniz's Prussian Academy," in *The Age of Projects*, ed. Maximillian E. Novak (Toronto: University of Toronto Press, 2008), 302.

65. *Gulliver's Travels*, 150.

66. Ibid.

67. Ibid.

68. James Scott, *Seeing Like a State: How Certain Schemes to Improve the Human Condition Have Failed* (New Haven, Conn.: Yale University Press, 1998).

69. *Gulliver's Travels*, 138.

70. Ibid., 152, 158.

71. Joad Raymond, *Pamphlets and Pamphleteering in Early Modern Britain* (Cambridge: Cambridge University Press, 2006), 54. *Gulliver's Travels*, 152, 163.

72. *Gulliver's Travels*, 161, 162.

73. Ibid., 157.

74. Ibid.

75. Ibid., 154.

76. Ibid., 155.

77. Ibid., 158.

78. Ibid., 151.

79. Ibid., 152.

80. Ibid.

81. Marjorie Nicolson and Nora M. Mohler identify two specific sources for the cucumber project: correspondence printed in the *Philosophical Transactions* on the respiration of plants and Thomas Shadwell's 1678 theatrical comedy *The Virtuoso*. Swift, they imply, was familiar with both project writing and *The Virtuoso*, a play that mocked the Royal Society through its depiction of a deranged scientist who contrived to store country air in vials that could be sold throughout London's underventilated wards. "Scientific Background," 301.

82. Robert Phiddian argues that Swift "calls up styles of language without fully or sincerely inhabiting them," in prose that grants these idioms "a sort of life, but sounds their hollowness at the same time." "A Hopeless Project: Gulliver Inside the Language of Science in Book III," *Eighteenth-Century Life* 22.1 (1998), 51. Peter Briggs suggests that Swift's occupation and evacuation of established modes of discourse imply a commitment to the possibilities of those rhetorics. "Parody," Briggs contends, "succeeds by establishing a recognizable kinship with an earlier work, and because kinship implies a relationship that necessarily runs both ways, parodies can never stand chastely apart from their sources, nor can parodists themselves ever be wholly disengaged from those whom they imitate, whether knaves or fools, enthusiasts or dreamers." Peter Briggs, "John Graunt, Sir William Petty, and Swift's *Modest Proposal*," *Eighteenth-Century Life* 29.2 (2005), 4.

83. Here, I am extending Jessica Ratcliff's observation that antiprojectors used literary invention to "question rhetorics that presented innovation as progress, and progress as apolitical," by suggesting that such questions arise in Swift's satire when a project's language and action are made simultaneous. "Art to Cheat the Common-Weale: Inventors, Projectors, and Patentees in English Satire, ca. 1630–70," *Technology and Culture* 53.2 (2012), 356.

84. *Gulliver's Travels*, 151.

85. Ibid., 153.

86. Ibid., 160.

87. Mary Poovey, *A History of the Modern Fact: Problems of Knowledge in the Sciences of Wealth and Society* (Chicago: University of Chicago Press, 1998), xii. Poovey, like Swift, is attentive to the axis between epistemology and statecraft in the seventeenth century, when "knowledge-making projects" were being presented "as an aid to—or even a mode of—effective state rule" (2).

88. Ibid., 1.

89. On the nineteenth-century "erosion of determinism" and rise of probability as a dominant epistemology, see Ian Hacking, *The Taming of Chance* (Cambridge: Cambridge University Press, 1990).

90. *Project for the Advancement of Religion*, 7.

91. *Gulliver's Travels*, 150.

92. *Jonathan Swift*, 213.

93. Samuel Fortrey, *England's Interest and Improvement* (Cambridge: John Field, 1663), 5-6, 12.

94. John Smith, *England's Improvement Reviv'd* (London: John Smith, 1670), A3v.

95. John Houghton, *Proposal for Improvement of Husbandry and Trade* (London: [s.n.], 1691), 1. Many more examples of this construction abound. T. Langford assures readers that "if he can get ripe Seeds . . . he need not doubt the success" in *Plain and Full Instruction to Raise All Sorts of Fruit-Trees* (London: Robert Chiswell, 1681), 20. Humphrey Mackworth boasts, "Doubtless we may aggrandize our Trade" if readers put into practice his idea for establishing a bank, in *England's Glory, by a Royal Bank* (London: Thomas Bever, 1694), A2v.

96. *Gulliver's*, 151.

97. Ibid., 154.

98. *Project for the Advancement of Religion*, 7.

99. *Gulliver's*, 154.

100. Samantha Heller, "Poets and Projectors: Profit, Production, and Economic Paradigms in Early Modern England," PhD diss., Columbia University, 1999, 7.

101. Carew Reynell, *The True English Interest; or, An Account of the Chief National Improvements* (London: Giles Widdowes, 1674), A4r.

102. Ibid., A6v.

103. Ibid., 51.

104. Chancellor, "Reynell, Carew (1636–1690)," *Oxford Dictionary of National Biography*, ed. Lawrence Goldman (Oxford: Oxford University Press, 2004). In a similar vein, Nicholas Barbon's 1685 *Apology for the Builder* lobbies for a relaxation of ordinances and attitudes constraining the growth of London. He answers the "fears and false conceptions" of rural landholders who worried that an expanding metropolis would drain the countryside of cheap labor by claiming that "the Builder ought to be encouraged in all Nations as the chief promoter of their Welfare." *Apology* does not disclose that Barbon sold fire insurance and understood how a larger London would generate greater policy sales. Nicholas Barbon, *Apology for the Builder* (London: Cave Pullen, 1685), 3.

105. Defoe, *Essay upon Projects*, ed. Joyce Kennedy, Michael Seidel, and Maximillian Novak. (New York: AMS, 1999), 9.

106. *Gulliver's Travels*, 151.

107. Ibid., 155.

108. Ibid., 157.

109. Ibid., 160.

110. Apletre, *Proposals for an Undertaking to Manage and Produce Raw-Silk . . . Pursuant to a Patent Granted to John Apletre, Esq: Under the Great Seal of England* (London: [s.n.], 1718), 3, 4.

111. Monsieur Bon, "A Discourse upon the Usefulness of the Silk of Spiders," *Philosophical Transactions of the Royal Society* 27 (1710–12), 6.

112. *English Improver Improved; or, The Survey of Husbandry Surveyed* (London: John Wright, 1653), 144.

113. Yarranton, *England's Improvement by Sea and Land* (London: R. Everingham, 1677), 195.

114. *An Impartial Account of the Nature, Benefit, and Design, of a New Discovery, and Undertaking, to Make a Pure Sweet, and Wholesome Oil, from the Fruit of the Beech Tree* (London: [s.n.], 1714), 7.

115. *Gulliver's Travels*, 152.

116. Ibid., 151n6.

117. Ibid., 220.

118. Ibid., 246.

119. Ibid., 257.

120. Ibid.

121. Swift almost certainly had in mind William Petty's *The Political Anatomy of Ireland* (1691), which proposed a "new Settlement in IRELAND" and "the Re-establishment of that Kingdom," as if no society existed there prior to this projection (London: D. Brown and W. Rogers, 1691), A3r. The modest proposer also targets the political arithmetic performed in works like John Graunt's *Natural and Political Observations Made upon the Bills of Mortality* (London: John Martin, James Allestry, and Thomas Dicas, 1662) and Gregory King's 1696 manuscript "Natural and Political Observations and Conclusions upon the State and Condition of England" in *Two Tracts by Gregory King*, ed. George Ernest Barnett, 12-56 (Baltimore: Johns Hopkins University Press, 1936). The dubious data claims, assumptions, and extrapolations made in these tracts "might allow a thinker to pursue a train of ideas into absurdity without quite noticing" according to Briggs in "John Graunt," 11. See also Louis Landa's claim that Swift sought "to put the onus on England of vitiating the working of natural economic law in Ireland by denying Irishmen 'the same natural rights common to the rest of mankind.'" "'A Modest Proposal' and Populousness," *Modern Philology* 40.2 (1942), 165.

122. *The Essential Writings of Jonathan Swift*, ed. Claude Rawson and Ian Higgins (New York: W. W. Norton, 2010), 297.

123. Ibid., 295.

124. Ibid., 296.

125. Ibid., 298.

126. Ibid.

127. *A Proposal for Giving Badges to the Beggars in All the Parishes in Dublin* (Dublin: George Faulkner, 1737), 14.

128. Ibid., 16.

129. *The Author's Works: Collected and Revised by Deane Swift, Esq. of Goodrich, in Herefordshire*, vol. 12 (Dublin: George Faulkner, 1765), 251–262.

130. Ibid., 261.

131. Swift's legacy of projection would extend beyond his death. He reserved a portion of his estate for purchasing land around Dublin to establish St. Patrick's Hospital for the "reception of as many idiots and lunaticks as the annual income of the said lands and worldly substance shall be sufficient to maintain." "Dr. Swift's Will," in *The Prose Works of Jonathan Swift*, vol. 6, ed. Temple Scott (London: George Bell and Son, 1907), 407. Whereas *Gulliver's Travels* presents an asylum of projectors, the will commits securing that institution's future in Ireland.

132. Two 1733 ballads, *The Projector in the Dumps* (London: [s.n.], 1733) and *The Projector's Looking-Glass* (London: T. Jonas, 1733), criticize Robert Walpole's disastrous attempt to levy new duties on tobacco and wine in order to reduce land taxes on rural nobility, an act that precipitated the Excise Crisis. Another work, James Puckle's *The Club*, first published in 1711 and recirculated through subsequent editions in 1713, 1721, 1723, and 1733, portrays the projector as someone who "made Ropes of Sand, built Castles in the Air, and talk'd as if capable of benefiting Mankind more than the Invention of Spectacles, tho' never yet oblig'd the World with any Thing so useful as a Mouse-Trap." *The Club; In a Dialogue Between Father and Son* (London: James Puckle, 1713), 33. See also William Hunt's unproduced play *The Projectors: A Comedy* (London: T. Cooper, 1737), which features a host of poor inventors named Drainwell, Sir Richard Landless, Air-castle, Shirtless, Machine, Sly, Tarrier, and Principle. This play was "intended to be acted at one of the theatres." Hunt promises in the prologue to expose "a Group of Figures to the Stage are new / Yet

to keen Satyr's Lash who've long been due," apparently unaware of England's long dramatic tradition of project parody. *The Projectors: A Comedy* (London: T. Cooper, 1737), A4r.

1. *A Tour thro' the Whole Island of Great Britain, Divided into Circuits or Journies*, vol. 1, letter 3 (London: G. Strahan, 1724), 47.

2. Ibid., 56.

3. *The Making of the English Working Class* (New York: Pantheon Books, 1964), 12.

4. Catherine Gallagher and Stephen Greenblatt, *Practicing New Historicism* (Chicago: University of Chicago Press, 2000), 16.

5. Philip Otterness shows that more than half of the so-called Palatines "came from principalities outside the control of the Palatine elector." *Becoming German: The 1709 Palatine Migration to New York* (Ithaca, N.Y.: Cornell University Press, 2004), 9.

6. For a complete account of the Palatine migration to England, see ibid., 7–57.

7. 7 Anne c. 5.

8. Hopeful German émigrés could also look to the example of a smaller Palatine migration that came to England in the summer of 1708 and received "generous treatment" from the Board of Trade. See Walter Allen Knittle, *Early Eighteenth-Century Palatine Emigration* (Philadelphia: Dorrance, 1937), xiii, 32–46.

9. Francis Hare, *The Reception of the Palatines Vindicated: In a Fifth Letter to a Tory Member* (London: [s.n.], 1711), 4.

10. *The Palatines Catechism; or, A True Description of Their Camps at Black-Heath and Camberwell. In a Pleasant Dialogue Between an English Tradesman and a High-Dutchman* (London: T. Hare, 1709), 4.

11. For summaries of these plans and others, see Knittle, *Early Eighteenth-Century Palatine Emigration*, 72–81.

12. *Defoe's Review*, vol. 6, ed. Arthur Wellesley Secord (New York: Columbia University Press, 1938), 154.

13. *A Brief History of the Poor Palatine Refugees Lately Arriv'd in England* (London: [s.n.], 1709), 42. For Defoe's dismissal of plans to send Palatines abroad, see 36–42.

14. *Defoe's Review*, vol. 6, 135. Defoe's diction echoes the preamble to the Naturalization Act of 1708, which asserts that "the increase of people is a means of advancing the wealth and strength of a nation" (7 Anne c. 5).

15. *Defoe's Review*, vol. 6, 149.

16. *Brief History*, 9.

17. *Defoe's Review*, vol. 6, 154.

18. Ibid., 158.

19. Defoe may have had the New Forest in mind when he lamented "how many parts of the World which have been peopled and planted, cultivated and improv'd have, by the fate of Nations been again laid wast, and have return'd to their primitive, undiscovered State," in *A General History of Discoveries and Improvements in Useful Arts* even though he drew his main examples from Greek, Asian, and Carthaginian culture. (London: J. Roberts, 1725–26), vi.

20. *Defoe's Review*, 150. Defoe published his satirical poem *The True Borne Englishman* in 1701.

21. Vittoria Di Palma, *Wasteland: A History* (New Haven, Conn.: Yale University Press, 2014), 178.

22. C. J. Cornish, *The New Forest* (New York: Macmillan, 1894), 7.

23. *Journal of the Commissioners for Trade and Plantations from February 1708–9 to March 1714–5 Preserved in the Public Record Office* (London: Her Britannic Majesty's Stationery Office, 1925), 39.

24. *Defoe's Review*, 154.

25. John Wise, *The New Forest: Its History and Its Scenery* (London: Smith, Elder & Company, 1863), 29.

26. A doggerel satire accused Defoe of trespassing on "Dominion; A sacred Thing no Pow'r could alter," including, presumably, the sacred power of the crown. See *Canary-Birds Naturaliz'd in Utopia: A Canto* (London: [s.n.], 1709), 9.

27. Otterness, *Becoming German*, 45.

28. Wise argues that historians of the New Forest have erred in attributing to William "one of the worst pieces of cruelty ever committed by an English sovereign" by wrongly presuming that "afforestation" meant that "villages were destroyed and inhabitants banished, or according to others, murdered." *New Forest*, 21, 26.

29. On August 24, the Board of Trade reported that it "took into consideration the settling of some Palatines upon Hudson's River at New York, and agreed upon several heads, and gave directions for preparing the draught of a letter to the Lord High Treasurer thereupon." *Journal of the Commissioners*, 65.

30. See chapter 5 of Otterness, *Becoming German*, "They Will Not Listen to Tar Making," 89–112.

31. *Tour*, vol. 1, iii.

32. Ibid., iv.

33. "Literary Art in Defoe's Tour: The Rhetoric of Growth and Decay," *Eighteenth-Century Studies* 6.2 (1972–73), 174.

34. *Tour*, vol. 2, v.

35. Ibid., vol. 1, viii.

36. Ibid., vi.

37. Ibid., letter 3, 47.

38. *Defoe's Review*, 138.

39. *Tour*, letter 3, 48.

40. Ibid., 48, 49, 50.

41. Ibid., 49.

42. Ibid., 150.

43. Ibid., 56.

44. Ibid.

45. See, for example, *An Essay upon Projects*, ed. Joyce Kennedy, Michael Seidel, and Maximillian Novak (New York: AMS, 1999), 10.

46. *Tour* makes several suggestions for improving Britain. In his London circuit, Defoe lists three "projects" that could benefit the metropolis: one for constructing a new bridge over the Thames, another for consolidating Southwark into the City, and a third for regulating the outgrowth of urban neighborhoods. The implication is that London will not only expand but advance through these designs and others. See vol. 2, letter 5, 119.

47. *Practicing*, 28.

48. *Essay upon Projects*, 7.

49. Ibid., 13.

50. Partial renditions of the Babel myth abound in English literature and art. William Wordsworth's "Michael: A Pastoral Poem" (1800) "appertains" to the site of an unfinished sheepfold; the preacher Edward Casaubon obsesses over his incomplete monograph "The Key to All Mythologies," in George Eliot's *Middlemarch* (1874); Keats found "unheard melodies" sweeter in "Ode on a Grecian Urn" (1820); the eighteenth-century painter Joseph Michael Gandy envisioned immense but collapsing edifices for banks and other institutions that were never meant to be built; the theoretical provocations of Italo Calvino's *Invisible Cities* (1972) underscores the literary possibilities of unexecutable plans; and more recently, the theme of the unbuilt has spurred a cottage industry of coffee-table books and gallery exhibitions. See Daniel M. Abramson, "Stakes of the Unbuilt," *Aggregate Architectural History Collaborative*, accessed January 16, 2017, http://weaggregate.org/piece/stakes-of-the-unbuilt.

51. *A Designe for Plentie, by an Universall Planting of Fruit-Trees* (London: Richard Wodenothe, 1652), 3.

Bibliography

Abramson, Daniel M. "Stakes of the Unbuilt." *Aggregate Architectural History Collaborative.* Accessed January 16, 2017. http://weaggregate.org/piece/stakes-of-the-unbuilt.

"An Account of Three Books." *Philosophical Transactions of the Royal Society* 11 (1676): 790–98.

Adams, John, and Gwen Averley. "The Patent Specification: The Role of Liardet v. Johnson." *Journal of Legal History* 7.2 (1986): 156–77.

Agamben, Giorgio. "On Potentiality." In *Potentialities: Collected Essays in Philosophy*, ed. Daniel Heller-Roazen, 177–85. Stanford, Calif.: Stanford University Press, 1999.

Aikin, John. *An Essay on the Application of Natural History to Poetry.* London: J. Johnson, 1777.

Albright Knittl, Margaret. "The Design for the Initial Drainage of the Great Level of the Fens: An Historical Whodunit in Three Parts." *Agricultural History Review* 55.1 (2007): 23–50.

A.M. *Thoughts of a Project for Draining the Irish Channel.* Dublin: [s.n.], 1722.

Anderson, Adam. *Historical and Chronological Deduction of the Origin of Commerce.* 4 vols. London: J. Robson and W. Clarke, 1787.

Angliae Tutamen; or, The Safety of England. London: [s.n.], 1695.

The Anti-Projector. London: [s.n.], 1646.

Apletre, John. *Proposals for an Undertaking to Manage and Produce Raw-Silk . . . Pursuant to a Patent Granted to John Apletre, Esq: Under the Great Seal of England.* London: [s.n.], 1718.

Appleby, Joyce. *Economic Thought and Ideology in Seventeenth-Century England.* Princeton, N.J.: Princeton University Press, 1978.

Armstrong, John. *The Art of Preserving Health: A Poem.* London: John Smith, 1744.

Ash, Eric. "Amending Nature; Draining the English Fens." In *The Mindful Hand: Inquiry and Invention from the Late Renaissance to Early Industrialisation*, ed. Lissa Roberts, Simon Schaffer, and Peter Dear, 117–43. Amsterdam: Edita, 2007.

———. *The Draining of the Fens: Projectors, Popular Politics, and State Building in Early Modern England.* Baltimore: Johns Hopkins University Press, 2017.

Ashton, T. H. *An Economic History of England: The Eighteenth Century.* Abingdon, Oxfordshire: Routledge, 2006.

Astell, Mary. *Serious Proposal to the Ladies.* London: R. Wilkin, 1694.

Aubrey, John. *Aubrey's Brief Lives*, ed. Andrew Clark. London: Henry Frowde, 1898.

Auricchio, Laura, Elizabeth Heckendorn Cook, and Giulia Pacini. "Introduction: Invaluable Trees." In *Invaluable Trees: Cultures of Nature, 1660–1830*, ed. Laura Auricchio, Elizabeth Heckendorn Cook, and Giulia Pacini, 1–21. Oxford: Voltaire Foundation, 2012.

Austen, Jane. *Mansfield Park*, ed. Kathryn Sunderland. New York: Penguin Books, 2003.

Austen, Ralph. *A Treatise of Fruit-Trees Shewing the Manner of Grafting, Setting, Pruning, and Ordering of Them in All Respects.* Oxford: William Hall, 1665.

Badeslade, Thomas. *The History of the Ancient and Present State of the Navigation of the Port of King's-Lyn, and of Cambridge*. London: Thomas Badeslade, 1725.

———. *A Scheme for Draining the Great Level of the Fens*. London: J. Roberts, 1729.

Baker, Samuel. "The Maritime Georgic and the Lake Poet Empire of Georgic." *ELH* 75.3 (Fall 2008): 531–63.

Barbon, Nicholas. *Apology for the Builder*. London: Cave Pullen, 1685.

———. *A Discourse of Trade*. London: Nicholas Barbon, 1690.

Barker, Jane. *The Galesia Trilogy and Selected Manuscript Poems of Jane Barker*, ed. Carol Shiner Wilson. New York: Oxford University Press, 1997.

Barrell, John. *English Literature in History 1730–80: An Equal, Wide Survey*. New York: St. Martin's, 1983.

Baston, Thomas. *Thoughts on a Trade, and Public Spirit*. London: Thomas Baston, 1716.

Bataille, Georges. *Inner Experience*, trans. Leslie Ann Boldt. Albany: State University of New York Press, 1988.

Baxter, Peter. "The East Coast Big Flood, 31 January–1 February 1953: A Summary of the Human Disaster." *Philosophical Transactions of the Royal Society* 363 (2005): 1293–312.

Beale, John. *Herefordshire Orchards, a Pattern for All England: Written in an Epistolary Address to Samuel Hartlib, Esq*. London: [s.n.], 1657.

Bedford, William. *A Particular of the Ninety Five Thousand Acres*. London: Richard Baddeley, 1653.

Behn, Aphra. *The Rover*. In *The Broadview Anthology of Restoration and Early-Eighteenth Century Drama*, ed. Douglas Canfield, 590–645. Toronto: Broadview, 2001.

Benedict, Barbara. "Collecting Trouble: Sir Hans Sloane's Literary Reputation in Eighteenth-Century Britain." *Eighteenth-Century Life* 36.2 (2012): 111–42.

Benjamin, Walter. *The Arcades Project*, trans. Howard Eiland and Kevin McLaughlin. Cambridge, Mass.: Belknap Press of Harvard University Press, 2002.

———. *Selected Works*, 4 vols., trans. Michael W. Eiland. Cambridge, Mass.: Harvard University Press, 2006.

Bentham, Jeremy. *Defence of Usury*. London: T. Payne, and Son, 1787.

Berg, Maxine. "From Imitation to Invention: Creating Commodities in Eighteenth-Century Britain." *Economic History Review* 55.1 (2002): 1–30.

———. "In Pursuit of Luxury: Global History and British Consumer Goods in the Eighteenth Century." *Past and Present* 182.1 (2004): 85–142.

Bernstein, Michael Andrew. *Foregone Conclusions: Against Apocalyptic History*. Berkeley: University of California Press, 1994.

Blanch, John. *Interest of England Considered*. London: Walter Kettilby, 1694.

Blith, Walter. *The English Improver Improved; or, The Survey of Husbandry Surveyed*. London: John Wright, 1652.

———. *The English Improver Improved; or, The Survey of Husbandry Surveyed*. London: John Wright, 1653.

Bon, Monsieur. "A Discourse upon the Usefulness of the Silk of Spiders." *Philosophical Transactions of the Royal Society* 27 (1710–12): 2–16.

Bond, T. Christopher. "Keeping Up with the Latest Transactions." *Eighteenth-Century Life* 22.2 (1998): 1–17.

Bowers, Toni. *Force or Fraud: British Seduction Stories and the Problem of Resistance 1660–1760*. Oxford: Oxford University Press, 2011.

Bowring, Julie. "Between the Corporation and Captain Flood: The Fens and Drainage after

1663." In *Custom, Improvement and the Landscape in Early Modern Britain*, ed. Richard Hoyle, 235–62. Burlington, Vt.: Ashgate, 2011.

———. "Exploring Landscape and Livelihood: The Bedford Level Corporation Collection and the Great Level of the Fens." In *Drowned and Drained: Exploring Fenland Records and Landscape*, ed. Susan Oosthuizen and Frances Willmoth, 29–34. Cambridge: Institute of Continuing Education, University of Cambridge, 2009.

Boyle, Frank. *Swift as Nemesis: Modernity and Its Satirist.* Stanford, Calif.: Stanford University Press, 2000.

Boyle, Robert. *Some Considerations Touching the Vsefulnesse of Experimental Naturall Philosophy Propos'd in Familiar Discourses to a Friend, by Way of Invitation to the Study of It.* Oxford: Richard Davis, 1663.

Bradley, Richard. *The Riches of a Hop-Garden Explain'd.* London: Charles Davis, 1729.

Breward, Christopher. *The Culture of Fashion: A New History of Fashionable Dress.* Manchester: Manchester University Press, 1995.

Brewer, John. *The Sinews of Power: War, Money, and the English State, 1688–1783.* Cambridge, Mass.: Harvard University Press, 1990.

Brewster, Dorothy. *Aaron Hill: Poet, Dramatist, Projector.* New York: AMS, 1913.

Briggs, Peter. "John Graunt, Sir William Petty, and Swift's *Modest Proposal.*" *Eighteenth-Century Life* 29.2 (2005): 3–24.

Broadway, Jan. "'A True and Perfect Plot.'" In *Drowned and Drained: Exploring Fenland Records and Landscape*, ed. Susan Oosthuizen and Frances Willmoth, 21–26. Cambridge: Institute of Continuing Education, University of Cambridge, 2009.

Brome, Richard. *The Court Beggar.* London: Richard Marriot and Thomas Dring, 1653.

Brown, Laura. *Fables of Modernity: Literature and Culture in the English Eighteenth Century.* Ithaca, N.Y.: Cornell University Press, 2001.

Brugis, Thomas. *The Discovery of a Proiector: Showing the Beginning, Progresse, and End of the Projector and His Projects.* London: [s.n.], 1641.

Bucknell, Clare. "The Mid-Eighteenth-Century Georgic and Agricultural Improvement." *Journal for Eighteenth-Century Studies* 36.3 (2013): 335–52.

Bullard, Paddy. "Pride, Pulpit, Eloquence, and the Rhetoric of Jonathan Swift." *Rhetorica* 30 (2012): 232–55.

Burrell, Andrews. *Brief Relation Discovering Plainely the True Causes Why the Great Levell of Fenns . . . Have Been Drowned and Made Unfruitfull for Many Yeares Past.* London: Francis Constable 1642.

———. *Exceptions Against Sir Cornelius Virmudens Discourse.* London: Robert Constable, 1642.

———. *An Explanation of the Drayning Workes vvhich have beene Lately Made for the Kings Maiestie.* London: [s.n.], 1641.

Butterfield, Herbert. *The Whig Interpretation of History.* New York: W. W. Norton, 1965.

Calendar of State Papers: Domestic Series, 1660–61. London: H. M. Stationery Office, 1860–1949.

Canary-Birds Naturaliz'd in Utopia: A Canto, London: [s.n.], 1709.

Carter, William. *England's Interest Asserted.* London: Francis Smith, 1669.

———. *The Case of the New Project for Bringing Water to London and Westminster, Considered.* London: [s.n.], 1725.

Cavendish, William. *The Country Captaine.* London: Humphrey Robinson, 1649.

Chalmers, Alan. *Jonathan Swift and the Burden of the Future.* Newark: University of Delaware Press, 1995.

Chancellor, V. E. "Reynell, Carew (1636–1690)." In *Oxford Dictionary of National Biography*, online ed., ed. Lawrence Goldman. Oxford: Oxford University Press, 2004.

Clarke, Ernest. "Yarranton, Andrew (1619–1684)," rev. P. W. King. In *Oxford Dictionary of National Biography*, ed. Lawrence Goldman. Oxford: Oxford University Press, 2008.

Cleland, Jonathan. *Fanny Hill; or, Memoirs of a Woman of Pleasure*, ed. Peter Wagner. New York: Penguin Books, 1985.

Clipsam, Robert. *The Grant Expedient for Suppressing Popery Examined; or The Project of Exclusion Proved to be Contrary to Reason and Religion*. London: William Freeman, 1685.

Codr, Dwight. *Raving at Usurers*. Charlottesville: University of Virginia Press, 2016.

A Coffee-House Dialogue; or, A Discourse Between Captain Y—— and a Young Barrester of the Middle Temple. [s.l.]: [s.n.], 1679.

The Coffee-House Dialogue Examined and Refuted. London: [s.n.], 1680.

Coke, Roger. *England's Improvements*. London: Henry Brome, 1675.

A Continuation of the Coffee-House Dialogue. London: [s.n.], 1680.

Cornish, C. J. *The New Forest*. New York: Macmillan, 1894.

Crawford, Rachel. "English Georgic and British Nationhood." *ELH* 65.1 (1998): 123–58.

———. "Forms of Sublimity: The Garden, the Georgic, and the Nation." In *A Concise Companion to the Restoration and Eighteenth Century*, ed. Cynthia Wall, 226–46. Malden, Mass.: Blackwell, 2005.

Damrosch, Leo. *Jonathan Swift: His Life and His World*. New Haven, Conn.: Yale University Press, 2013.

Darby, H. C. *The Changing Fenland*. Cambridge: Cambridge University Press, 1983.

———. *The Draining of the Fens*. Cambridge: Cambridge University Press, 1940.

Davenant, Charles. *An Account of the Trade Between Great-Britain, France, Holland, Spain, Portugal, Italy, Africa, Newfoundland*. London: A. Bell, W. Taylor, and J. Baker, 1715.

———. *An Essay upon Ways and Means of Supplying the War*. London: Jacob Tonson, 1695.

Davis, Lennard. *Factual Fictions: The Origins of the English Novel*. New York: Columbia University Press, 1983.

De Bruyn, Frans. "From Georgic Poetry to Statistics and Graphs: Eighteenth-Century Representations and the "State" of British Society." *Yale Journal of Criticism* 17.1 (2004): 107–39.

Defoe, Daniel. *A Brief History of the Poor Palatine Refugees Lately Arriv'd in England*. London: [s.n.], 1709.

———. *Defoe's Review*, vol. 6, ed. Arthur Wellesley Secord. New York: Columbia University Press, 1938.

———. *An Essay upon Projects*, ed. Joyce Kennedy, Michael Seidel, and Maximillian Novak. New York: AMS, 1999.

———. *A General History of Discoveries and Improvements in Useful Arts*. London: J. Roberts, 1725–26.

———. *A Journal of the Plague Year*, ed. Louis Landa. Oxford: Oxford University Press, 2010.

———. *Moll Flanders*, ed. G. A. Starr. Oxford: Oxford University Press, 1971.

———. *A Plan of the English Commerce*. London: Charles Rivington, 1728.

———. *Robinson Crusoe*, ed. Evan R. Davis. Toronto: Broadview, 2010.

———. *Roxana*, ed. John Mullan. Oxford: Oxford University Press, 1996.

———. *A Tour thro' the Whole Island of Great Britain, Divided into Circuits or Journies*, vol. 1. London: G. Strahan, 1724.

De Krey, Gary S. *Restoration and Revolution in Britain: A Political History of the Era of Charles II and the Glorious Revolution*. New York: Palgrave Macmillan, 2007.

A Designe for Plentie, by an Universall Planting of Fruit-Trees. London: Richard Wodenothe, 1652.

Di Palma, Vittoria. *Wasteland: A History.* New Haven, Conn.: Yale University Press, 2014.

Dodson, William. *The Designe for the Perfect Draining of the Great Level of the Fens.* London: [s.n.], 1665.

Doležel, Lubomir. *Heterocosmica: Fiction and Possible Worlds.* Baltimore: Johns Hopkins University Press, 2000.

Dove, Patrick Edward. *Account of Andrew Yarranton: The Founder of English Political Economy.* Edinburgh: Johnston and Hunter, 1854.

Dryden, John. *Annus Mirabilis.* London: Henry Herringman, 1667.

———. *Astraea Redux: A Poem on the Happy Restoration & Return of His Sacred Majesty Charles the Second.* London: Henry Herringman, 1660.

———. *The Works of Virgil Containing His Pastorals, Georgics and Aeneid: Adorn'd with a Hundred Sculptures.* London: Jacob Tonson, 1697.

Dugdale, William. *The History of Imbanking and Draining of Divers Fens and Marshes, Both in Foreign Parts and in This Kingdom, and of the Improvements Thereby.* London: [s.n.], 1662.

Dyer, John. *The Fleece: A Poem. In Four Books.* London: J. Dodsley, 1757.

———. *Poems.* London: R. and J. Dodsley, 1761.

Dymock, Cressy. *A Discoverie for Division or Setting Out of Land.* London: Richard Wodenothe, 1653.

Edgar, William. *Vectigalium Systema; or, A Complete View of that Part of the Revenue of Great Britain.* London: William Edgar, 1714.

Eniaytos Terastios Mirabilis Annus. London: [s.n.], 1661.

England's Improvements Justified. London: [s.n.], 1680.

"Enquiries Concerning Agriculture." *Philosophical Transactions of the Royal Society* 5 (1665): 91–94.

An Essay on the New Project for a Land-Mint. London: [s.n.], 1705.

Evelyn, John. *Pomona; or, An Appendix Concerning Fruit-Trees in Relation to Cider.* London: [s.n.], 1664.

———. *Sylva; or, A Discourse on Forest-Trees and the Propagation of Timber in His Majesty's Dominions.* London: Royal Society, 1664.

———. *Sylva, or A Discourse of Forest-Trees, and the Propagation of Timber in His Majesties Dominions.* London: Royal Society, 1670.

Exchange-Alley; or, The Stock-Jobber Turn'd a Gentleman. London: T. Bickerton, 1720.

The Eyes of Ireland Open: Being, a Short View of the Project for Establishing That Intended Bank of Ireland. London: J. Roberts, 1722.

Fabricant, Carole. "Geographical Projects in the Later Eighteenth Century: Imperial Myths and Realities." In *The Age of Projects,* ed. Max Novak, 318–43. Toronto: University of Toronto Press, 2008.

Fairer, David. " 'The Year Runs Round': The Poetry of Work in Eighteenth-Century England." In *Ritual, Routine, and Regime: Repetition in Early Modern British and European Cultures,* ed. Lorna Clymer, 153–71. Toronto: University of Toronto Press, 2006.

Feather, John. "The Commerce of Letters: The Study of the Eighteenth-Century Book Trade." *Eighteenth-Century Studies* 17.4 (1984): 405–24.

Feuerbach, Ludwig. *Essence of Christianity,* trans. Marian Evans. London: John Chapman, 1854.

Fielding, Henry. *The History of Tom Jones a Foundling,* ed. Fredson Bowers. Middletown, Conn.: Wesleyan University Press, 1975.

Flower, Philip William. *History of the Trade in Tin.* London: G. Bell and Sons, 1880.

Fortrey, Samuel. *England's Interest and Improvement*. Cambridge: John Field, 1663.

———. *The History or Narrative of the Great Level of the Fenns Called Bedford Level*. London: Moses Pitt, 1685.

Freud, Sigmund. *The Origins of Psycho-Analysis: Letters to Wilhelm Fliess, Drafts and Notes, 1887–1902*, trans. James Strachey. London: Imago, 1954.

F.S. *The Anatomy of a Project for Raising Two Millions*. London: [s.n.], 1698.

Funkenstein, Amos. *Theology and the Scientific Imagination from the Middle Ages to the Seventeenth Century*. Princeton, N.J.: Princeton University Press, 1986.

Gallagher, Catherine. "The Rise of Fictionality." In *The Novel*, vol. 1, *History, Geography, and Culture*, ed. Franco Moretti. Princeton, N.J.: Princeton University Press, 2006.

Gallagher, Catherine, and Stephen Greenblatt. *Practicing New Historicism*. Chicago: University of Chicago Press, 2000.

Gaskell, Philip. *A New Introduction to Bibliography*. New Castle, Del.: Oak Knoll, 1995.

Gay, John. *Rural Sports*. London: Jacob Tonson, 1713.

———. *Trivia; or, The Art of Walking the Streets of London*. London: Bernard Lintott, 1716.

Genovese, Michael. "An Organic Commerce: Sociable Selfhood in Eighteenth-Century Georgic." *Eighteenth-Century Studies* 46.2 (Winter 2013): 197–221.

Gentles, Ian. "The Management of the Crown Lands, 1649–60." *Agricultural History Review* 19.1 (1971): 25–41.

Gerrard, Christine. *Aaron Hill: The Muses' Projector, 1685–1750*. Oxford: Oxford University Press, 2003.

Gierl, Martin. "Science, Projects, Computers, and the State: Swift's Lagadian and Leibniz's Prussian Academy." In *The Age of Projects*, ed. Maximillian Novak, 297–317. Toronto: University of Toronto Press, 2008.

Gilmore, John. *The Poetics of Empire: A Study of James Grainger's* The Sugar Cane *(1764)*. London: Athlone, 2000.

Glanvill, Joseph. *Plus Ultra; or, The Progress and Advancement of Knowledge Since the Days of Aristotle*. London: Iames Collins, 1668.

Goodman, Kevis. *Georgic Modernity and British Romanticism: Poetry and the Mediation of History*. Cambridge: Cambridge University Press, 2004.

Goodridge, John. *Rural Life in Eighteenth-Century English Poetry*. Cambridge: Cambridge University Press, 1995.

Graunt, John. *Natural and Political Observations Mentioned in a Following Index, and Made upon the Bills of Mortality*. London: John Martin, James Allestry, and Thomas Dicas, 1665.

G.S. *Anglorum Speculum; or, The Worthies of England, in Church and State*. London: Thomas Passinger, 1684.

Hacking, Ian. *The Taming of Chance*. Cambridge: Cambridge University Press, 1990.

Haines, Richard. *Aphorisms upon the New Way of Improving Cyder, or Making Cyder-Royal*. London: Richard Haines, 1684.

Hale, Thomas. *An Account of Several New Inventions and Improvements Now Necessary for England*. London: James Astwood, 1691.

Hare, Francis. *The Reception of the Palatines Vindicated: In a Fifth Letter to a Tory Member*. London: [s.n.], 1711.

Harries, Walter. *An Enquiry into the Caledonian Project*. London: John Nutt, 1701.

Harris, Michael. "London Newspapers." In *The Cambridge History of the Book in Britain*, vol. 5, ed. Michael Suarez and Michael L. Turner, 413–33. Cambridge: Cambridge University Press, 2009.

Hartlib, Samuel. *The Compleat Husband-Man; or, A Discourse of the Whole Art of Husbandry.* London: [s.n.], 1659.

———. *Samuel Hartlib: His Legacy.* London: Richard Wodenothe, 1655.

Hawksmoor, Nicholas. *Remarks on the Founding and Carrying on the Buildings of the Royal Hospital at Greenwich.* London: [s.n.], 1728.

H.C. *A Discourse Concerning the Drayning of Fennes and Surrounded Grounds in the Six Counteys of Norfolke, Suffolke, Cambridge with the Isle of Ely, Huntington, Northampton, and Lincolne.* London: [s.n.], 1629.

Heidegger, Martin. *Being and Time*, trans. John Macquarrie and Edward Robinson. New York: Harper and Row, 1962.

Heinzelman, Kurt. "Roman Georgic in the Georgian Age: A Theory of Romantic Genre." *Texas Studies in Literature and Language* 33.2 (1991): 182–214.

Heller, Samantha. "Poets and Projectors: Profit, Production, and Economic Paradigms in Early Modern England." PhD diss., Columbia University, 1999.

Herbert, Thomas. *Newes Out of Islington.* London: [s.n.], 1641.

Hervey, John. *Some Materials Towards Memoirs of the Reign of King George II*, ed. R. Sedgwick, 3 vols. London: Eyre and Spottiswoode, 1931.

Heylyn, Peter. *Cosmographie in Four Books.* London: Ann Seile, 1669.

Heywood, Thomas. *Hogs Character of a Projector, Being a Relation of His Life and Death, with His Funerall.* London: [s.n.], 1642.

Hill, Aaron. *Account of the Rise and Progress of the Beech-Oil Invention.* London: [s.n.], 1715.

———. *The Dedication of the Beech-Tree.* London: John Morphew, 1714.

———. *The Fatal Extravagance.* London: T. Jauncy, 1721.

———. *An Impartial Account of the Nature, Benefit, and Design, of a New Discovery.* London: [s.n.], 1714.

———. *An Impartial State of the Case Between the Patentee, Annuitants, and Sharers, in the Beech-Oil Company.* London: Aaron Hill, 1716.

———. *Proposals for Raising a Stock of One Hundred Pounds; For Laying Up Great Quantities of Beech-Mast for Two Years.* London: [s.n.], 1714.

Hill, Christopher. *The Century of Revolution, 1603–1714.* New York: Routledge, 2002.

Holmes, Clive. "Drainers and Fenmen: The Problem of Popular Political Consciousness in the Seventeenth Century." In *Order and Disorder in Early Modern England*, ed. Anthony Fletcher and John Stevenson, 166–95. Cambridge: Cambridge University Press, 1985.

Houghton, John. *Husbandry and Trade Improv'd: Being a Collection of Many Valuable Materials Relating to Corn, Cattle, Coals, Hops, Wool, &c.*, vol. 4. London: Woodman and Lyon, 1727.

———. *Proposal for Improvement of Husbandry and Trade.* London: [s.n.], 1691.

Hume, David. *A Treatise of Human Nature*, ed. David Fate Norton and Mary J. Norton. New York: Oxford University Press, 2000.

Hunt, William. *The Projectors: A Comedy.* London: T. Cooper, 1737.

Hunter, Phyllis Whitman. *Purchasing Identity in the Atlantic World: Massachusetts Merchants, 1670–1780.* Ithaca, N.Y.: Cornell University Press, 2001.

Irvine, Robert P. "Labor and Commerce in Locke and Early Eighteenth-Century English Georgic." *ELH* 76.4 (Spring 2009), 963–88.

Jago, Richard. *Edge-Hill; or, The Rural Prospect Delineated and Moralized.* London: J. Dodsley, 1767.

James, Nicholas. "The 'Age of the Windmill' in the Haddenham Level." *Proceedings of the Cambridge Antiquarian Society* 98 (2009): 113–20.

———. "The Making of the Bedford Level: Archives and Archaeology." In *Drowned and Drained: Exploring Fenland Records and Landscape*, ed. Susan Oosthuizen and Frances Willmoth, 6–12. Cambridge: University of Cambridge Institute of Continuing Education, 2009.

Jardine, Lisa. *Ingenious Pursuits: Building the Scientific Revolution*. New York: First Anchor Books, 1999.

Johnson, Samuel. *An Account of the Life of Mr Richard Savage, Son of the Earl Rivers*. London: J. Roberts, 1744.

———. *Dictionary of the English Language*. London: J. and P. Knapton, T. and T. Longman, C. Hitch and L. Hawes, A. Millar, and R. and J. Dodsley, 1755.

———. *The Idler and the Adventurer*, ed. W. J. Bate, John Bullitt, and L. F. Powell. In *The Yale Edition of the Works of Samuel Johnson*, 18 vols. New Haven: Yale University Press, 1958–2005.

Jonson, Ben. *The Devil Is an Ass*. London: [s.n.], 1641.

Journal of the Commissioners for Trade and Plantations from February 1708–9 to March 1714–5 Preserved in the Public Record Office. London: Her Britannic Majesty's Stationery Office, 1925.

Kaul, Suvir. *Poems of Nation, Anthems of Empire: English Verse in the Long Eighteenth Century*. Charlottesville: University of Virginia Press, 2000.

Keller, Vera. *Knowledge and the Public Interest, 1575–1725*. Cambridge: Cambridge University Press, 2015.

King, Gregory. "Natural and Political Observations and Conclusions upon the State and Condition of England" in *Two Tracts by Gregory King*, ed. George Ernest Barnett. Baltimore: Johns Hopkins University Press, 1936.

Kirkwood, James. *A Copy of a Letter Anent a Project, for Erecting a Library, in Every Presbytery, or at Least Every County in the Highlands*. Edinburgh: [s.n.], 1702.

Kishik, David. *The Manhattan Project*. Stanford, Calif.: Stanford University Press, 2015.

Knittle, Walter Allen. *Early Eighteenth-Century Palatine Emigration*. Philadelphia: Dorrance, 1937.

Korthals-Altes, J. *Sir Cornelius Vermuyden*. New York: Arno, 1977.

Koselleck, Reinhart. *Futures Past: On the Semantics of Historical Time*, trans. Keith Tribe. New York: Columbia University Press, 2004.

Kramnick, Jonathan. *Actions and Objects from Hobbes to Richardson*. Stanford, Calif.: Stanford University Press, 2010.

Labelye, Charles. *The Result of a View of the Great Level of the Fens*. London: [s.n.], 1745.

Landa, Louis. "'A Modest Proposal' and Populousness." *Modern Philology* 40.2 (1942): 161–70.

Langford, T. *Plain and Full Instruction to Raise All Sorts of Fruit-Trees*. London: Robert Chiswell, 1681.

Latour, Bruno. *Aramis; or, The Love of Technology*, trans. Catherine Porter. Cambridge, Mass.: Harvard University Press, 1996.

Lawrence, Anthony. *Nurseries, Orchards, and Profitable Vineyards Encouraged*. London: Henry Brome, 1677.

Leaford, John. *Some Observations Made of the Frequent Drowned Condition of the South Level of the Fenns*. London: [s.n.], 1740.

Leslie, Michael. "The Spiritual Husbandry of John Beale." In *Culture and Cultivation in Early Modern England*, ed. Michael Leslie and Timothy Raylor, 151–72. Leicester: Leicester University Press, 1992.

A Letter to a Livery-Man, Occasion'd by His Commencing Projector. London: Author, 1737.

Lewis, M. J. T. *Early Wooden Railways*. London: Routledge and Kegan Paul, 1970.

L.G. *A Project, Humbly Offered to Both Houses of Parliament, for the Ready Raising of a Million*. London: L.G., 1693.

Lindley, Keith. *Fenland Riots and the English Revolution*. London: Heinemann Educational Books, 1982.

Little, Edward. *A Project of a Descent upon France*. London: Rich. Baldwin, 1691.

Low, Anthony. *The Georgic Revolution*. Princeton, N.J.: Princeton University Press, 1985.

Lupton, Christina. *Knowing Books: The Consciousness of Mediation in Eighteenth-Century Britain*. Philadelphia: University of Pennsylvania Press, 2011.

Macaulay, Thomas. *The History of England*, ed. Hugh Trevor-Roper. New York: Penguin Books, 1986.

Mackworth, Humphrey. *England's Glory, by a Royal Bank*. London: Thomas Bever, 1694.

MacLeod, Christine. "The 1690s Patents Boom: Invention or Stock-Jobbing?" *Economic History Review* 39.4 (1986): 549–71.

Macpherson, Sandra. *Harm's Way: Tragic Responsibility and the Novel Form*. Baltimore: Johns Hopkins University Press, 2010.

Mantoux, Paul. *The Industrial Revolution in the Eighteenth Century: An Outline of the Beginnings of the Modern Factory System in England*. Abingdon, Oxfordshire: Routledge, 2006.

Marvell, Andrew. *The Complete Poems*. London: Penguin Books, 2005.

Massinger, Philip. *The Emperour of the East*. London: Iohn Waterson, 1632.

Maurice, Henry. *Project for Repealing the Penal Laws and Tests*. London: [s.n.], 1688.

Maynard, John. *The Picklock of the Olde Fenne Project*. London: [s.n.], 1650.

McCusker, John. *Essays in the Economic History of the Atlantic World*. London: Routledge, 1997.

McKenzie, D. F. "'What's Past Is Prologue': The Bibliographical Society and History of the Book." In *Making Meaning: "Printers of the Mind" and Other Essays*, ed. Peter D. McDonald and Michael F. Suarez, 259–75. Amherst: University of Massachusetts Press, 2002.

McKeon, Michael. *The Origins of the English Novel, 1600–1740*. Baltimore: Johns Hopkins University Press, 1987.

———. *Theory of the Novel: A Historical Approach*, ed. Michael McKeon. Baltimore: Johns Hopkins University Press, 2000.

McRae, Andrew. "Husbandry Manuals and the Language of Agrarian Improvement." In *Culture and Cultivation in Early Modern England*, ed. Michael Leslie and Timothy Raylor, 35–62. Leicester, UK: Leicester University Press, 1992.

Milton, John. *John Milton: The Complete Poems*, ed. John Leonard. London: Penguin Books, 1998.

Mirabilis Annus Secundus; or, The Second Part of the Second Years Prodigies. London: [s.n.], 1662.

Mitchell, B. R. *Abstract of British Historical Statistics*. Cambridge: Cambridge University Press, 1962.

Moore, Sean. *Swift, the Book, and the Irish Financial Revolution: Satire and Sovereignty in Colonial Ireland*. Baltimore: Johns Hopkins University Press, 2010.

Morson, Gary Saul. *Narrative and Freedom: The Shadows of Time*. New Haven, Conn.: Yale University Press, 1994.

Mounsey, Chris. *Christopher Smart: Clown of God*. Lewisburg, Pa.: Bucknell University Press, 2001.

Myers, Joanne. "Defoe and the Project of 'Neighbours Fare.'" *Restoration: Studies in English Literary Culture, 1660–1700* 35.2 (2011): 1–19.

Nalson, John. *The Project of Peace*. London: Jonathan Edwin, 1678.

Nethersole, Francis. *A Project for an Equitable and Lasting Peace*. London: [s.n.], 1648.

A New Project to Make England a Florishing Kingdom. London: [s.n.], 1702.

Nicolson, Marjorie, and Nora M. Mohler. "The Scientific Background of Swift's 'Voyage to Laputa.'" *Annals of Science* 2 (1937): 299–334.

The Nevv Projector; or, The Privileged Cheat. London: William Gilbertson, 1662.

A New Project Humbly Offer'd to the Consideration to the Honourable House of Commons for the More Effectual Encouragement of a General Trade. London: [s.n.], 1695.

N.N. *A Narrative of All the Proceedings in the Drayning of the Great Level of the Fenns, Extending into the Counties of Northton: Lincoln, Norffolk, Suffolk, Cambridge, and Huntington, and the Isle of Ely; From the Time of Queen Elizabeth Untill This Present May, 1661.* London: N.N., 1661.

Novak, Maximillian. *Economics and the Fiction of Daniel Defoe.* Berkeley: University of California Press, 1963.

———. Introduction. In *The Age of Projects*, ed. Maximillian Novak, 3–29. Toronto: University of Toronto Press, 2008.

O'Brien, Karen. "Imperial Georgic, 1660–1789." In *The Country and the City Revisited: England the Politics of Culture, 1550–1850*, ed. Gerald MacLean, Donna Landry, and Joseph P. Ward, 160–79. Cambridge: Cambridge University Press, 1999.

Otterness, Philip. *Becoming German: The 1709 Palatine Migration to New York.* Ithaca, N.Y.: Cornell University Press, 2004.

Overton, Mark. *Agricultural Revolution in England: The Transformation of the Agrarian Economy 1500–1850.* Cambridge: Cambridge University Press, 1996.

The Palatines Catechism; or, A True Description of Their Camps at Black-Heath and Camberwell. In a Plesant Dialogue Between an English Tradesman and a High-Dutchman. London: T. Hare, 1709.

Palomo, Dolores. "The Dutch Connection: The University of Leiden and Swift's Academy of Lagado." *Huntington Library Quarterly* 41.1 (1977): 27–35.

Pasanek, Brad. *Metaphors of the Mind.* Baltimore: Johns Hopkins University Press, 2016.

Patey, Douglas Lane. "Swift's Satire on 'Science' and the Structure of *Gulliver's Travels*." *ELH* 58.4 (1991): 809–39.

Patterson, Annabel. *Censorship and Interpretation: The Conditions of Writing and Reading in Early Modern England.* Madison: University of Wisconsin Press, 1984.

———. "Dryden and Political Allegiance." In *The Cambridge Companion to John Dryden*, ed. Steven N. Zwicker, 221–37. Cambridge: Cambridge University Press, 2004.

———. "Hard Pastoral: Frost, Wordsworth, and Modernist Poetics." *Criticism* 29.1 (1987): 67–87.

Paulson, Ronald. *The Fictions of Satire.* Baltimore: Johns Hopkins University Press, 1967.

Pearl, Jason. *Utopian Geographies and the Early English Novel.* Charlottesville: University of Virginia Press, 2014.

Pellicer, Juan. "Georgic." In *A Companion to Eighteenth-Century Poetry*, ed. Christine Gerrard, 403–17. London: Wiley-Blackwell, 2006.

———. "John Philips (1676–1709): Life, Works, and Reception." PhD diss., University of Oslo, 2002.

Penn, William. *One Project for the Good of England.* Ware, London: Andrew Sowle, 1679.

Pepys, Samuel. *The Concise Pepys*, ed. Tom Griffith. Ware, Hertfordshire: Wordsworth Editions, 1997.

Petty, William. *The Political Anatomy of Ireland.* London: D. Brown and W. Rogers, 1691.

Phiddian, Robert. "A Hopeless Project: Gulliver Inside the Language of Science in Book III." *Eighteenth-Century Life* 22.1 (1998): 50–62.

Philips, John. *Cyder: A Poem. In Two Books.* London: H. Hills, 1708.

———. *The Poems of John Philips*, ed. Mary Gwyneth Lloyd Thomas. Oxford: Blackwell, 1927.

Picciotto, Joanna. *Labors of Innocence in Early Modern England*. Cambridge, Mass.: Harvard University Press, 2010.

Pitt, Moses. *England's Improvement Reviv'd*. London: Moses Pitt, 1670.

Plat, Hugh. *A Discouerie of Certaine English Wants*. London: William Ponsonby, 1595.

Pollock, Della. *Exceptional Spaces: Essays in Performance and History*. Chapel Hill: University of North Carolina Press, 1998.

Poovey, Mary. *Genres of the Credit Economy: Mediating Value in Eighteenth- and Nineteenth-Century Britain*. Chicago: University of Chicago Press, 2008.

———. *A History of the Modern Fact: Problems of Knowledge in the Sciences of Wealth and Society*. Chicago: University of Chicago Press, 1998.

Pope, Alexander. *The Dunciad, in Four Books*. London: M. Cooper, 1743.

———. *The Temple of Fame: A Vision*. London: Bernard Lintott, 1715.

———. *Windsor-Forest*. London: Bernard Lintott, 1713.

Povey, Charles. *The Unhappiness of England*. London: Charles Povey, 1701.

A Project for Establishing the General Peace of Europe. London: [s.n.], 1712.

The Projector in the Dumps. London: [s.n.], 1733.

The Projector's Looking-Glass. London: T. Jonas, 1733.

Projectors Downfall; or, Times Changeling. London: Thomas Paine, 1642.

Puckle, James. *The Club; In a Dialogue Between Father and Son*. London: James Puckle, 1713.

Ratcliff, Jessica. "Art to Cheat the Common-Weale: Inventors, Projectors, and Patentees in English Satire, ca. 1630–70." *Technology and Culture* 53.2 (2012): 337–65.

Raymond, Joad. *Pamphlets and Pamphleteering in Early Modern Britain*. Cambridge: Cambridge University Press, 2006.

Rees, Christine. *Utopian Imagination and Eighteenth-Century Fiction*. New York: Longman, 1996.

Reeves, Anne, and Tom Williamson. "Marshes." In *The English Rural Landscape*, ed. Joan Thirsk, 150–66. Oxford: Oxford University Press, 2000.

Remarques upon the New Project of Association. London: Walter Davis, 1682.

Reynell, Carew. *The True English Interest; or, An Account of the Chief National Improvements*. London: Giles Widdowes, 1674.

Richardson, Samuel. *Clarissa; or, The History of a Young Lady*, ed. Angus Ross. London: Penguin Books, 1985.

———. *Pamela; or, Virtue Rewarded*, ed. Thomas Keymer and Alice Wakely. Oxford: Oxford University Press, 2001.

Rivlin, Elizabeth. *The Aesthetics of Service in Early Modern England*. Evanston, Ill.: Northwestern University Press, 2012.

Roach, Joseph. *Cities of the Dead: Circum-Atlantic Performance*. New York: Columbia University Press, 1996.

Rogers, Pat. "Gulliver and the Engineers." *Modern Language Review* 70.2 (1975): 260–70.

———. "John Philips, Pope, and Political Georgic." *Modern Language Quarterly* 66.4 (2005): 411–42.

———. "Literary Art in Defoe's *Tour*: The Rhetoric of Growth and Decay." *Eighteenth-Century Studies* 6.2 (1972–73): 153–85.

———. *The Symbolic Design of* Windsor-Forest: *Iconography, Pageant, and Prophecy in Pope's Early Work*. Newark: University of Delaware Press, 2004.

Rooke, Church. *An Olde Thrift Newly Reuiued VVherein Is Declared the Manner of Planting, Preserving, and Husbanding Yong Trees of Diuers Kindes*. London: Richard Moore, 1612.

Rotherham, Ian. *The Lost Fens: England's Greatest Ecological Disaster*. Stroud, Gloucestershire: History Press, 2013.

Rubright, Marjorie. *Doppelgänger Dilemmas: Anglo-Dutch Relations in Early Modern English Literature and Culture*. Philadelphia: University of Pennsylvania Press, 2014.

Sartre, Jean-Paul. "Existentialism Is a Humanism." In *Existentialism from Dostoevsky to Sartre*, ed. Walter Kaufmann, 287–311. New York: Meridian Books, 1966.

Schechner, Richard. *Performance Studies: An Introduction*. New York: Routledge, 2002.

Scholar, Richard. "Montaigne's Forays into the Undiscovered Country." In *The Uses of the Future in Early Modern Europe*, ed. Andrea Brady and Emily Butterworth, 39–53. New York: Routledge, 2010.

Schumpeter, Elizabeth Boody. *English Overseas Trade Statistics 1697–1808*. Oxford: Clarendon, 1960.

Scott, James. *Seeing Like a State: How Certain Schemes to Improve the Human Condition Have Failed*. New Haven, Conn.: Yale University Press, 1998.

Scott, William Robert. *The Constitution and Finance of English, Scottish and Irish Joint-Stock Companies to 1720*, 3 vols. Cambridge: Cambridge University Press, 1910–12.

Scotten, Edmud. *A Desperate and Dangerovs Designe Discovered Concerning the Fen-Countries*. London: Robert Constable, 1642.

Shapin, Steven, and Simon Schaffer. *Leviathan and the Air-Pump: Hobbes, Boyle, and the Experimental Life*. Princeton, N.J.: Princeton University Press, 2011.

Shirley, William. *The Triumph of Peace*. London: Iohn Norton, 1634.

Siskin, Clifford. "Novels and Systems." *NOVEL: A Forum on Fiction* 34.2 (2001): 202–15.

Skeen, Catherine. "Projecting Fictions: *Gulliver's Travels*, *Jack Connor*, and *John Buncle*." *Modern Philology* 100.3 (2003): 330–59.

Skempton, A. W. *A Biographical Dictionary of Civil Engineers in Great Britain and Ireland: 1500–1830*. London: Thomas Telford, 2002.

Slack, Paul. *From Reformation to Improvement: Public Welfare in Early Modern England*. Oxford: Clarendon, 1999.

———. *The Invention of Improvement: Information and Material Progress in Seventeenth-Century England*. Oxford: Oxford University Press, 2014.

Slush, Barnaby. *The Navy Royal; or, A Sea-Cook Turn'd Projector. Containing a Few Thoughts, About Manning Our Ships of War with the Best of Sailors, Without Violences, and in the Most Pleasing Manner*. London: B. Bragge, 1709.

Smart, Christopher. "The Hop-Garden: A Georgic." In *Poems on Several Occasions*. London: Christopher Smart, 1752.

Smiles, Samuel. *Lives of the Engineers: Vermuyden-Myddelton-Perry-James Brindley*. London: John Murray, 1904.

Smith, Adam. *The Wealth of Nations*, ed. Edwin Cannan. New York: Modern Library, 2000.

Smith, Courtney Weiss. *Empiricist Devotions: Science, Religion, and Poetry in Early Eighteenth-Century England*. Charlottesville: University of Virginia Press, 2016.

Smith, John. *England's Improvement Reviv'd*. London: Thomas Newcomb, 1670.

Smith, Pamela, and Benjamin Schmidt. "Introduction: Knowledge and Its Making in Early Modern Europe." In *Making Knowledge in Early Modern Europe: Practices, Objects, and Texts, 1400–1800*, ed. Pamela Smith and Benjamin Schmidt, 1–18. Chicago: University of Chicago Press, 2008.

Smith, Simon. *The Golden Fleece; or, The Trade, Interest, and Well-Being of Great Britain Considered*. London: [s.n.], 1736.

Smollett, Tobias. *The Adventures of Peregrine Pickle*, ed. James L. Clifford. London: Oxford University Press, 1964.

South Sea Bubble, and the Numerous Fraudulent Projects to which it gave Rise in 1720. London: Thomas Boys, 1825.

Spacks, Patricia Meyer. *The Varied God: A Critical Study of Thomson's The Seasons*. Berkeley: University of California Press, 1959.

Spiller, Elizabeth. *Science, Reading, and Renaissance Literature: The Art of Making Knowledge, 1580–1670*. New York: Cambridge University Press, 2004.

Sponsler, Claire. "Writing the Unwritten: Morris Dance and Theatre History." In *Representing the Past: Essays in Performance Historiography*, ed. Charlotte M. Canning and Thomas Postlewait, 84–116. Iowa City: University of Iowa Press, 2010.

Sprat, Thomas. *The History of the Royal Society of London for the Improving of Natural Knowledge*. London: J. Martyn and J. Allestry, 1667.

Spratt, Danielle. "Gulliver's Economized Body: Colonial Projects and the Lusus Naturae in the *Travels*." *Studies in Eighteenth-Century Culture* 41 (2012): 136–59.

Stage-Players Complaint. London: Thomas Bates, 1641.

Stanford Encyclopedia of Philosophy, ed. Edward N. Zalta. Stanford, Calif.: Metaphysics Research Lab, Center for the Study of Language and Information (Stanford University), accessed January 13, 2017, https://plato.stanford.edu/.

Stewart, Larry. *The Rise of Public Science: Rhetoric, Technology, and Natural Philosophy in Newtonian Britain, 1660–1750*. Cambridge: Cambridge University Press, 1992.

Stubbe, Henry. *Legends, No Histories: A Specimen of Some Animadversions upon the History of the Royal Society*. London: [s.n.], 1670.

———. *A Specimen of Some Animadversions upon a Book Entituled, Plus Ultra; or, Modern Improvements of Useful Knowledge Written by Mr. Joseph Glanvill, a Member of the Royal Society*. London: [s.n.], 1670.

Stubbs, Mayling. "John Beale, Philosophical Gardener of Herefordshire: Part I. Prelude to the Royal Society (1608–1663)." *Annals of Science* 39 (1982): 463–89.

Suarez, Michael F. Introduction to *The Cambridge History of the Book in Britain*, vol. 5, ed. Michael F. Suarez and Michael L. Turner, 1–36. Cambridge: Cambridge University Press, 2009.

Swift, Jonathan. *Correspondence of Jonathan Swift*, 5 vols., ed. Harold Williams. Oxford: Clarendon Press, 1963–65.

———. *The Drapier's Letters to the People of Ireland*, ed. Herbert Davis. Oxford: Clarendon Press, 1965.

———. *Gulliver's Travels*, ed. Albert J. Rivero. New York: W. W. Norton, 2000.

———. "A Modest Proposal." In *The Essential Writings of Jonathan Swift*, ed. Claude Rawson and Ian Higgins, 295–303. New York: W. W. Norton, 2010.

———. *A Project for the Advancement of Religion and the Reformation of Manners*. London: Benjamin Tooke, 1709.

———. *A Proposal for Correcting, Improving, and Ascertaining the English Tongue*. London: Benjamin Tooke, 1712.

———. *A Proposal for Giving Badges to the Beggars in All the Parishes in Dublin*. Dublin: George Faulkner, 1737.

———. *A Proposal for the Universal Use of Irish Manufacture*. Dublin: E. Waters, 1720.

———. *Proposal That All the Ladies and Women in Ireland Should Appear Constantly in Irish Manufactures*. In *The Author's Works: Collected and Revised by Deane Swift, Esq. of Goodrich, in Herefordshire*, vol. 12, 187–94. Dublin: George Faulkner, 1765.

———. *The Prose Works of Jonathan Swift*, ed. Temple Scott, 12 vols. London: George Bell and Son, 1907.

———. *A Tale of a Tub: Written for the Universal Improvement of Mankind*. London: John Nutt, 1704.

Taylor, Christopher. "Fenlands." In *The English Rural Landscape*, ed. Joan Thirsk, 167–87. Oxford: Oxford University Press, 2000.

Taylor, Diana. *The Archive and the Repertoire: Performing Cultural Memory in the Americas*. Durham, N.C.: Duke University Press, 2003.

Taylor, John. *The Complaint of M. Tenter-Hooke the Projector*. London: Francis Coles, 1641.

———. *The Praise of Hemp-Seed*. London: H. Gosson, 1620.

Thick, Malcolm. *Sir Hugh Plat: The Search for Useful Knowledge in Early Modern London*. Totnes, Devon: Prospect Books, 2010.

Thirsk, Joan, ed. *The Agrarian History of England and Wales*. Cambridge: Cambridge University Press, 1985.

———. "Agricultural Policy: Public Debate and Legislation, 1640–1750," in *Agricultural Change: Policy and Practice, 1500–1750*, ed. Joan Thirsk. Cambridge: Cambridge University Press, 1990.

———. *Economic Policy and Projects: The Development of a Consumer Society in Early Modern England*. Oxford: Clarendon, 1978.

———. "Vermuyden, Sir Cornelius (1590–1677)." In *Oxford Dictionary of National Biography*, ed. Lawrence Goldman. Oxford: Oxford University Press, 2006.

Thompson, E. P. *The Making of the English Working Class*. New York: Pantheon Books, 1964.

Thomson, James. *The Seasons*, ed. James Sambrook. Oxford: Clarendon, 1981.

Tighe, R. R., and J. E. Davis, *Annals of Windsor Forest*, vol. 2. London: Longman, Brown, Green, Longmans, and Roberts, 1858.

Treadwell, J. M. "Jonathan Swift: The Satirist as Projector." *Texas Studies in Literature and Language* 17.2 (1975): 439–60.

Trevers, Joseph. *An Essay to the Restoring of Our Decayed Trade*. London: Giles Widdowes, 1675.

Tricks of State; or, More Westminster Projects. London: [s.n.], 1648.

Upton, Chris. "Andrew Yarranton the Forgotten Visionary." *Birmingham Post* (UK) August 17, 2011, accessed August 14, 2015, http://www.birminghampost.co.uk/lifestyle/andrew-yarran ton-the-forgotten-visionary-3918876.

Vaughan, Rowland. *Most Approved, and Long Experienced Water-Workes*. London: [s.n.], 1610.

Verity, Victor. *The Royal Project; or, A Clear Discovery of His Majesties Design in the Present Treaty*. London: [s.n.], 1648.

Vermuyden, Cornelius. *A Discourse Touching the Draining of the Great Fennes*. London: [s.n.], 1642.

Virgil. *The Georgics*, ed. L. P. Wilkinson. New York: Penguin, 1982.

Warde, Paul. "The Idea of Improvement, c. 1520–1700." In *Custom, Improvement and the Landscape in Early Modern Britain*, ed. Richard W. Hoyle, 127–48. Burlington, Vt.: Ashgate, 2011.

Watt, Ian. *The Rise of the Novel: Studies in Defoe, Richardson, and Fielding*. Berkeley and Los Angeles: University of California Press, 1962.

Watts, Martin. *Water and Wind Power*. Buckinghamshire: Shire, 2005.

Webber, William. *The Consequences of Trade, as to the Wealth and Strength of Any Nation*. London: [s.n.], 1740.

Webster, Charles. *Samuel Hartlib and the Advancement of Learning*. Cambridge: Cambridge University Press, 1970.

Wells, Samuel. *The History of the Drainage of the Great Level of the Fens*, 2 vols. London: Samuel Wells, 1828–30.

Weston, Richard. *A Discours of Husbandrie Used in Brabant and Flanders*. London: [s.n.], 1650.

Wildman, John. *Putney Projects; or, The Old Serpent in a New Forme*. London: [s.n.], 1647.

Williams, Raymond. *Keywords: A Vocabulary of Culture and Society*. New York: Routledge, 2011.

———. *Marxism and Literature*. Oxford: Oxford University Press, 1977.

Willmoth, Frances. "Fens Maps and Moore's Mapp of the Great Levell." In *Drowned and Drained: Exploring Fenland Records and Landscape*, ed. Susan Oosthuizen and Frances Willmoth, 13–20. Cambridge: University of Cambridge Institute of Continuing Education, 2009.

———. *Sir Jonas Moore: Practical Mathematics and Restoration Science*. Rochester, N.Y.: Boydell, 1993.

Wilson, John. *The Projectors*. London: John Playfere, 1665.

Wise, John. *The New Forest: Its History and Its Scenery*. London: Smith, Elder, and Company, 1863.

Wittkowsky, George. "Swift's Modest Proposal: The Biography of an Early Georgian Pamphlet." *Journal of the History of Ideas* 4.1 (1943): 75–104.

Woodcroft, Bennet. *Subject-Matter Index of Patents of Invention from March 2, 1617 (14 James I.) to October 1, 1852 (16 Victoriae) Part II*. London: George Edward Eyre and William Spottiswoode, 1854.

Woodland, Patrick. "Beale, John (*bap.* 1608, *d.* 1683)," in *Oxford Dictionary of National Biography*, ed. David Cannadine. Oxford: Oxford University Press, 2004.

Worlidge, John. *Systema Agriculturæ: The Mystery of Husbandry*. London: Samuel Speed, 1669.

———. *Vinetum Britannicum; or, A Treatise of Cider, and Such Other Wines and Drinks That Are Extracted from All Manner of Fruits Growing in This Kingdom*. London: [s.n.], 1676.

Wycherley, William. *The Country Wife*. In *The Broadview Anthology of Restoration and Early-Eighteenth Century Drama*, ed. Douglas Canfield, 1038–100. Toronto: Broadview, 2001.

Yamamoto, Koji. "Piety, Profit and Public Service in the Financial Revolution." *English Historical Review* 126 (2011): 806–34.

———. "Reformation and the Distrust of the Projector in the Hartlib Circle." *Historical Journal* 55.2 (2012): 375–97.

Yarranton, Andrew. *England's Improvement by Sea and Land*. London: R. Everingham, 1677.

———. *A Full Discovery of the First Presbyterian Sham Plot*. London: Francis Smith, 1681.

———. *The Improvement Improved by a Second Edition of the Great Improvement of Lands by Clover*. London: Francis Rea: 1663.

Zevenbergen, Jaap. *Systems of Land Registration: Aspects and Effects*. Delft: Nederlandse Commissie voor Geodesie, 2002.

Zucker, Adam. *The Places of Wit in Early Modern English Comedy*. Cambridge: Cambridge University Press, 2011.

Index

Acknowledgments

Mentors, colleagues, friends, and family made this book possible. Over the past decade, I have had the privilege of learning from some of the most insightful and generous scholars imaginable, first at the University of Pennsylvania and then at SUNY-Buffalo. Toni Bowers supported my "project of projects" from the start with unflagging enthusiasm and inspiring confidence in what early drafts could become. Suvir Kaul and Chi-ming Yang challenged me to establish the theoretical stakes of researching human endeavor within and beyond early modern British studies. Through their searching questions and candid criticism, Toni, Suvir, and Chi-ming have taught me volumes about the trying but vital art of sharing scholarly ideas.

My research, writing, and overall academic life have been enriched and sustained by conversations with my colleagues Rachel Banner, Marina Bilbija, Alyssa Connell, Daniel DeWispelare, Joe Drury, Anna Foy, Greta LaFleur, Phil Maciak, Alice McGrath, Sarah Nicolazzo, Marissa Nicosia, Katie Price, Jared Richman, Christopher Taylor, Sarah Pierce Taylor, and Simran Thadani. Special thanks to Chris Taylor for his sharp-eyed reading of an early draft of my introduction, and to Marissa Nicosia and Simran Thadani for bringing their book history chops to bear on Chapter 2. I have found in the world of eighteenth-century studies several colleagues who have taken time to offer their wisdom and camaraderie, and I would like to thank especially Tita Chico, Michael Gamer, Michael Genovese, Danielle Spratt, Cynthia Wall, and Gena Zuroski.

With its mixture of ruin and revival, nostalgia and futurism, Buffalo, New York, was the perfect place to write the bulk of this book. In the English Department at SUNY-Buffalo, I owe greatest thanks to Ruth Mack, who read this entire manuscript multiple times, offering comments and questions on each iteration. I count myself lucky to have a senior colleague working in eighteenth-century studies, let alone one who models exemplary citizenship in the department, university, and discipline. Carla Mazzio and Graham Hammill offered helpful feedback on the contents of the manuscript and on my numerous proposals for library fellowships and travel grants that made possible its research. Thanks to my departmental colleagues Rachel Ablow, Judith Goldman, Walter Hakala, James Holstun, Jang Wook Huh, Damien Keane, and Randy Schiff for conversation and good cheer, and to the SUNY-Buffalo historians Jim Bono, Hal Langfur, Adam Malka, and Erik Seeman for taking interest in my work and for suggesting ways to broaden its audience. Special thanks to Eric Ash, historian at Wayne State University, who read and commented on Chapter 3 despite knowing me only through one unsolicited e-mail.

I presented an early version of my introduction and coda to students and faculty in the McMaster University English and Culture Studies Department. Thanks to Gena Zuroski for the invitation and to her students and colleagues for engaging with my work. Likewise, I am grateful to Erik Seeman and Elizabeth Otto, co-coordinators of the SUNY-Buffalo Humanities Institute's faculty fellowship program, which gave me a forum in which to present my research and a semester of leave to facilitate its completion. At Indiana University, Rebecca Spang and Jesse Molesworth organized the 2016 Bloomington Eighteenth-Century Workshop, which pushed me to fathom British projecting's epistemological analogues in French, Dutch, and German culture. My thanks for these lively and timely exchanges and for the warm hospitality.

This book received financial support from the National Endowment for the Humanities in the form of a Summer Stipend, which enabled me to examine manuscripts in the United Kingdom. The Huntington Library's Mayers Fellowship afforded me one sun-drenched and intellectually exuberant month in San Marino in 2014. A subvention through SUNY-Buffalo's Julian Park Fund subsidized my acquisition and reproduction of three illustrations from materials in the Huntington's collections. I am grateful to the librarians and archivists who have assisted me over the course of this project at the Huntington, Folger, and Houghton Libraries, the British Library, the UK National Archives, the Cambridgeshire Archives, and the Nottingham University Manuscripts and Special Collections. I also wish to thank John Pollack in the Special Collections of the University of Pennsylvania's Van Pelt–Dietrich Library, and Laura Taddeo, head of the Arts, Humanities, and Social Sciences Team in SUNY-Buffalo's Lockwood Library.

At Penn Press, Jerry Singerman placed my manuscript in the hands of expert and unstinting readers. Their comments improved my manuscript immensely, and I owe them gratitude for subjecting my work to peer review at its best. I am grateful to Jerry and Penn Press for their long-standing commitment to publishing first-time academic authors.

A portion of Chapter 5 appeared originally in *Eighteenth-Century Studies* 47.3 (Spring 2014), copyright Johns Hopkins University. Thanks to ECS's editors for allowing me to republish this material here.

My parents-in-law, Henry and Nancy Rowan, have supported me and this book for many years. Most recently, they provided childcare at two pivotal moments, which allowed me to travel to conduct research and deliver conference presentations. My own parents, Dave and Lorraine, have offered me constant encouragement (and occasional consolation) over the long process of composing this book. I am grateful for my father's willful curiosity pertaining to matters historical, religious, economic, and political, and my mother's adventurous interest in exploring new places. I hope both inclinations are evident here. Thank you to my sister, Christine Alff, and brother-in-law, John Rowan, for their continued love and support.

Over her first two years in the world, Mira Rowan Alff has managed to inspire and divert me each day. Through her resolute indifference to my work, Mira has given me every motivation to complete this project, and with Lucy, her partner in crime, even better reasons to set it aside. I could not have begun, let alone finished, this book without the tireless love, compassion, intelligence, and fortitude of Katie Rowan. She is my first and last reader, and my deepest debts are to her.